I End With My Pen,
But Not With My Heart

Dutch immigrant letters, memoirs and travel journals

Compiled by Mary Risseeuw

Published by the Sheboygan County Historical Research Center,
518 Water Street, Sheboygan Falls, WI 53085
2008

Funded in part by The Netherland-America Foundation, Inc.
New York, NY

Introduction

These letters, memoirs and travel journals span a hundred year period and offer a fascinating view into the lives of the immigrants and their families. Some provide remarkable detail about their journey to America and their struggles to establish a new life. Others offer little beyond the basics: weather, health, crops, births and deaths. Most are grateful for the blessings of God and the fact that they are still 'fresh and healthy' (alive and well, in more modern terms!). But, in reality, has letter writing changed a great deal in the last 100 years? For those of us who still write letters, aren't these some of the same issues that concern us today? Inquiring about the health of family and friends, explaining the latest job challenges, telling the tale of the latest snowstorm are as prevalent today as they were 150 years ago. The criterion for selecting the contents of this book was to present an overview of different settlements in Wisconsin and to provide a glimpse into the differences and similarities between the various immigration waves.

There are vivid tales of crossing the Atlantic Ocean and personal glimpses into the Civil War, World War I and World War II. This collection is not presented as an academic assessment of an immigrant letter collection. Some of these letters can also be found in the highly regarded publications of Dr. Herbert Brinks; *Write Back Soon: Letters from Immigrants in America* and *Dutch American Voices: Letters from the United States, 1850-1930* and Henry S. Lucas' *Dutch Immigrant Memoirs and Related Writings*. The editor of this volume does not have the scholarly background of Drs. Brinks and Lucas, and this publication is not intended in any way to equal their scholarly contributions to the study of Dutch immigration. It is, instead, an effort to encourage further examination of Dutch immigration to Wisconsin. Historians use many sources in their attempts to reconstruct the past and immigrant letters have the ability to give character to the facts of immigration. They can also challenge the genealogist to move beyond the gathering of names and dates to uncover the stories behind the people.

The impetus for writing letters was most often in the hands of those who immigrated. They were prompted to write for many reasons. Most importantly, they knew that their family and friends would be anxious to hear the facts about their new homeland. The possibilities of owning land and prospects for employment were important stimulus for encouraging further immigration. Immigrants also wrote letters to reaffirm family connections and announce important events. Most immigrants knew it was unlikely they would see family and friends who had stayed behind, but many held on to the hope that they would be reunited one day.

Between 1840 and 1890, Wisconsin was a major center of Dutch immigration. Before 1845 there were about 200 Dutch immigrants annually arriving in the U.S. 1845 saw an immigration wave of nearly 800 and for the next decade it averaged about 1,100 yearly. The 1845-46 potato famine and religious and economic factors were large contributors to the increase. The division in the Reformed Church between the conservative Calvinists and the liberal State Church forced many to leave in search of freedom to worship. During this immigration wave, three clergymen organized followers and established colonies in the mid-west. Two conservative clergy, Albertus van Raalte and Hendrik

Scholte, founded respectively, Holland, Michigan and Pella, Iowa. Dutch immigrants to Wisconsin were easily divided into two basic groups based on religious affiliation-- Protestants and Catholics. The Protestants were the first to arrive in Wisconsin and settled mainly in Milwaukee, Sheboygan, Fond du Lac and La Crosse counties. This first group established the town of Alto in 1845, one of the first Dutch communities in the Midwest. By the late 1840s a community had been established in Milwaukee and was often referred to as Dutch Hill. For many the city was seen as a temporary stop to earn enough money to purchase land further west or to the north. The sinking of the ship *Phoenix* off the shores of Sheboygan in 1847 greatly affected immigration to Wisconsin in the 1850s and 1860s.

Father Theodore Johannes Van den Brock was an early promoter of Dutch Catholic immigration to Wisconsin and, beginning in 1848, he helped to bring 40,000 Catholic Dutch to Wisconsin. Most Dutch immigrants to the Fox River Valley came by way of the Erie Canal and the Great lakes. This migration route was also favored by those settling in other areas of Wisconsin. Dutch communities in Albany and the Rochester, New York areas provided stopping points for immigrants needing to work to finance the rest of their journey. Later Dutch settlements in Wisconsin were generally small agricultural communities.

Although Protestant clergy were arriving in Wisconsin in this decade, none arrived with large numbers of followers. The colonies established by Van Raalte in Michigan and Scholte in Iowa were not to be duplicated in Wisconsin. The emigrants to Wisconsin seemed to have been a far more independent group. Another wave of immigration occurred after the turn of the century. As some of these letters will indicate, conditions were as bad in 1909 as they had been in the 1850s. Another wave of immigration occurred after World War II when the Netherlands was left with a badly damaged economy and housing crisis. Approximately 80,000 immigrants came to the U.S. after the war.

Because these letters and journals represent a hundred year time span, the language used in these letters and journals varied greatly. The older Dutch language and dialects proved challenging for many of the translators. Some of the translations may be awkward to read, but all attempts were made to keep the translations true to the original intention of the writer. Punctuation and sentence structure has been added judiciously in order to provide clarification.

The letters, memoirs and travel journals included in this publication were provided by Calvin College Archives, Grand Rapids, MI; Evert Smilda, Willem Wilterdink, Jean Reese, Alice Hoffman, Sharol (Hesselink) Stessman, Twilah DeBoer, Mary Risseeuw and the Van Der Hyden family. Many of the letters in the Calvin College collection were already translated. Translation for other material was provided by Evert Smilda, Aalten, Gelderland, Netherlands; Adriana E. (Smilda) Delfgou, Sault Ste. Marie, Canada; Louisa Rank, WI; Nel Prins-Serier, Emmen, Groningen, Netherlands; Alice Hoffman, WI and Mary Risseeuw, WI.

Travel journals and memoirs

[The first Dutchman to arrive in Alto, WI in 1845 was Albertus Meenk. By 1847 the number of settlers had steadily increased and in the fall of that year a new log church was built. Although there was not a formally organized congregation, a call was made to Rev. Gerrit Baai (Baay) in Het Loo, Gelderland, Netherlands. He and his family arrived in the spring of 1848 and this letter was written not long before his death on 7 November 1849. This letter is from the Dutch Immigrant Letters Collection, Archives, Calvin College, Grand Rapids, MI, Box 4, Folder 5.]

Fond du Lac County   Alto, 4 January 1849

My dear friends in Netherland:

I have written to a few friends and relatives in Netherland. To satisfy all the requests to write is absolutely impossible for me. So I concluded to write in general, and, if possible, in print, to hand to such as are unknown to me, so that others may make of it on their journey to America. In a previous, brief account, I have mentioned some things; now I shall write a little more to the point.

Toward the end of February last year, we departed from Apeldoorn for Rotterdam. We have no reason, whatever, to complain about H.H. Wambersie and Crooswyk, and yet, we would have saved at least f.50 if we had chosen Amsterdam to take ship. I would advise, (if anyone can get there just as easily from their home place) to make use of the services of H.H. Wehlburg and Breuker, on the outskirts of Amsterdam. I have every reason to recommend them, no doubt, they will give good service. One should know that the ship in which our passage to Rotterdam took place had to be towed from Gouda in order to be in Rotterdam in time; for this alone f.40 had to be paid. On March 7 we left with the Bremer ship *Wichelhausen* under Captain H. Warnke from Hellevoet into sea.

It was a favorable occasion. The people were in good spirit. But before long, we had a strong wind. For a long time we cruised to and fro. We saw England, then France, until finally we passed through the channel. We were sixty-four days on the ocean. Three bodies had to be lowered into the sea. One was a Wurtemburger, it was said this was the result of overeating and drinking. The other two, a father and a son, were leaving a widow with seven children. At the lowering into the sea of the father, I gave a brief discourse on Heb. 11:9, 10. I can mention with praise Captain Warnke and his whole crew. They conversed with our people in the most and the best of harmony and were helpful, particularly during stormy weather. So far as was possible, we held a public service each day. On the second day of Easter at 2 o'clock in the afternoon, our bowsprit, pole of the foremast, broke in consequence of which we floated more backward than forward. After struggling eight days in which our people took an active part, we were able to set sail again and made fairly good progress. Finally, we saw the American pilot boats, one of them cruising to our side. How we rejoiced in getting a pilot on board, one can better feel than describe. And we rejoiced not less when

1

we saw New York in front of us. And, above all, when the anchor was lowered in the harbor, we joined in a thanksgiving prayer unto God. Yes, to the praise of our faithful Covenant God and Leader; I can truly say, our joy ended in Him! And here I cannot omit to advise all who intend to follow us, to care especially for cleanliness and temperance. The condition of our health thus far had been as desired. The father and son I mentioned above had been sick the whole winter in Rotterdam; the father died, believing. However touching a funeral at sea may be, the truth of God comforted us: "And the sea gave up its dead that were in it." Rev. 20: 13.

<u>At anchor.</u> Would I were able to give a sketch of the view of New York with its hundred thousands of inhabitants! Thousands of ships, whose mast tops with thousands of flags and pennants made the most agreeable sight and indicated that America has relation with the whole world. How the believer in Jesus will rejoice when his vessel sails into the haven of eternal rest and into the city which hath foundations whose Builder and Maker is God!

<u>In the city.</u> What a stir! And yet, tiresome for a Christian who has been used to a quiet country life. On board, and especially when stepping on shore, an emigrant is surrounded by various countrymen. One makes an appeal, to some minister, another shows several letters, still another asks whether this or that person is known to you, while a fourth slips cards into your hand, etc. Was I glad when I saw New York and not less so when I was on the steamboat *Newton*. The best advice I can give here is to pay no attention to anyone. I regret that I am compelled to warn against some of my own countrymen most of all. According to Mr. Ed Forrester, Bleeker Street 202, the Netherland Emigration, in Cedar Street, is the best; therefore, we have made use of this company at the advice of Mr. Forrester. For the rest, it is best to let one's baggage be brought to the steamboat that leaves New York every evening for Albany.

<u>On the steamboat.</u> At the outset I would make the remark here; if anyone arrives in New York and still has left some of his food, don't sell it. You might just as well give it away for you get very little for it. Along the canal there is offered plenty food for sale but they ask a high price for it and one must calculate on two or three weeks for the inland trip.

I had never been able to form an idea of such winter-castles as the *Newton*. Dining rooms, men's and women's sleeping rooms, everything is splendid. The uppermost room gives you almost the impression that you are in the church at Gouda, by reason of the windows with painted ceilings. I noticed a Bible lying on the table of many rooms. Various black servants are soaring as if on wings back and forth. Our people were in the steerage; and while I had a cabin, I could not sleep and spent the night mostly with them. There was room enough to walk back and forth. It is said that the Newton is three hundred fifty feet long. On May 14, in the morning at four o'clock we arrived in Albany. A man came on board with a plate on his forehead, runner, etc. It soon dawned on me this man was concerned mostly in favor of his own hotel than looking after the interests of the emigrants. With the help of the agent Quintus, we went with him to his home. I cannot recommend him, however; his name is Willem Smith, a German.

Canalboat. After I had talked with several of my former Holland friends, and had preached to a tolerably large audience on Sunday in the neat school building of the Presbyterian Church, we left Albany for Buffalo. While we rejoiced greatly in meeting brethren in Albany who were well situated there, the bidding farewell of them was touching. The religious condition of those who live in cities is far from ideal. This is the reason why we like to be where the Hollanders live more unitedly together.

We had made arrangements on the canal boat to have at least twice a day boiling water. At first the captain, not a very friendly person, had refused. But when I had reminded him of his duty, things improved. We were on the canal boat eight days. In several cities, through which the canal flows, we met Holland friends. One cannot describe the noise along the canal. At a distance of three hundred sixty-three miles, you have canal boats before and behind, and freighted with flour, meat, etc. You see them night and day. Then we were advised to inquire in Albany for Reverend Wyckoff. At my arrival this Reverend was at a church meeting in New York, so that, to my regret, I did not meet him.

The trip on a canal boat is not very convenient for the emigrant. One should not think that one can live at ease there like at home. But nevertheless the Lord has been good to us.

Buffalo. On the 29th day of May we were glad to arrive in Buffalo. We had to bury a child on a farmstead, for the rest we were all in good health. Here, once more, let me advise to get on a steamboat, to bring you to the interior where you want to go. The reason for this word of advice is the same as I gave before at New York. If one should ask: are all people bad in North America? My answer is: far from it! But the case is this: with the best of intentions, one can hardly escape a course that one may rue afterwards. Here is an example: in New York we had agreed with the True Netherland Society where we had deposited 2 dollars a person. Arriving at Buffalo we were told that we had paid large enough in that deposit. We agreed in Buffalo to go to Chicago or Michigan for 6 dollars. And when I came stepped on the steamboat, the Oregon, the captain told me that had I paid on the boat, he would have brought us over with our baggage for 3 dollars.

In Buffalo there was a letter from Rev. A.C. van Raalte, giving a further explanation of his Rev., that our misconception was the cause why several had changed their plans to go to Wisconsin. For several reasons, the place of our destination was not the best. Since Oregon remained for an hour in Milwaukee, I used this opportunity to meet some friends to convince myself more fully in the matter. I soon learned that in this country, there was not a single Roman Catholic or German who controlled the land as we understood matters. Then I had my baggage brought from the boat to follow my own inclination, leaving others entirely to their choice. It was a painful moment. The folk had become attached to me and to me there were dearer than ever before. But the choice had to be made soon. Two families followed me, and after bidding farewell in tears, the rest left for Michigan.

Milwaukee. A new city, already counting a population of 14,000. Many Germans and about 500 Hollanders are living here. I was eight days among them, preaching and speaking concerning the kingdom of God. During my stay here I was dwelling on a mountain, in a

3

house built out of stone. From there I had a most beautiful view of the city and of Lake Michigan. The Hollanders are nearly all living on an elevation, near together. They are doing well, in things temporal. Rev. Zonne, formerly living and serving here, has settled with a number of Hollanders in Sheboygan, so they are now without a pastor. If there should be a brother in Netherland, who were willing to come on faith and for the Lord's sake, not loving greatness or ease, but only taking to heart the interests of his congregation, I should account this a blessing for my countrymen in Milwaukee, if such a pastor was with them. In spite of their sincere wish and my own also, I cannot serve them except by letter! May the Lord provide for his people according to his mercy! Though my sojourn with them was brief, I enjoyed it. Two wagons came from Alto, my present charge, to call for me and my family. Leaving in Holland was for me very painful, especially with the thought in mind: "We will not see one another again this side of the grave." But to leave believers and Holland folk in America too, is hard indeed! Nevertheless, the will of the Lord be done! After we had commenced one another to the Lord in prayer, we left on Monday morning, at 6 o'clock, June 5, on the wagons.

The first day we rode through nothing but woods, yet the road was not lonesome. We met many wagons with various products, until in the evening we came to a German and real Christian family, which entertained us in a very agreeable way. We had much fellowship in conversation, prayer and singing of old High German songs. On the day following, we resumed our journey and on Wednesday evening we arrived safely at Alto. This journey had been pleasant to us. Now I viewed the land covered with a variety of fruit, alternating with green (grass) that abundantly provides feed for cattle. For those who are thinking of coming here, it will be well to consult the Hollanders in Milwaukee and there also buy oxen and wagons. Then they can take their belongings with them and save freight expenses. The expense for travel in Milwaukee to us is ordinarily from 16 to 18 dollars a family. Otherwise, if people here could be notified in time before their arrival in Milwaukee, someone might call for them for less money. Little use is made here of firesides; stoves are quite common. I was advised to buy a stove in Buffalo; also kettles, pots, etc. or in Milwaukee. I hear there is little difference in price, if any. Earthenware is here expensive. Wrapping it between clothes one can safely carry it along. I advise to take with you as much as you can. But your chests should not be too large. When two men can carry them, they suffer the least. Otherwise they turn them over, and throw them from one ship into another. There is here also a great need of Holland Bibles and psalm books. Whoever can take a few along will render a real service to Hollanders.

<u>My station and work at Alto.</u> Our dwelling here was not quite ready when we arrived. So we lived with D.A. van Eck until the Sunday following. It is a large place, and also is the place where we meet for service. It was a privilege for me and my family to kneel in it before the throne of Grace, thanking Him who had been our faithful Guide on the journey of more than three months. I turned my thoughts back to Netherland and felt the tie of relationship. But did not wish to return. I rather prayed that the Lord might lead many to this good land. On the first day of Pentecost I preached my first sermon here, which now regularly happens every Sunday. Fully thirty families are living here together. When I say together one should realize that each family owns at least eighty acres of land, and some 3 or

4 times eighty, so they live quite apart. But it is not difficult to visit each other, which often happens, especially in winter. No one need to ask anxiously: "Do I have enough to feed them all?" and wishing secretly the visitors to leave. The abundance, shared by all, makes one wish at times for a guest to come. And, though the winters here are usually more severe than in Holland, they are not felt that way on account of abundance that is shared by all. The stoves have different sizes. I would advise from numbers 1, 2, 3 and 4 to choose one of the latter, the larger ones. They are easier for baking bread, etc. than the smaller ones. And then the wood can be used in larger pieces than for smaller stoves.

Nor is it necessary to be sparing in wood as in any other necessity. Our neighbors are Americans and they gladly sell out. Near our dwelling there are a few farms for sale, one for about 800 dollars; another for 1600 dollars, more or less. I would count many of my friends happy, were they living here. The calculation is that two families can have a good living here on one of these farms. This is the reason why people with means hire their farms out for one half of the products and they can have a good living. It is not necessary, therefore to know and do the work of a farmer, if one deals the way I have just explained.

The city of Fond du Lac will be our staple town 7 or 8 hours from here. I look upon this country as one of the most agreeable and profitable in North America. For a Hollander, it is specially surprising that this soil, by proper cultivation, can produce so much. The tax to be paid is only 2 dollars or a little more per acre. The simple, rural administration keeps taxation down. Before this is was a surprise to me that one meets no beggars in North America at all. And the only wish I hear concerning the poor, is: "Alas, could he only share with so many in Netherland who are in need!" In Holland it has happened that our clothes hanging on the line while we were eating our dinner, were stolen in that time. What is the reason for this great difference? The abundance in which all share makes them content with what they have.

Oxen are mostly used for labor and transportation. Also many keep horses. There is little woods here. Enough, however, to mark off one's land and to be protected against fire. This is the way they mark off their property. They cut down the trees and split the straight lumber into rails. Then they lay seven rails on top of each other around the property. These give it good protection and last for many years. And this protection is not for people but to prevent cattle from injuring the crops. There are few fruit trees here, but many produced by the soil itself. Also fragrant flowers grow here. The climate is very healthy. You who have known my spouse in Holland will recall that she had been ailing for 28 years. Here she feels healthy and strong. And all of us, so far as I know, are as healthy, or healthier than in Netherland.

Most of the men who possess 800 acres today, had nothing but a claim when they first settled here.

With moderate labor which pays here well, (usually 1 dollar per day) they are independent and cheerful. Those who can work, I can invite freely to come and to enjoy the good of the land! Here is much demand for Holland laborers and maid-servants. Here is also need of Holland wives. American wives are not advisable for Hollanders for several reasons. A

Holland wife, though she may not be sitting in a rocking chair and plan on what clothes she will wear, can live here happier than in Holland. No father need ask here: "What can I do for my children when they grow up? For they can hardly make a living when they grow up."

The temptations of youth are less here. The celebration of American Independence is held here annually. But no one thinks in that connection of a kermis (fair) or anything of that kind.

In addition to two sermons on Sunday, I also preach in various homes during the week. And I may state to God's glory of his Grace: my preaching has not been in vain! When I came here my acre was somewhat like a natural ground at the first settlement. I could begin my work with prayer, and the heavenly husbandman gives me good hope on fruitage which will be to his glory!

<u>Concerning church life.</u> Following the regular course, preaching on Sunday and at the homes during the week, I had decided first to meet every Wednesday. I soon noticed who were showing the best interest in the general welfare. I believe, however, that there is much coming to the surface that I might proceed to the organization of a congregation. A prepared "Regalement," which was read at the last meeting, has been adopted and will be signed in the near future. The principle contents of it are: "Jesus Christ is our King and Lawgiver. His word is the only rule for faith and practice. Baptism and the Lord's Supper are the signs and seals of God's Covenant of Grace: the privileges of believers. The sign and seal of Holy Baptism, is administered to the children of the congregation; Holy Communion is the food for them who can discern the body of the Lord. The acceptance of members in the church takes place after they make a confession of their faith, etc. etc."

The Lord, I hope, will bless my feeble efforts. May He come down with his grace and Spirit to live and work within us. May He make us jointly to grow and flourish in our glorified Head, Jesus Christ! I trust that our friends in the Netherlands will support us with their prayers. From a distance we witness the struggles in Europe and we will not cease to pray for our people amid what is approaching for them. May many seek a protection in Christ for their lives. Oh, that they may know what pertains to their peace! May they also, in departing for North America, heed the admonition of the Lord, Luke 17: 82: "Remember Lot's wife." I too, have declared in solemn oath, to act in that same manner, from today on and in every way. But, as citizen of the United States, I cannot forget the country of my birth, my natural and spiritual birth. And in particular not those, who with me are looking for Him who is about to come and who will announce himself, as the only King of his church, even by them who have not been willing that He, the true and eternal King of God, be King over them. May He also bless the efforts of many in the Netherlands (thanks be to God) who are still standing faithful against the apostasy. We know that, the Lord willing, some intend to come this year. May the Lord guide them and bring them in his own time to us.

G. Baai

[Oepke Bonnema was born 26 May 1825 in Wonseradeel, Friesland, Netherlands to Haitse Eeltjes Bonnema and Stijntje Jelles Fopma. The village of New Amsterdam (present day La Crosse) was laid out on land he purchased shortly after arriving in Wisconsin. He built the first store in the Town of Holland (LaCrosse County) and in 1855 a post office was established with Bonnema as postmaster. In 1856 he donated land on which the first schoolhouse in the township was built and in 1857 he erected the first sawmill on the Black River. His travel journal was published in the Netherlands at Harlingen by S. Housma for the benefit of his father. These travel journals are from the Dutch Immigrant Letters Collection, Archives, Calvin College, Grand Rapids, MI, Box 8, Folder 18; Box 27, Folder 17 and Box 336, Folder 16.]

Adventures of Oepke H. Bonnema
and his travel companion
on the trip from Friesland to the United States of America.

Described by the bookkeeper
B.B. Haagsma (formerly assistant teacher at Arum)

Chapter 1
1. Presumed reason for emigration. Various reports. Farewell.

It was during the closing day of February, 1853, that a total of 92 individuals in Friesland organized to leave as emigrants for America. The reports which were circulating at the time, and the conversations concerning the subject would provide ample material to fill twenty booklets such as this one. Some lauded the decision as enterprising, and regarded it to be something which alone could enable people to escape the fetters of poverty and want, and open up a source of prosperity.

Others, on the other hand, viewed the matter in a less favorable light. They denied the advantages which America offered to the emigrant, they labeled us as individuals who were wanting in patriotism. They said: "Many ships went down and if they make the harbor, then we still do not always receive better. A few even allowed these rumors to stop them and they stayed at home, most likely to be a victim of poverty in the near future. This must, however, have been the main incentive of those emigrants that they wished to free themselves from that general retrogression which was so evident in our fatherland.

That thought gave them ability to leave relatives and friends, to bid them farewell, probably forever, and that country to which they were bound with ties of national affection, where Friesian virtue and loyalty were always gloriously displayed.

2. Departure from Harlingen. The North Sea. Storm. The sick, Lowestaft, Liverpool.

The day of our departure was scheduled for February 26 at 9 o'clock in the morning. The steamboat, *City of Newark*, lay prepared to take us to Lowestaft. The scene we witnessed

7

there was heart rending. Those tense moments between those thousands of relatives and friends, in which people once more bade each their farewell, and we left the soil of Friesland, we will never forget. I never hovered between hope and fear more than I did during those moments.

Driven by a strong northeasterly wind the crowd soon vanished from our sight and only the coast of Friesland was visible. It was covered with snow and looked like a bank of chalk. As to the arrangements on the boat, they were far from what we might have desired. They might be called fit for cattle, but for people between decks they were very poor. When the trip lasts 13 hours, it is not so bad, but how often a longer passage is to be dreaded. At least this was true in our case.

At 11 o'clock, we were passing the steamboat, the *Magnet*. We were prevented from continuing our course by a snow and hail storm and the anchor was cast out. It was not until 5 o'clock in the evening before the air cleared up and the anchor was hoisted. After sailing for an hour and a half, we felt a shock which caused several anxious cries. We had run into the shallow waters of the North Sea and were obliged to stay there all night. After a tiresome night we left at 7 o'clock in the morning and the next morning we found that we were in the "New Deep." It is a beautiful place, which, since the days of Napoleon, has acquired such a prosperous appearance, and is very well located for trade. After we had loaded on some cattle we sailed for some ten hours on the North Sea.

The winds blew harder and the wave rose higher and higher, and because of the rocking of the ship, almost every one became seasick. In the evening the storm increased, and I can assure you that we did not spend a pleasant night. On February 28th, between 1 and 2 o'clock in the morning, we were driven about, the prey of the waves, and because of the darkness, we could not enter the harbor of Lowestaft. As a result of the skilled management of the young captain, however, we reached it after the bright beams of the moon had dispelled the darkness of night. Here at Lowestaft we immediately left the ship, and then went to the railroad station. Here we found a warm room to stay in and warm coffee for our refreshment.

In the morning we left by train and rode past the beautiful village of Reed Udm. where wonderful landscapes, and Norwich, picturesquely located on the slope of a mountain. There, on the east coast of England, we still saw snow and ice, but none of the west coast. At 12 o'clock we were at Eli. Here the cattle, intended for the market in London, were to be transported along another track, and probably had to travel another 4 to 6 hours by train. We had to remain there until two thirty, and meanwhile toured the city, to the great amusement of the residents. The wooden shoes and silver ear ornaments caused people to stare at us.

At the appointed time we left there and at 5 o'clock we were at Peterborough, where they had a station 160 feet in length. The beautiful scene across hills and valleys, along woods and creeks soon disappeared. They were covered by the dark evening fog, which alas prevented the inquisitive traveler from seeing any more. But I know this, that we passed through tunnels three times, which are the result of the iron will of English enterprise. During the night we sped along the east coast of England and by the morning of March 1 we found ourselves in the Liverpool station at about 5 o'clock.

3. Liverpool

Immediately after our arrival in Liverpool efforts were put forth to find a suitable hotel which we succeeded in doing. We came across a fairly good German place and soon recovered from the cold we endured on the train. Because of the long trip from Harlingen to Lowestaft we arrived too late to be able to leave on the March 2 steamboat. All the places had been reserved, so we were obliged to remain 2, or possibly 3, weeks.

During that time we purchased the necessary provisions and cooking equipment, while the city provided some diversion to shorten the time. So we visited the English races. We passed through a tunnel, a half hour in length, on the train. They can still be properly called races, while thousands of pounds sterling are spent in betting. The rule is that four horses run a great distance at the same time and the first to arrive is the winner. We also visited several places of amusement, where we were usually surprised by English inventiveness, but very seldom by beautiful music and song. A harshness pervades English music.

Across the Mersey River which flows past the city there is the beautiful fortress of Brighton, and also a park which is outstanding because of its fine location and here and there by its beautiful historical monuments, among others that of Walter Scott. In the city there is a market 600 feet long and 100 feet wide, besides beautiful churches, a large stock exchange with a beautiful statue of the famous Admiral Nelson, etc. You can well imagine that our people saw many things of interest. I often heard them say as we passed beautiful stores, "Oh look here, green colors, blue colors, red colors, all kinds of colors." The Friesian women with their bonnets aroused the pity of the English, and they said, "O, God, those women have no hair."

The most wonderful of all, for the stranger is the police in England, so that he is protected everywhere against the sometimes rough and immoral resident. In Liverpool 9,000 police are on guard and provide matchless order and quiet, and also the strict observance of the Sabbath. In the second largest center of the world a deathlike silence reigns, which enables a citizen to honor his God in a proper manner.

It is also a city, which has a large amount of shipping, with docks which are not inferior to those of London. As a result there is a stream of emigrants who there board ships for America or Australia. I just read (March 6) in a German newspaper, that in Liverpool there are 34 ships in Liverpool, and 50 in London prepared to sail for America or Australia with emigrants, also that between June 16 and December 31 of 1852 that many have sailed from English harbors with 221, 068 individuals. Besides the docks are crowded with ships. On March 6 someone counted 11,000.

The area surrounding Liverpool is also scenic and worth visiting. We made a little trip to Aigburth, three hours from the city, along beautiful hills and valleys, glittering in fresh greenery, affording the traveler opportunity to admire the wonderful works of Providence.

We were at least awed by the wonderful locations where the cattle grazed. We rode back in a carriage drawn by four horses which galloped back to the city. And what do you think a regal visit like that cost? Thirty cents, my friend. On a little tour like that one must stand amazed to see the many beauties he observes. A person sees a variety of colors near a city. As Lady Henrietta glides by dressed in finery on her spirited steed, a little farther on you see the poor Anna, with a little pipe in her mouth, stumbling by on her donkey.

On the evening of March 11, we had a experience which worried everyone. We had just returned when the fire alarm sounded in our ears. People streamed in from all directions and we too went to the scene of the fire. It was a sugar factory about 300 feet long, 50 feet wide and 40 feet high which was ablaze. The flames rose in a terrifying manner, but it was more terrifying to discover a person on the roof of the factory, who had little choice, either to be burned alive or to meet almost certain death by jumping down. The unfortunate victim chose the latter, jumped down and lay dead on the spot. Three others lost their lives there. With the use of a fire hose, and as a result of the exemplary actions of the police, the fire was, however, soon extinguished and the damage was limited to the upper part of the factory.

Finally the day approached upon which we left for the ship, to be taken aboard, the account of which we wish to begin the next chapter.

Chapter II
1. Boarding. Departure. The beginning of the sea journey. Storm.

Early in the morning of March 21 we were taken aboard. Our baggage was not handled as well as we might have wished, but that is the usual manner of the sea folk. As far as the ship is concerned, it was a fine 3-master, called *William and Mary*, 500 English ton, and famous for its speed. But between decks we really had poor light, which is quite common for those large ships. The name of the Captain was Stinson, a man with a fine seaman's appearance; but in his bearing there was something which I might properly call American pride which was apparent and often noticed in the seamen.

The cargo consisted of iron ore which certainly could be most easily stored, and also our baggage and provisions, of which every emigrant on a ship must take an ample supply, because such a journey by sea can be very uncertain as to its duration.

Among the ship's company there were 86 Friesians, a hundred English and Irish, and 12 Germans. The Friesians and Germans were separated from the others. The number of Friesians had been reduced by 6 persons, and I surely do not have to tell you who they were. You only need to know that they were a man and his wife and four children who had been advised in Liverpool to return to the Fatherland. For what reason they decided to do so I do not know; but I suppose it was because they did not like the trip to Liverpool, or most likely it was a whim of the moment. At least I know that the Captain and crew of the ship *Jupiter* conducted themselves very badly in this matter.

On the morning of March 23 we were towed from the dock up the river by a steamboat. There a doctor came aboard who declared all passengers to be fit to make the trip. We left on the 24th, again towed by a boat and left that city, whose only means of support is its trade. In the forenoon the boat returned and we sailed along with a good northeaster along the chalk cliffs on the coast of England, which displayed a profusion of lights and shadows.

It was the first time we saw the sun disappear behind the waves, which is one of the most beautiful sights one can imagine in nature. The following morning it reappeared beautifully in the waves to the east, and we floated along slowly because there was almost no wind. The motion of the ship soon caused people to become seasick but I and a few others were spared.

In the evening we went to bed to go to sleep very soon as if we were rocked in a cradle. But, no! At three o'clock at night there was a cry, "Oh, Lord, we perish! To the life rafts! To the life rafts!" Such was the cry of distress in the dead of night. Almost all of the passengers were awakened, and in what kind of situation do you suppose we found ourselves? Eight strong muscular young fellows sleeping on four upper berths rolled among those sleeping below them and paid them an unexpected visit. They raised the cry mentioned above.

The next morning (March 26) we lost sight of the coasts of England and Ireland and we were on the Atlantic Ocean. The important event of that day was that an Irish woman gave birth to a healthy daughter, of whom the father was being sought. Our doctor and mid-wife came in handy then.

It is really no wonder that in England the people label the Irish as cattle. At least, this woman did not exhibit much in the way of human traits, because when our doctor asked her about her condition the next morning, and if she needed anything, he received the answer that she was in need of nothing. She had an abundant supply of something to drink. But what do you suppose she had to drink? Whiskey, my reader, being a very intoxicating drink, which she had been drinking like water. That evening we were entertained again as two Germans humorously reviewed the scene of the previous night.

Truly, a person faces entirely different circumstances and has different reflections on a trip, for, as we awoke in the morning, the sun rose with great splendor on the eastern horizon. The immeasurable expanse of water appeared calm and smooth and it seemed that nature was making every effort to add to the luster of the Lord's resurrection. Gradually the keel turned to the south. Toward evening, however, the wind became stronger so that we could soon call it a moderate storm.

The next morning the waves increased gradually until they became enormous masses of water, which worried the inexperienced passenger. Then one finds a faint description of the entire scene in the following poem:

On March 29 we had two people suffering from nerve fevers and a few with bad colds. For the former the sea is not much of a help because of the constant tossing of the ship. The following morning we awoke with alarm, when one of those who were ill was snatched away by death from his mourning family. The crying of both of the parents, brothers and sisters was too heartrending for my pen to describe. In time we lost more members in our party. You will find a list of the names at the end of this booklet.

2. Hurricane. Arguments regarding the long trip. Fighting.

On the morning of March 31 we had to cope with another storm. In the afternoon then it turned northwest followed by a hurricane too terrible for me to describe adequately with my pen. Under such circumstances the emigrant has many inconveniences, since it is almost impossible to be on deck, and much less prepare anything to eat or drink. And one person can make adjustments much more readily than another.

At least, on April 6 my attention was drawn to the wife of a man, who people call "?" and a couple who were a good match. The appearance of the man is not very pleasant. With Chinese eyes, a somewhat crooked Napoleonic nose, he assumes the attitude of someone, who, according to Lavater's physiognomy, was not guilty of the July revolution of Paris. Of the 24 hours, he lies in bed 22. The other two he spends eating and drinking and, of course, taking care of natural necessities.

On April 7 we were at 45 degrees north latitude and 20 degrees west longitude from Greenwich. From this you can infer that our trip was not too prosperous. We made better time during the day. We sailed 10 English miles per hour, that is 240 in a day, being a distance of 80 hours or 4 degrees.

On April 10 my attention was drawn to the quiet movements of the crew. No work was done on the ship and the sailor sat quietly reading his testament. From this you can conclude that the Sabbath is observed in quiet reverence by English crews. The next day we were near the Azores Islands. Again our number was increased, when an Irish gave birth to a healthy daughter. Those Irish! Those Irish, they are certainly a peculiar people. I recently read the following in a book by a famous English author, "a group of Irishmen were driven to the coast by a barbaric government 200 years ago, and have as a result of hardships or rough treatment developed the following characteristics: repelling facial features, protruding jaws, a broad open mouth, stubby nose, bulging cheek bones and bow legs." And it would not surprise me but what we had some of these creatures in our ship's company.

On April 12 the captain said we had covered 900 English miles in 5 days. Notwithstanding we heard a great deal of argumentation about the duration of the passage. One of our people, not exactly the inventor of the steam engine, says: We will arrive in New Orleans on Sunday night and from here it is eight more days of travel to Michigan. This is according to a laborer. The next day ship's rations were distributed. You know we had ordered half of our board for as long as the trip lasted. Once a week provisions were distributed, and in such a way that a half of the ordered portion stuck to the fingers of those doing the distributing which was all loot for the Captain and mates. This time one of our people was not satisfied and he accused the first mate of being a thief which prompted the latter to start a fight.

Another member of our party joined in, and he received a greeting which was not welcome. He placed his hand on his knife but at that moment the captain interfered and the parties were more or less satisfied. The emotions varied greatly during the fight, because some women cried: "He will get killed, he will get killed" while several young men took advantage of the sugar barrel which had been left unguarded by the sailors in order to help the mate. We had more of such scenes so you, my readers can conclude that in America such things are not taken seriously while in the Netherlands the law makes it practically impossible to engage in them.

Sometimes the people had enjoyable moments also when we entertained ourselves with music or in other ways. One evening, at the request of the Captain, a Friesian girl was dressed in national or rather provincial clothing, and presented to him, which he, the mates and others enjoyed very much. They were especially impressed by the gold ear pieces with the lace bonnet. The Captain called her "a soldier with a southwester." The gold ear piece he said was the helmet and the southwester, that you can easily guess.

On April 24 we were at 41 ½ degrees north latitude and 52 ½ west longitude from Greenwich. I noticed that the Captain does a great deal in the way of caring for the sick. The man had little or no knowledge of natural science nor chemistry; but his practical ability was dependent upon a small book, which among other things contains the statement that in case of a fever it is sometimes advisable to eat bacon. Before he would visit his patients he would study in this his trustworthy guide. Herewith I close the paragraph and wish to begin another, richer in the reporting of events, but sadder as to contents.

3. Land. Shipwreck. The night the Captain leaves us. The second night. Severe weather. Rescue. Bahama Islands

That night of May 2 and 3 was one of joy and fear. It was 12 o'clock when the ship's guard was on the alert. And why? Because they expected to sight land at any moment. We were sailing straight west with a strong north wind and had only 3 or 4 ship lengths to go before striking the Bahama shore, and face certain death. But as soon as land was in sight, the Captain rushed to the helm, and in a moment turned to prow to the southwest and we were saved.

I thought about the responsibility a seaman has at a time like that, and for the first time realized how important it is to abstain from the use of strong drink. I was glad the Captain did not have liquor on the ship for the crew, because, how many shipwrecks are caused by human indulgence in that beast-like lust, is a secret which some day will be revealed (Footnote: the author is a member of the society for the abstinence from the use of liquor, being the former secretary of the Arun division. Publisher)

But you ask (with the map available for the reader), "How could you have the Bahamas before you?" You must realize, my friend, that the crew had continued to go south, so that it was not possible to sail along the north side of the island, into the New Bahama Canal, but where the gulf was available to us. I just said that the wind was from the north so we could not reach the proper channel without difficulty. The only approach possible would be to turn back and then sail in. But, alas, the captain did not wish to turn back, so he followed a southeast course in order to enter into the New Bahama canal.

On the morning of May 3 we saw a few islands, including a coast of elbow key, but, of course, at our right, and then headed west, when we found ourselves in the Providence canal. It was certainly hazardous for the Captain to enter a canal 20 ft. deep with a vessel drawing 17 ft. of water. Only one hidden rock at 3 feet would be enough to determine our eternal destiny. And, sure enough, we discovered that our Captain had miscalculated, when the keel scraped along the hard sand of Isaac's bank at 9 o'clock in the evening with a loud crackling sound, in my estimation near the Bemin islands. We noticed that the bottom was clearly damaged. Everyone expected to perish at once. The cries and scramble were terrible. Then some people leaped into the lifeboat, so that the iron sides, with a diameter of 5 Netherland inches, bent like a reed, others climbed into the masts, at another point a lifeboat was lowered, in order to inspect the damage, as they said, and between decks people almost crowded one another in order to rush up the stairs.

At around midnight the shocks of the keel lessened somewhat and we reached open water. The damage to the bottom was not so serious that we could not keep the vessel afloat with pumps for quite some time. The Captain seemed to think otherwise, at least he tried all night to get into the lifeboat which was drifting in the sea a short distance from us. He was continually prevented by the crowding of the people.

The pumping was zealously continued throughout the night which saved our lives, because, when the Captain left us the next morning, this was our only chance for survival. He conducted himself in a very selfish manner. He has said a short time before that, "If you pump you will live, if you do not pump, I will leave you to your fate." And in spite of the fact that they all continued to pump enthusiastically, he got into the lifeboat which had cruised around the ship all night. He took advantage of a suitable opportunity, namely, at the very moment when the large boat was being lowered into the water - at the very moment when many were eager to leap into it – at the very moment that a man drowned – at the very moment that another young man who missed the boat but still attempted to climb into it, lost his fingers when a rude crew member made use of an axe, and drowned as a result – at the very moment that a woman was thrown from the boat into the water, who was bewailing the fate of those who were drowning, with sympathetic tears, and similarly became the victim of those monsters – at the very moment when a man parted from his wife and children forever – at the very moment.....but why recall more of the horrors? Only because I wish to write in detail, I must do so.

Three Friesians jumped into the large boat, namely, O. Wagenaar from 't Heerenveen, U. Bergsma from Kimswerd, and J. Roorda from Dantumawoude, plus 17 Irish and Englishmen, 3 Germans, and 4 sailors. (Footnote: these people were shortly thereafter picked up by an American ship, the Pulluck, Captain Entyre, and on June 6, 1853 brought to Liverpool.)

Before the Captain left, he had dropped the anchor in order that we might not be witnesses of his evil deed, having become victims of the waves. Soon both lifeboats were out of sight and there were only 4 sailors left who could be of great service to us. But we soon discovered they had little regard for us, as they had lost their common sense. They had, that is, partaken freely of that liquor, which turns a person into a beast. One of the Germans had been foolish enough to give it to them.

We cut the anchors and considered it to be wise, under the circumstances, to make rafts on which we could spend our final moments, when the ship sank. We raised the distress signal and looked around to see if we could discover land or a ship here or there. Finally we saw a 3- master; but, alas, as happy as we were to see it appear, we were disappointed to see it disappear. Then evening approached, as the weather became more unfavorable. The scene became more dreadful as the storming elements were covered by the drape of the night, when the thunder rolled, the lightning flashed, the storm wind howled, and the rain pelted down. The anxiety of the passengers was so great that many tied themselves to the raft with ropes, awaiting death there. Among others there was a young English woman who greatly aroused everyone's pity. During the previous morning her husband had disappeared with the lifeboat, at the time when she, during the anxious moments gave birth to a child prematurely. We decided to see our lives at the highest possible price and pumped on.

Finally May 5 dawned, the day commemorating the Lord's ascension. And it was upon that day that we experienced His wise, invisible hand extended in a wonderful way. Namely, when we were filled with gratitude, as we saw land in the early morning, and later a ship. Oh! How eagerly every eye was fixed upon the horizon from whence help was anticipated. And a few moments later you should have seen the tears of joy flow as the aforesaid ship turned toward us. It was an English wreck master, the schooner the *Oracle*, Captain Roberts Sands (a negro) from the Bahama Islands. The women and children were immediately transferred and afterwards the men.

We were obliged to abandon all of our baggage but that was a matter of minor concern. Our only aim and desire was to save our lives and to that end Providence granted evident aid. The crew cruised around the irretrievable ship all day to salvage as much as possible, all of which would be loot for the Captain of the schooner.

In the evening the Friesians and Germans were put ashore on the Great Bahama Island, the island we had discovered in the morning. We wish to close this paragraph herewith, the contents of which remain vividly in our memory, and begin the one following.

4. Stay on Great Bahama Island. Boarding and trip to Nassau. Stay there and trip to New Orleans.

"Where are we?" That was the first question we asked each other, because at that time we did not know the name of the island. Each person armed himself with something with which to defend himself in case of need. Some of the people rested under the open sky while the others kept watch. And, behold, soon we were surrounded by enemies. Unashamed they attacked our camp from all sides, and, regardless of how we defended ourselves, still several were wounded. But I do not wish to prolong your curiosity any longer – those enemies were not human. Mosquitoes, a kind of fly, which in a warm climate often attack a traveler, so that the entire head and hands are covered by their somewhat poisonous stings.

On the morning of May 6 a few of us went on a reconnoitering trip, and, because of the density of the underbrush, which covered the entire island, following the rocks along the shore. Soon we met someone on the other side of the island who approached us peacefully. It was fortunately an agent of the chief officer of the island who apparently had been informed about our situation. He accompanied us to our lodging place and inquired further about what had taken place. Our water and ship's biscuits were soon supplied, which was a treat for us, such as we had never tasted before. Frequently, fishermen came by who furnished some refreshing food.

In the afternoon we made another little trip along the coast and found buildings which are like those in some areas of North Brabant. They were occupied by white and negroes, all of them being friendly toward us serving us hospitably with meal cake, fish and pork, and refused to accept anything for it. I was especially amused by a woman who was sitting on a rocking chair, rocking herself with one foot and her child with the other.

On that day our deserted ship really sank. The people who had remained on it to pump, Friesians among them, leaped into one of the lifeboats of the schooner. One of our people, had because of confusion, not followed the others and sank with the ship into the sea. He surely would have drowned had he not been grabbed immediately when he came up unconscious.

At night we again camped under the open sky, and the next morning a few were called for, who, at the request of the aforesaid agent, sailed to the city of Nassau (on the island of New Providence) where several consults lived. Their route is shown on the map by the letter B. The rest of the people (myself among them), a total of 44, remained on the island that day, and refreshed themselves with oysters and clear spring water. The next night we were taken on two vessels to follow the course indicated on the map by the letter c.

Provisions were bought from time to time, although there is not much to be had anywhere; it must all be brought from Nassau. The inhabitants of the Bahama Islands live very poorly so there are no wealthy merchants. All of the Bahama Islands are under British rule. There are no slaves; the negro is just as free and independent as the white resident.

The meals on our little ship consisted of buckwheat and bacon, fish and turtle soup. Occasionally we were allowed to go ashore once in a while, where a white inhabitant, among other things, told me that there 215 people had been shipwrecked in two months, all of whom were taken to New Orleans by way of Nassau. From that ship the Captain was not the first but the last to leave the ship.

So we progressed until the evening of May 12 when we sighted Nassau. The view of the newly built city was beautiful, undoubtedly enhanced by the sparkling evening sun – for us who had been separated from social life for fifty days. On the morning of May 13 we were put ashore and conducted to a well organized building where we were refreshed with food and drink. Then we were glad we had not leaped into the boat, because our situation was certainly more favorable than that of the three Friesians. Besides, we had a few extra clothes, while I had seen one of those who left dressed in trousers held up by a rope, without a coat or vest, with one and a half of a wooden shoe, and without provisions for such an uncertain trip.

The island of New Providence belongs to the Bahama Islands and belongs to the English government. The inhabitants belong to the white and negro races, or rather copper colored, and make a good living. They showed a very generous attitude toward us and provided for needs with money they had collected. Everyone there seems to take pride in doing something for others, and their deeds have the mark of a Christian religion which they profess. There are Baptists, Episcopalians, Quakers, etc. On Sunday, May 15, we visited one of the churches and on Pentecost we were able, with the congregation to offer our silent prayers to Him who had so remarkably saved us when our souls were oppressed by the fear of death.

Among the interesting things to see in the city is the statue of Columbus. On the base is inscribed "Columbus" and just below it "1492" the year in which that great man discovered America and as a result opened a rich source of prosperity for the inhabitants of the old world. It was a little to the east where we first set our foot on the coast of the island of St. Salvador. A bit farther on there was the fort called "Charlotte" which had been completely hewn from a rock with a number of underground passages and rooms and certainly may be called a masterpiece of fortress architecture. I was shown, among other things, the underground room in which the governor hid when the fort was surrendered to the English.

The expense of our stay was charged to the account of the owner of the lost ship, and that amounted to quite a total, when you figure: 1 pound of bread, 1 pound of beef or pork, 3 ounces of rice, 1 ounce of sugar and ½ ounce of coffee per person, per day for 200 people. Besides the inhabitants distributed to each individual: 1 white jacket and trousers, 1 shirt, 1 hat and 1 pair of shoes, and in addition to all of that we received 1 dollar a piece when we left.

June 1 was the day of our departure and, after having had the doctor on board, we set out to sea with a strong north east wind. It was then a great deal more peaceful on the ship than usual since the Irish left on another schooner. Some twenty Irish and German, who were to be picked up later, remained. During the night of June 1 and 2 we sailed around the northern corner of the Barbary Islands and then followed a course to the southwest, as you will see on the map, the line marked with the letter d.

The following night we passed a lighthouse located on one of the group of islands of the Salk Key Banks, and by noon on June 3 we were in its Gulf of Mexico. The next night at about 3 o'clock we sailed around the last of those islands which surround Florida, when we sailed straight northwest up the Mississippi. I must include at this point something which is reprehensible for every Friesian in the 19th century. June 5 was, that is, the Lord's Day which it behooves every human being to spend in quiet reverence. And what do you suppose the captain said to me? "It surprises me that your people are not reading the Bible today." You probably wonder what our people were really doing. Well, they were lying on the deck practically all day, like cattle in a pasture. In the case of only a few did a sense of religion have sufficient power to move them to take the best of all books, the faithful guide on the often difficult pathway of live, in hand. Truly, my reader! I have often remarked that we are far behind the English in the matter of strictly observing the Sabbath. Even many a colored person puts us to shame in this respect.

On Tuesday, June 7 we saw a lighthouse on the Mississippi in the quiet of the morning when we were still 2 or 3 hours from it. A river boat was cruising around to take ships up the river, and took us in tow. Soon we reached the desired shores, and herewith we wish to end this chapter, being the end of the sea journey, and begin another.

Chapter III
1. The Mississippi River. Orleans. Trip to St. Louis.

It was, as I have stated, on June 8 that we sailed into the Mississippi River. Its mouth is almost 400 feet wide there and covered with reeds or other green growth. We were towed up the river for about three hours, when the boat returned to find other ships. There we cast out the anchor and stayed until evening when the boat returned with a 3 master. 3 ships were taken up the river.

We stared about at the beautiful river bands, which were there decked in a luxurious green and lovely woods, presenting a beautiful scene. Now and then we would collide with a large tree trunk many of which float down the river, when the women would moan, again, thinking that the rocks of the Bahama Bank were also found in the Mississippi. During the night the machine stopped but that was soon remedied. In the meantime the boat became so entangled in the branches of a gigantic willow that axes had to be used to free it.

The following morning I heard from the Captain that the small boat with the crew of the William and Mary had been rescued and that the people were in an American port. The Captain had made a report regarding the shipwreck, and the following appeared in the newspaper: "The ship William and Mary went aground near the Bahama Islands. A total of 200 passengers died in the waves. Only the captain and a few members of the crew saved themselves in life boats. The ship sank so fast that the Captain had difficulty in leaving it." As soon as we heard that, our Captain sent a telegram to New Orleans reporting that the so-called lost passengers were coming up the river.

On June 9 we again came into picturesque areas, interspersed with sugar plantations and beautiful woods, while here and there new villages arose or were being enlarged. There was evidence everywhere of wealth and prosperity. I have as yet not seen poverty in America. If one has ambition he need have no fear of want, because a laborer or tradesman earns twice as much here as he does in Friesland and can live just as cheaply.

So we traveled on into the night until we arrived at New Orleans. When the morning of June 10 dawned, that capital of the business of the southern states lay before us. In the golden rays of the morning sun the scene was beautiful. Those colossal, mostly white buildings, those hundreds of gigantic steamboats, and those luxurious banks on each side of the winding river, presented an unsurpassable scene.

There is a great deal of activity on the river bank. Often you are carried away in your imagination to former times or other countries, and you think of yourself as being in places, of which history alone speaks, when a boat lies prepared to leave for Alexandria, Cairo, Memphis or Bethlehem in one place, and in another one is leaving for Amsterdam, Waterloo or Moscow, all of the cities located in the United States, and yonder another of 250 horse power sailing for Rome and Milan. We were taken further into the city where we looked for an opportunity to leave for St. Louis.

There is a German society which aids immigrants there, of which a representative was very helpful to us, so that we were able to leave the city the following day. As a result of his services we each received $5.50 and provisions for the trip from the municipality, amounting to a total of $440.

On the evening of June 11 everyone was busy preparing to go aboard. It is an interesting sight to see such a busy moment. The free American, the staid Englishman, the congenial German, the vivacious Frenchman and the lumbering Spaniard there loose all their characteristics and look for a place on the boats. Here one will see a group of immigrants arriving, and there an American hunter with a ham on his shoulder with a fine dog walking at his side, who has his eye on the ham rather than on its master.

New Orleans has real clean streets and beautiful buildings. Among others, I was shown a building which was being erected to serve as a stock exchange and a bank, etc. The cost amounted to 25 million dollars, one million for the laying of the foundation. However, where the city is not as built up, there are also streets which seem to call to the traveler, "Come and help us!" At six o'clock the boat whistle announced the time for departure and we left this first of the southern states in good spirits.

We saw beautiful scenery during the following days along the river banks, which were adorned everywhere in the beautiful green of spring. At one time we would see fine plantations and then stately oak forests and then once again dense woods down to the river band, yes, even 20 to 30 feet into the river. I did not tire of that river voyage; those thousand turns each presented something of interest every minute. First we came to the city of Baton Rouge with its 3000 inhabitants, situated on a hill 30 to 40 feet high, the prosperous village of Waterloo, where we took on wood for the boat. There I witnessed something interesting. A few Americans were urging a slave who was working there to flee with the boat in order to enjoy a life of freedom. And the latter took advantage of the opportunity, about which many of the people were pleased; because every American says, "a person is a free being," and

19

many attempt to promote that by word and deed. Others on the other hand agree with a former famous American who said, "I will devote every heart beat to abolition" but they frequently forget to act accordingly. And, that is why slave trade continues in the southern states.

On June 13 we passed the city of Natchez, a French settlement with 8000 inhabitants. The river is from 90 to 300 feet deep there. The boat stopped there temporarily, so we had an opportunity to enjoy some refreshments. We noticed that the merchants here not only make a living but have a profitable business – because in New Orleans a person would pay 12 cents for a bottle of wine and here 25 cents.

On the morning of June 14 we did not have 300 feet of water under the keel but only 5 to 6 feet, when we became stuck on a sand bank. Soon we were freed from it, and we found ourselves a short time later at Vicksburg, a city with 5000 inhabitants, romantically situated on a hill 300 feet high. There the people have rich plantations. On the evening of the next day we came to the prosperous little cities of Napoleon and Victoria in the following morning to Helena. During the night of June 16 and 17 we passed Memphis, a very prosperous city of 12,000 inhabitants.

A short time prior to that a passenger had been caught stealing. He had very cleverly taken a wallet from the pocket of a person who was sleeping, which the mate fortunately saw and had him tied up. After he had been given a stern lecture about the dastardly nature of what he had come, he was freed upon condition that he would not leave the boat. But he did not seem to feel comfortable, because when we were near shore the next morning he jumped into the river and swam to shore.

On that day the boiler was out of order, and also the propeller, which suffers a great deal of damage because of the tree trunks which float down the river and often get under it. We were obliged to stop all night until it had been repaired. There are members of many different trades on a ship who earn a good wage. Among others, the carpenter earned $40 a month.

On the evening of June 18 we were at New Madrid, a small city of 500 inhabitants, which was formerly located high on a rock, but in an earthquake in 1800 it sank down. The next day we passed along lime and iron banks on the latter of which the city of Columbus is located. In the forenoon we were at the Ohio River and landed at Cairo. On June 20 we traveled on all day along hills 300 to 400 feet high covered by tall and shorter woods and in the early morning of June 21 reached the city of St. Louis.

2. St. Louis. The further trip on the river. Galena. Prairie la Crosse.

There lies the new city with its beautiful buildings to which a total of 200 ships have connections. This is the center of the trade of the great Mississippi, which can possibly soon equal the sea traffic of Liverpool. Among its numerous hotels we moved into a German inn, where we were not treated very cordially. It was even so bad that the manager wished to have his money in advance, after which we went to a French hotel and enjoyed far better treatment.

A person always notices that the native American is the most honest man of all the nationalities which are found all over the country. The younger immigrants think too much of the American motto "To make money" and often expect too much from the advantages of the country.

St. Louis can certainly be called a beautiful city, especially when one considers that it was originally built in 1764 (??). On the many cross streets here are colossal and exceptionally beautiful buildings which were constructed according to its own architectural plan. The ordinary barbershop, in its beauty, rivals that of Sinkel in Leeuwaarden. The population totals 82,744. In 1840 it had 16,000 inhabitants.

On the way up the river we met several steamboats, one larger than the other. The river boats do not look much like vessels when you see them lying at a distance. Only by the colossal smoke stack would you identify it. Imagine a large flat bottomed boat with its highest point 2 or 3 feet above water level, upon which a castle had been built, for which the beloved French emperor would not have to be ashamed, then you can form somewhat of an idea of what these steamboats look like.

Of all the steamers the *Isaac Newton* is the largest in the world. It is 445 feet long and 85 feet wide, which corresponds to the Albany and New York. A person is surprised at the speed of some of the river boats which you can infer from the following: The distance from St. Paul to Galena is 385 English miles or 128 hours and 20 minutes, and this distance is covered by the *West Newton* in 24 hours and 7 minutes.

We stayed there 5 days, and, after having purchased necessary supplies, we left on June 25 with a boat to the city of Galena, in Northern Illinois. By the morning of June 26 we had already passed the Missouri River, and we were in the clear Mississippi water, which up to that time had been effected by the muddy waters of that branch. We passed the beautiful cities of Hannibal, Quincy, and the adjoining Nauvoo, settled by Jews.

On the 27th of that month we were in Burlington, the former capital city of Iowa, being favorably and beautifully situated for trade. The following morning we passed by Davenport, a new city with 2000 inhabitants, where someone standing on the river bank asked us, "Where are you from?" I knew very well where he was from and answered his unexpected question. "I am from Wolvegae," he said. He was the first Friesian we met in America. We had already met many Hollanders in the different cities.

We reached Galena early in the morning of June 29, where we remained for some time. The city is located on the Fever River, being a branch of the Mississippi. There are several hills in and around it which give it a romantic appearance, and which contain lead mines and assure the residents of a good living.

The next day (June 30) we left, the wives and children remaining there in order to look for a suitable place for a settlement and to build a few cabins. We passed Dubuque, beautifully situated between high bluffs and the river and at noon the next day were in Prairie la Crosse. It is a new city or only the plan for one, with a church, several stores and other buildings. Until 7 years ago it was an uninhabited prairie. A Mr. Levi, a Jew, bought this area at a small price and now is playing a money-making role selling it.

In the evening we looked over part of the area, but found it to be more favorable as a place to build a city than it would be for farming, because of the amount of sand found in the soil. Because of Mr. Bonnema's illness we could not make another trip until July 5.

Across the Mississippi a person would enter Minnesota, which was not as yet surveyed, and the next evening news arrived that exceptionally good land had been found, but unsuited for the shipment of products. On the 7th another area, south of the city, on this side of the river was visited. There also a lack of communication was noted. On the 9th Minnesota was visited again and Mr. Bonnema bought a house with 80 acres of land, 3 miles from the river, upon the advice of a German.

On July 13th I meanwhile went to the city of Anna Losky, seven miles to the north on the Black River. It is a beautiful location, on a high level, situated between bluffs and the river, two hours eastward. At a distance of three miles from here there is still exceptionally good land which has not yet been sold. A Dutch gentleman regulates matters here where a year ago there was no one. Our plan is to move to the new land on July 15, and in this we have reached the end of our pilgrim's journey, with which we wish to bring our booklet to its close.

According to later news received from Hendrickus de Boer, dated July 25, Mr. Bonnema has purchased an additional 800 acres.

From the Dutch colony of Sheboygan (North America) someone wrote on August 2 that the 66 Friesians who remain of the 86 who were on the ship *William and Mary* when it was wrecked on the coast of Florida, have bought farms in the fertile area at Black River, in La Crosse County, and have settled there. That is the 5th Dutch settlement in Wisconsin; La Crosse is situated on the township and county of the same name on the Mississippi River, and since a few years ago has arisen as if by magic out of the wilderness.

◆◆◆◆◆◆

[The following two letters were written by other passengers on the voyage with Oepke Bonnema.]

1853
Dear parents, brothers and sisters!

I can inform you that by God's grace I am still healthy and well, and hope you will receive this letter in good health. I think you have probably been looking eagerly for a letter. It is fortunate that you can receive these letters from me, for we have experienced a great deal during our immigration from Lowestoft on February 28. From there we went by train to Liverpool, and arrived and Liverpool on Mary 1. Then, as planned with Mr. Bonnema, we were to go by steamboat to North America.

The steamboat was not able to take on more passengers, so we had to stay in Liverpool three weeks. Then we left on a sailing vessel for New Orleans. The name of our ship, a three-master, was *William and Mary*. We left on March 24, through the English Channel, and everything was fine until May 3.

In the evening the ship struck a rock, and soon there was some leakage, and we could already see the water. Everyone was terribly frightened about such a collision against a rock, and we were all in fear of death. We saw nothing in store for us than death. For if there was no escape we would all have our grave in the waves, and no one saw a chance of being rescued.

On May 4, at 2 o'clock in the afternoon, we saw a ship in the distance, but unfortunately it did not see us and it sailed on. You must realize, and I can assure you, that anyone who is in that kind of danger does not escape, for we would have to be rescued by another ship or drown – this we realized very well.

But, we had better see what we can do. We had better pump as long as we can. Our captain seemed to be such a fine man judging outwardly. But on May 4, at 5 o'clock in the morning, the captain and eight sailors got into a life-boat, set out on the ocean, took off his hat and said, "Friends, may you fare well." Then we saw another life-boat with four sailors, and seven natives and three Germans and three of our people. One of them was Ulbo Bergsma from Kimswert, one was from 't Heerenveen, and one was from Wouden. But, where they landed we do not know.

But between the night of May 4 and 5 we had a severe storm with heavy thunder and rain. Suddenly God caused the wind to die down and we had the finest weather in the world, and the sea was as smooth as glass. On the same day, May 5, at 11 o'clock, we saw a ship approaching in the distance, and fortunately it saw us and knew we were in trouble. It rescued us from danger.

Now you will wonder what became of our things. Our trunks and all of our clothes are partially gone. There were approximately 200 passengers on the ship, and now we were on the other ship, and it brought us to the island of the Bahamas where there was not much to eat. Then we were on the island for two days, and from there to Nassau where we had to stay for three weeks. There we all received clothing and free board for three weeks, and each a pair of shoes, and besides, each one of us 2.40 cents because a collection had been taken in the churches. For all of us $400, and for each an English testament, for the people are very religious everywhere. They sell nothing on Sunday, and worship faithfully in the churches and in the homes. Yes, in our Friesland they would have had to clothe 200 people and in addition raise two gulden and forty cents, you must understand. And it is such a small island; and I know this very well, that anyone in Friesland who has much cannot spare much, but we had better add: more and more, to satisfy the money chest is the desire of most people

We met several black people on that island and they are the best people of all. They would give the clothes off their backs for poor seamen. Then we left Nassau on two ships for New Orleans. There each individual received $5.50 and food for ten days on the steamboat going to St. Louis. Ten dollars is equivalent to two gulden and 50 cents in Dutch money. Our larger three-master suddenly sunk on May 6, where there was 200 feet of water and it was wrecked.

Now our belongings were all gone, but it is better to lose our things there than to have all of us lose our lives. Boat trips like that, to my mind, do not leave one unaffected, for we have suffered a great deal from the cold, and also from a lack of food. For in the island of Bahamas there was not enough for so many people. Now we were on a ship 4 or 5 days on the way to Nassau. Things looked quite bad there. But our crew soon began fishing and soon had large quantities of fish. We arrived in Nassau with little difficulty. Where I stepped ashore the ship had more than 20 feet of water, and some of the trunks were already floating around, and it was a completely mixed up mess, as you can well imagine. We have all had an expensive trip. But, I do believe that if God will give us health, we will soon recover.

Then we went to New Orleans, and from there to Galena, and from Galena to Le Gras (LaCrosse), where we will probably settle, but that I do not know for sure. We lost sixteen individuals, adults and children, at sea, all unknown. Johannes Steema and his wife and children are all well. And, Piet Zalverda also, and Jan Janssen too, and also G.J. Jansonius. I think I will like living here. Americans eat pork three times a day, and beef, and that is a bright prospect for me.

Write to me about all circumstances, and how the crops look in Friesland, and the flax lands. I read in the papers that the Catholics have increased in number considerably and their influence is being felt.

The trip was quite difficult as everyone can truthfully say. But it is not for a single person. I know also that all emigrants do not have the experience like we had, and I also know this, that it could be much worse for many lost their lives at sea, and we are all still alive, except for three natives. As they attempted to jump into the life boats, they jumped into the ocean and drowned. For they all wanted to get into the life boat and that did look rather dangerous to me, due to being without food and water in the boat, and then to let it drift before God's wind and weather. So we decided to remain in our larger boat as long as possible, and God

24

rescued us all.

Now I will stop with the pen but not with the heart.

Your son,
Hendrick Jans Kas

You may tell Karel Spanjer that Hendrik Spanjer died on the ship.
Regards to all friends and acquaintances.

◆◆◆◆◆◆

Dear brothers, sisters, uncles and aunts:

I wish to inform you that I am healthy and well and wish the same of you. You will certainly know about the shipwreck, but the good God saved us all.

I now plan to write you a letter when we are at our destination, for where we settle we still do not know. You can well imagine that we are eager to hear any news from Friesland; what the situation is there. Then I can give you the address you must use when you write. Regards to friends and acquaintances. The pens are not as good here as in Friesland.

Your sister,
Grietje Jans Jansonius

◆◆◆◆◆◆

Record of Voyage from Netherlands to Milwaukee
By Grandpa John Remeeus
Translated by Herman Bottema, February 1928

Short description of our trip from Middelburg, province of Zeeland, Kingdom of the Netherlands, to Milwaukee, State of Wisconsin, United States of America, in the year 1854.

[Johannes Remeeus was born in 3 February 1815 in Veere, Zeeland to Karel Remeeus and Helena Hulst. On 13 May 1836 in Middelburg, Zeeland he married Jacoba Helena Burck. Jacoba was born 1 January 1815 in Amsterdam to Jan Fredrik Burck and Leijntje Schietekatte. This diary was first published in *Wisconsin Magazine of History*, XXX (1946).]

Members of the family were as follows:
Father: Johannes Remeeus – age 39
Mother: Jacoba Helena Remeeus (Burck) – age 39
Five children:
Anna Caterina Remeeus – age 17 (b. 6 May 1837 Middelburg)
Helena Johanna – age 11 (b. 21 December 1843 Middelburg)
Caterina Jacoba – age 5 (b. 30 December 1848 Middelburg)
Dina Antonia – age 3 (b. 26 April 1851 Middelburg)
Jan Frederick – age 6 months (b. 25 November 1853 Middelburg. Birth record lists his name as Frederik Karel)

In memory to our children.

It was in the evening of May 30th, 1854, that we left Middelburg for Flushing, after having taken leave of absence of our dear and kind friends one cannot easily forget. The reason we left in the evening was because the steamer for Antwerp leaves early in the morning. We slept that night on board the steamer. The next morning at 4 o'clock the boat left for Antwerp (Belgium), at which port we arrived the same morning at 10 o'clock.

When we arrived at Antwerp, servants were already waiting for us. They brought us to the office of the steamship company. However, we soon found out that they did not have so very much respect for emigrants. Soon I saw that they imposed upon us by charging us 7 guilders each more for the trip across the ocean, and there was no redress. Albeit, Mr. Straus and I had in the month of April, entered into a verbal agreement as to the price to be paid for our passage. You can imagine that this was a great hardship for me because our purse was very slender. Money became scarce, indeed later in traveling through America we were in actual want of it. Meanwhile, our baggage was brought from the steamer's hold and piled with others on the dock to be stowed away on the ship which was to bring us to the promised land.

In the afternoon, we repaired to a hotel which was built exclusively for emigrants. 2700 people, mostly Germans, were there at the time waiting for ships to take them to America. The winds had been blowing for weeks out of the wrong direction, hence no boats had entered the harbors of Holland, Belgium or Germany.

After we had enjoyed our meat, every man had to help to bring the trunks, boxes, etc. on board the ship. We got the authority to provide our sleeping quarters in as suitable a manner as we chose. The ladies in company of Messrs. Westvan, Snoep and the agent of the line, Messieur Vermeulen, went to see the sights of the town. I was kept busy all afternoon fixing up my berth. I used a course wallpaper for this purpose. Then, I put curtains around the bed and otherwise I did everything in my power to make it as agreeable and comfortable for my family as I could. The captain and helmsman observed me while thus engaged and laughed kindly, showing that they, too, were pleased with what I was doing. After I got through, I went to the hotel to get Mother and the children. The same night we slept in the ship that was to bring us to America. It was the bark *Fedes Koo* from Portland, in charge of Captain H. Higgins.

The next morning, June 1st, they were engaged in bringing the provisions for our long sea trip on board. Later on, when all this labor was accomplished, our names were called from a list and two men were distributing the food according to the size of each family. The provisions consisted of green peas, navy beans, rice, flour, ham, salt and a small quantity of coffee and sugar. Everything we received was measured and weighed and had to be signed for. Potatoes and ship biscuits we were to receive every week. We also got enough fresh bread to last us for about five days. In the afternoon we had to appear with our families before an office who examined our papers and when he found everything to be in good order, only then did we receive our ship's papers.

Once more we went together to see some more of Antwerp. In the evening we returned on board the ship. We were often in a brown study, our thoughts were of a grave nature, as you might surmise. The children, however, soon fell asleep – a peaceful sleep – but with Mother and I it was different. The following morning, June 2nd, we again went our way to the hotel to eat. In the afternoon we had to be on board again because the other passengers were going to get their places on board the ship. It was so arranged that the Hollanders were placed on one side and the Germans on the other side of the ship. The total number of passengers were 130.

In the evening, we again ate at the hotel and then went aboard. The children played on shore near the boat for a while. Of course, they were in good and trusty hands. There was not any too much room in our "cabin" for all of us, but we were contented and tried to arrange matters as well as we could.

We left the basin in the night and soon were in the road stand of Antwerp. In the morning of June 3rd, the water bailiff, police and doctors came on board. We all had to go on deck – everyone that was on the ship – nobody was allowed to remain below. Lanterns were lighted and the whole ship below was looked through. The sleeping places were counted and examined thoroughly in order to convince themselves that there were no stowaways on board. The doctors looked us over and then one by one we had to go down in the hold to our "cabins." They were very strict in regard to two things, n.1. that no person with any contagious disease, and also that n.2. not too many passengers were on board the ship. According to the practice of the ship companies, many a ship in those days was overcrowded, hence the strict surveillance of the Belgian police to prevent this occurrence.

One family, consisting of Father, Mother and four children, who hailed from the Goesch Land (a district of Zeeland, Holland) were brought to a hospital. The disease they suffered from, a kind of exanthema, was considered to be dangerous to the fellow travelers. Of course, it was bad for them to be left behind, but it goes to show how well they guarded the health of those on board the ship. After this family had left the ship, with the aid of the tug, De Klok, we went down the river Scheldt (waterway between Holland and Belgium) and at six o'clock we dropped anchor at Terneuzen.

27

In the afternoon there had been a quarrel between the Captain and helmsman, and the ship's carpenter. The cause of it we did not know, because we could not understand their language. The result was that as soon as we dropped anchor, the ship's carpenter left the ship with his chest of tools. Thus, a very valuable man, whose service every ship is in need of, was there no more.

The wind was blowing from the right direction and there certainly was no better opportunity than to sail away. The Captain sent for the Belgian pilot, who asked the passengers if there was anybody among us who understood the trade of ship carpenter. No, there was none. Soon, he came back and asked us if there was a house carpenter among us to help out in case his services were required. A German and I told him that we were willing to help. He thanked us. The German, however, asked the pilot, who acted as interpreter, how much he was going to get for it during the trip. They did not like the idea of paying for it, according to the pilot, and he was told to remain a passenger.

I never mentioned anything in regard to financial remuneration, but at the same time I told the pilot that I had never sailed on any boat and was not used to going up in mast and rigging, but was willing to help whenever and wherever my help was needed. The first helmsman, who had taken charge of the carpenter work on board, approached me right away, gave me his hand, and in broken Holland told me that this offer would not be forgotten by them. Indeed, I was never sorry for having rendered this service, because during the whole trip over we were always treated with politeness and kindness, which brought about no little jealousy among the fellow passengers.

Before darkness set in, the helmsman and I were already busy fastening the boxes to put them in frames, and now I learned from the first time how to drive an American nail into the wood without previously having to drill holes or split the wood.

On June 4th, at 6 o'clock in the morning, we heaved anchor and soon left Terneuzen behind and sailed with a strong east-north-east wind. Soon Flushing and Westkapelle were out of sight and we entered the North Sea. Now, all those happy and healthy people on board became seasick. The rocking of the boat caused this all of a sudden. We celebrated Whitsuntide (Pentecost) in the true sense of the word. All of us – Hollanders, Germans, men, women and children, only a few did not take part. There was something else that distracted their attention. At six o'clock we were in the English Channel – the dunes of Holland were out of sight but not in return we saw the chalk mountains of England. I had been well so far and tried to write a few letters to be taken along with the pilot, when I, myself, felt the seasickness coming over me. I went on deck once in a while, but did not like the idea of Mother and the children being left alone. Coming on deck again, the helmsman came over to me, took me by the arm and put me between two kettles, near the bowsprit. He advised me to take good hold of the kettles and breathe enough pure air. This agreed with me. Other passengers tried the same with good results. Soon I was able to work all day at some very agreeable occupation. Before evening, we passed Dover Castle, the Isle of Wight, and the light tower, Don Jones. Here we saw a brig (ship with large square sail) which had been all day on starboard side (right side of ship), also a bark and two koffs (two masted ships).

In the morning of June 5th, we had sailed out of the English Channel and as far as our eyes could see, we saw no land – nothing but water. We now were on the Atlantic Ocean. Here we sighted a steamboat bound for Plymouth. We got kind of used to the rolling of the ship, and as the seasickness was not so general, consequently there became life among the people on board. We got better appetites and every one of us in turn started to cook something. We still have a favorable wind.

June 6th, we had nice weather and there was blowing a stiff breeze. Our Cate was the first child that came on deck. She found a piece of rope and started to jump rope, the same as she used to do at home on the street. But she could not understand why she could not do it here. The Captain made a swing for her. Soon more children got on deck. The Goessche farmers, towards evening, fried pancakes with bacon.

In the morning of June 7th, we spoke to a schooner which was en route to Lisbon. This ship approached us so close that we could plainly hear the crew speaking. Everything that was on deck was visible. We lowered a boat and when the captain came back, he had bought a box of lemons and a box of dried prunes. Till now, we had had nice weather. Towards evening we had contrary winds, which began to blow very hard, and we saw immense schools of fish, which according to the sailors, was a sign of an approaching storm.

June 8th. Nothing extra. We passed a bark, a schooner and a brig.

June 9th. Ditto. This day there was a boy born on board to German parents. As soon as it was known, the captain and helmsman made the necessary arrangements to help them and provide separate quarters for them. And considering the conditions and circumstances in which we were on board, soon we had fixed up things in a comfortable way. Of course, it was far from being a chamber in which the Dutch mother delivers her baby. Without the aid of a doctor, the child was born. And our Holland ladies were surprised at the manner the baby was taken care of. In Holland these things were done in an entirely different way. This, of course, gave much material for the Holland women to talk about.

June 10th. During the day the weather was calm, but towards evening, the wind started to blow hard.

June 11th. Today we had the hardest wind we had had as yet. Many got sick again and among them Mother, who, albeit feeling so much better the last days, was compelled to go to bed for several days. The ship was rocking violently. Now we saw what a terrific force water is when brought in motion by a gale. The ship did not listen to her sails, but only and alone to the immense body of white capped waves. Our boxes and coffers got loose from their crates and were thrown from one side of the vessel to the other. Consequently I did not have a chance to fasten them with ropes. You have to witness the havoc a storm causes on board a vessel in order to believe it fully. Kettles, bottles, high chambers, etc. and all else that was not nailed tight was constantly thrown from larboard to starboard. The wind varied – now it would die out a little and then shortly increase in strength. There was much rain till

29

the 15th of June. In the meantime there was a quarrel between the Hollanders and Germans about the time of their respective cooking. But it did not amount to much. As soon as the helmsman was notified, he gave orders that from now on the Hollanders would be first the following morning, noon and evening; and the next day the Germans first, and the Hollanders afterwards to do their cooking. And, he who forgot his time to cook, had to help clean everything between deck. This rule worked splendidly. Everywhere below was spick and span, and it was kept up till we finally landed. We saw only one bark that day, a lot of fish and sea swallows. Our first helmsman, who was an expert harpooner, tried to catch some of those fish. Twice he was almost successful; he hit them with the harpoon but when hauling them on board they slipped off against the side of the vessel, which regretted us very much.

June 16th. Nice weather. Sea calm. At six o'clock in the morning, a three masted ship got in sight, which came from North America. Late in the evening, we witnessed how strong discipline is on board. Our first helmsman, a man of strong character and capable of keeping order among a body of 300 or 400 men, had had plenty of time of late to know his passengers. There was a loving couple on board – they were Germans. He had teased them many times and we often had to laugh, as he spoke a better broken Dutch than German. Well, this couple had evidently thought that the officer would not molest them. It seemed that they had exchanged their sleeping places. It had not drawn our attention, but other people had told him so. Be this as it may, when the helmsman, as was his wont, hung the ships lantern in its place late one evening below decks, he wanted to convince himself whether it was true. He called one of the sailors who stood watch, and with some difficulty they removed her from her berth. Mr. Smit, as he was called on board, was placed in the coal bin in the bow of the vessel and our Dora was locked up in the back part of the ship. There they had to stay all night long.

June 17th. Very agreeable weather. Too bad. It hurt me that Mother could not come on deck and it is understood that our little Frederick, who was too young to eat any other food but Mother's milk, suffered greatly. The poor child cried day and night. At 10 o'clock, Smit and Dora, the two lovers, were led out of their places of confinement and had to appear before the Captain. A sailor acted as interpreter. The Captain lectured them most severely and told them from now on to lead a more moral life. So, they were set at liberty again, but for several days they remained between decks, being ashamed to face their fellow passengers. In the afternoon of the same day, the helmsman caught a big fish, a so-called sea hog. This provided us with some entertainment. After it was killed (it was butchered in the same manner as a hog), it was cut into pieces and the parts which were suitable for consumption were eaten. A layer of meat of a reddish nature was salted. The fish was so strong that when it was hoisted on board, it hit with its tail a privy, which was standing in the bow, and threw it overboard. Now, I had to make a new one, which gave me for a while something to do.

June 18th. In the morning, agreeable weather, but there was a contrary wind. Every passenger got a portion of the fish we had caught. We had to cut it in slices, beat it and carve it. About the same way that you treat beef steak. Then we fried it with a piece of ham and the whole including fried potatoes tasted very delicious. Towards evening one of the sailors was put in the lockup. He had been seen talking to one of the passengers, which is against

30

the rule of the ship. When the officers took him to task for it he became very mean and insulting.

June 19th. This was the first Sunday since we were on board that we had fine weather. In the afternoon, the Hollanders asked permission of the Captain if they could not conduct their religious ceremony. Mother Westven prayed and many a psalm concerning our situation was sung. Towards evening, the weather became raw and cold; but during the night the weather was quieter.

June 20th and 21st. Quiet weather. Snoep and I were still on deck at 12 o'clock and we witnessed a conflagration at sea. It seemed as our ship was sailing through a mass of fire (supposedly a Saint Elmo fire). A beautiful, imposing phenomena which even the heart of the weakest amongst us much touch and fill with respect for Him who said: "Mine is the sea, etc."

June 22nd. Was again a bad day for all those that could not get rid of sea sickness, for in the morning the weather was stormy, and during the day a little calmer, but the ship was rocking violently, nevertheless. Today a brig and a bark were visible. Our Dientze had, without our having noticed it, drunk out of the hot coffee pot which was brought downstairs, and the result was that she had scalded her mouth.

June 23rd. Good weather all day, and the ship sailed more steadily. Saint John was celebrated among the Germans in the evening, and there was one among them whose 25th birthday it was. Consequently, both these two occasions were celebrated at one and the same time. He was escorted among hurrahs of the crowd to the rear part of the deck, and here his sister presented him with a bottle of Rhine wine, of which they had a large stock. In the neck of the bottle was a palm instead of a Saint John branch, and to the palm everything was tied – a piece of sausage, dried prunes, one lemon, etc. After having congratulated him, we drank to his health with many bottles of beer, which the captain had in store. Not only his health we drank, but also we proposed a toast to the Captain, the officers of the ship, and in fact to everybody and everything. We were convinced that evening that the Germans beat many nations when it came to singing.

June 24th. Nothing extra during the day. Towards evening we saw flying fish and noticed the same Saint Elmo fire.

June 26th. Nice cool weather, but the wind stayed west too much in order to make a fast passage possible. Toward evening, a ship was coming our way, but she passed us on our bow and starboard side. She seemed to be a frigate.

June 27th. Nice weather, really for the first time a nice warm day. All kinds of games were played among the passengers and also the children amused themselves. Mother came on deck that day, but could not stand it very long. That day I repaired the chicken coop and the hog's pen.

June 28th. Again nice weather, but we did not sail very fast. The Germans celebrated Saint Peter day. They sang, played the violin and drank a glass of wine. We heard the blowing of a big fish when it was already dark, but to our regret we did not see it.

June 29th. We had beautiful weather in the morning. In the afternoon the wind got blowing more and more increasing the violence towards evening, and we had our thoughts as to the danger that confronted us. The hatches were closed and secured, and the sails were hauled down. Our bark was rolling on top of the white capped waves, and then the next moment to be dropped down. Everything was lying helter skelter between decks and we could not sleep in our berths. It was a bad night for Mother and our poor little boy.

June 30th. This day the sea was much calmer. The Captain called Snoeps and my attention to a big yellow sea turtle, but our efforts to catch it were in vain. Maybe through the strong momentum of the ship. In the afternoon a sail was approaching us from the rear, and came so close to our starboard side that the signs of the ship were hung out by means of a speaking tube they spoke to each other. This was packet ship *Robert Wiltrop*, from Liverpool, bound for Baltimore, and she had 50 passengers on board.

July lst. Early in the morning the Captain called our attention to a big shark which was swimming alongside the ship. In the afternoon the wind started to blow stronger and we again had a stormy night.

July 2nd. Ditto. Nothing new; a ship in the distance.

July 3rd. Good weather in the forenoon. We still have a view of the ship, perchance the same we say yesterday, without knowing her. This day the two black pigs which were still on board were slaughtered by a German, who was a butcher. Hot water was used to clean it and afterwards hung up on the after deck. Again there was a ship in sight.

July 4th. Declaration of Independence which is celebrated by every American. We also did our bit. Early in the morning, flags were displayed on our bark, and at 8 o'clock the crew fired salutes in honor of the day. Also a Spanish family who had a cabin on deck, and the man who was a dealer in fireworks, got permission to open a box of fire weapons. Now everyone who had a liking for shooting could indulge in this sport as much as he wanted to. At 10 o'clock, one of the slaughtered hogs was distributed among the passengers.. We saw many fish and a ship. We had a fresh breeze; the evening was nice, but cold. At the request of Mr. Westven to the Captain, the Hollanders were allowed to sing psalms. Even the Captain took part in singing the last psalm with us. We had now sailed westward to the end of the ocean and were at the banks.

July 5th. The weather was very cold. The Captain and the helmsman were making observations in the rigging and with instruments. The helmsman had wakened Snoeps and I as soon as the day dawned as he wanted to show us something in which we would be interested. And no wonder! It was an iceberg. With our bare eyes we could see it plainly. The day was cold, but the men remained on deck all day long because several icebergs were passing by that same day, on both sides of the ship. One of them had the form of a village church, something like this drawing. The last one was measured by the officers and was estimated to be about 160 feet high.

We were overawed, and as I was standing near the railing and observed the big masses of ice on which just now the sun shone brightly, gradually floating by, well, I must admit like feeling as having a cold fever. I was shivering at the thought of how many ships which just now were in their path to be crushed to pieces. We saw many monstrous fish which spouted water. (Whales we supposed). We had a cold but otherwise beautiful evening and night. All night long they had lanterns in front of the bow and keeping watch.

July 6th. This was a happy day for us. Early in the morning we counted more than a hundred small vessels which were catching codfish, and we sailed between and among them. Soon, we left them behind. Later in the day the weather became foggy and rainy. Towards evening the wind shifted toward the east. Soon it cleared up again, and it was a beautiful sight to see the sun set. Imposing was the rising of the moon, and as the sea was so calm we could not conclude or make up our minds to go to bed. Late in the night there was still one fishing boat a stone's throw from our vessel.

July 8th & 9th. Nothing new. The wind steady but west-south-west head wind. Our delicacies, which we had taken along, were getting less and less. Want of sugar and vinegar were being felt daily. The potatoes became worse every day and event the drinking water was getting brackish. Everyone on board became tired of eating peas and beans.

July 10th. Nothing interesting. We are now actually drifting on the Grand Banks. The total population of the bark is on deck. Some are sewing, darning or knitting; others are reading, writing or playing; still others are busy cooking their meals or having become so lazy during the trip, did not know what to do. Mother and little Frederick were also on deck that afternoon.

July 11th. Much rain – weather. A schooner came in sight.

July 12th. The helmsman harpooned a big fish. Again the flesh was divided among us all, which we appreciated very much. In the evening we saw a big fish which spouted streams of water.

July 13th. Still the same contrary wind. In the morning dreary and cloudy – wet; in the afternoon the weather was clear and bright. Now we thought to see land on the horizon ahead of us. We soon hoped to reach land. There was that evening a fisher boat on starboard side, and a bark on our starboard side. The evening was extremely beautiful and no painter or writer has as yet given an adequate picture of the same.

July 16th and 17th. Below it is misty and higher up the sun is shining. We could hardly see three ship lengths ahead of us. A quarrel has broken out between the Germans and the cook who had told them not to light a fire after 6 o'clock in the evening.

July 18th. Weather is still. In the evening it is clear. Again we have seen sharks near the ship. When the moon rose we noticed clouds in the south which were visible signs of a nearing thunder storm. Again we saw Saint Elmo fire. We sailed so close to a ship as never happened as yet.

July 19th. Weather calm. It seemed as if our ship went backwards instead of forward against the strong current. In the morning as well as in the afternoon, many big ships and small ones were near us. In the evening a large English steamer passed us.

July 20th. Now we had a stiff breeze blowing south east. We got new courage and many said rather be seasick another two days if the ship only went ahead.

July 21st. As we woke this morning, we saw the beautiful sun rising. Also many ships and at 8 o'clock in the evening we saw a light in the distance, supposed to be a lighthouse. After we had sailed another hour it was truly observed to be one.

July 22nd. Today the weather is warm, actually too suffocating to be between decks. We can hardly sleep any more. The same wind or no wind! We were nearing the shore and soon a changed view greeted us after such a long trip. During the morning, at about 11 o'clock, we dropped anchor. Opposite us was an island on which the quarantine station stood, in the mouth of the Bay of Boston. There we had to remain the day and were given orders. Anything which we did not need and was useless we were to throw overboard. Yes, even the helmsman threw the caps of the girls of Goes and Yerseke and their sabots (wooden shoes) overboard. They told us to clear up as well as we could, to scrub the deck downstairs, and also to make ourselves look respectable. When we woke up the next morning, we put on our best suit of clothes. The health commissioners came on board early in the morning and examined everyone. They complimented the Captain and officers for the cleanness on board and the passengers and went with the Captain to the island. After having remained there an hour, we saw our Captain on a boat approaching the ship. Loud hurrahs went up from all of us; hats and handkerchiefs were waved, and he was literally carried from the boat to the ship and into his cabin. We could see that he was proud of having received such an ovation. Soon a tug got alongside of us and we entered the bay beside which the city of Boston is built. Many steamers and sailing vessels encircled us. There were also many pleasure boats, nicely gilded and painted. We saw steep cliffs on top of which were light towers. In the afternoon, at 1 o'clock, we arrived in Boston. On account of it being Saturday, and no trains were running in the New England states on Sunday, we got permission to remain on board till Monday morning. I must mention here that more than once had I told the officers on board my disappointment and objection to being landed in Boston instead of New York, because our tickets called for the latter port. We only had been on board a short while that we learned the ship's destination was Boston. I told him that I was afraid to miss my goal entirely, because I had a letter of recommendation from the commissioner of emigration at New York, not only to see that we traveled as soon as possible, but also as cheap as could be arranged and to protect us against swindlers. The helmsman promised me to see the Captain about it, which promise he kept faithfully. Before we were near Boston, the Captain called me in his cabin and it was difficult to understand each other, but he let me know that in case we wanted to consent to him mapping out and regulating our inland trip - the way he stipulated doing it n.l. that we should not listen to anybody else be he English, German, Irish or Hollander; no matter how elegant they were dressed or what fine manners they had. I made this known to my fellow passengers, and with a few exceptions, they agreed to it. Our bark was towed to the dock and several people tried to get aboard, but none of them gained admission. But, in spite of this, they again tried to get on board the ship. The Captain went on shore and soon came back with a police officer who stood watch and everyone who had nothing to do on board was refused admission. In the afternoon the Captain came on board with an official of the railway. The heads of families and other men were called one by one in the cabin and we paid for our tickets, including boat and railway from Boston to Milwaukee. Those who went to other places also got their tickets here. Children below ten years paid half fare. Our tickets were on the Boston Railway. As I was the first one who had gotten my tickets and Snoeps, who soon afterwards got his, we went ashore to get fresh milk and soft bread. We had never gotten used to black coffee. Then we purchased in one of the stores a straw hat each because the heat in those days was great. Although we had not put on all our clothes – had taken some off – still we were not used to such a heat. I wrote a letter to Mr. Broecke in Rochester telling him that his father and mother, instead of New York, had arrived in Boston. I made the letter as short as possible and dropped it right away in a letterbox. Snoeps and I were out early Sunday morning to see as much of the sights of Boston as the heat of the day would permit. Boston is one of the oldest and wealthiest commercial cities of the United States. She is built like a half circle like an amphitheater along the bay. Imposing elevated streets running the height of the rocks on which they are laid out. There are many springing fountains, beautiful parks and elegant houses built of red pressed bricks, and some constructed of rough hewn stone and blue colored hard stone. Also thousands of houses built of wood, but none the less nice and attractive – master creations of architecture. In the afternoon and evening, we had to pack up everything in order to be ready the next morning to leave with the first immigrant train westward.

Monday morning at 6 o'clock we left with our belongings the ship which had been the last fifty days our home. And albeit how poor and miserable had been our first impression on board. Our long stay, however, had changed our views and we left no hard feelings behind. Early in the morning – Monday morning – a boy was born on board. Henderik was the father. He hailed from Kattendyk, South Beverland, and his destination was the same as ours – Milwaukee. But, they were well taken care of, both in regard to lodging and treatment during their stay, till they could continue their journey. When we arrived at the depot our baggage was scaled in the presence of our helmsman who acted as interpreter for us. Our personal effects were too heavy and it cost me $18 more than I had ever expected. This caused such an emptiness in our purses that we were downhearted. Whether we were deceived or not treated right, I cannot maintain. A few said no, others again claimed to have been swindled out of money. I asked for a receipt and paid for our freight to Milwaukee. We got our tickets for steamer and train and at 12 o'clock we left Boston. Springfield was the first station we stopped at. But a bad accident happened as we left the Springfield depot. A child from one of the German passengers, who had made the trip across with us on the same boat, had been thrown, through the sudden starting of the train, out of the passenger coach and landed under the wheels of the car, with the result that both arms were cut off. The sorrowful father had to take his child to a hospital. At four o'clock in the morning we arrived at Worchester. A good sized factory town, among them foundries. Here we stayed on the train, albeit we were at liberty to leave our coaches as the train did not leave before 12 o'clock. We were very much annoyed during the hours of darkness by curious Irish people who seemed to belong to the dregs of the population. A low class of people who had attained only a low degree of civilization. Shortly before we started, they hitched about eight coaches back of our train, all crowded with emigrants. I observed that the cars which contained our baggage, and were loaded at Boston, were not back of our train anymore. However, I had taken precautions and had taken the number, also written down the color of the car on a piece of paper.

Now were riding through the state of Massachusetts. All the wonders of nature we saw here is not possible to describe adequately. Not for one like me because I had made but one trip to Gelderland (one of the eleven provinces of Holland) and had seen heretofore nothing but level land. But here were giant rocks against which sides a road bed has been built, which must have cost an enormous amount of labor and money. We went through tunnels cut out of solid rock, which took us more than a quarter of an hour to pass through. We sat that length of time in darkness, going through them seeing nothing but the sparks of the locomotive. We also passed bridges high up between the mountains where away below the water with a thunderous noise was forcing its way. Early in the morning of July 25th, we arrived in the state of New York. Here was a different view. This state (how beautiful is nature here!) has progressed, as human hands have built cities and villages on mountain sides and in the valleys. There were any number of hamlets and small settlements which had their own railroad station where the train stopped to take in water. We passed through many of them. At 12 o'clock we were in Albany. Here we had to leave the train. The world renowned Hudson River was crossed by steamer (ferries) which continually crossed back and forth between the two shores. They served as bridges. Those boats are divided into three parts – compartments for ladies and gentlemen on the sides with nice seats all roofed over, and the center of these boats is roomy enough to carry carriages of every description. I must admit that I was not very fortunate when I arrived at Albany. In the morning I had gotten a cinder in my eye. It happened as we sent through a tunnel. It bothered me so much that the moment we were out of the train, we hunted for a doctor who in a few minutes relieved me of it and my pain. But it cost me $1. That goes to show that the American doctors want sufficient remuneration for their services.

The first boarding place, or hotel, in America in which we stayed was here. A German was the proprietor. We considered ourselves to be fortunate, as we and the children were the first arrivals. (Three more Dutch families from Walcheren). The other Hollanders and their families had gotten quarters elsewhere. We could not find fault with the meal which was served us. Mother and our dear little sick child were craving – after so much travel and endurance – for a good night's rest. But how we were disappointed! During the evening the boarding house was filled with boarders. The heat was unbearable. Constantly they were going up and down the steps, trying to open our bedroom door. Out of fear that some harm might be done us, we slept little or not at all that night. That same evening and the following,

36

we were visited by many Hollanders who were living there, and who gave us good advice in regard to our railroad trip. A former Amsterdammer said, "Don't be afraid for your baggage. This is put on the car in Boston and will arrive in Buffalo in good order, but there you shall have to take care of it, as soon as it gets there, before it is shipped across the lakes." We also received bad news – the cholera was still raging in the western states and claimed many victims. These tidings deeply affected us, and you can imagine that after these bad prospects, I was elated when about 10 o'clock in the morning a well dressed man came rushing into our boarding place and in the Zeeland tongue hollered: "Is Remeeus here?" I said, "Here am I." And, indeed, it was Van Den Broeke from Rochester who stood before me. "Where are my Father and Mother?" he asked. His parents had taken a short walk. They must have attracted the attention and curiosity of the children on account of their odd clothes. They were surrounded by youngsters. Van Den Broeke forced his way through them and alternately took his Father and Mother in his arms. Such a welcome! Now we had a guide to Rochester, and I as their agent and advisor was thankful for it. Now, here we learned the truth of the Holland adage: "He that reckons without his host, must reckon over again."

After we had hunted up a few old acquaintances, we went our way to the depot to board the train which was to bring us to Rochester. At 12 o'clock the emigrant train left and we passed many a place, many a settlement and others that were growing and spreading out. Surprising and startling it is, after having seen so many strange names of places, one cannot pronounce, to notice the familiar names of Amsterdam and Haarlem. During the evening we passed alongside a large city called Syracuse, who counts her inhabitants by the thousands. The following morning, July 27th, we arrived at Rochester. Here I had wished to stay a day to visit some old acquaintances from our home town Middelburg. But the train stopped here only half an hour. Rochester is a very large city. There are in this city more foundries than in Holland combined, also an immense commerce in flour. Many mills have steam engines, but many more use water as native power. From our car windows we could see the waterfall of the Genesee River which has a fall of 90 feet. But the most interesting is the Erie Canal. There are great locks which regulate the water. It looks as if the canal is higher and is going over the city. Through this waterway hundreds of draw barges pass off and on from Albany to Buffalo.

Now we were en route to Buffalo. The heat was unbearable. We passed Batavia and Utica and arrived at about 2 o'clock in the afternoon in Buffalo. Here we had to leave the train and could not proceed until our baggage had arrived. On account of the high prices they charged in the boarding houses, our fellow travelers, farmers from Zierikzee and Goes (districts of the province of Zeeland, Holland) decided to leave each one member of their family behind and to cross Lake Erie in the evening. Here we were! We had to travel nearly one thousand miles and I had not money enough left to pay a night's lodging for my family. In those days there were no emigrant stations. I went out to buy bread and butter, and we three, Mr. Westven, Snoeps and I went to town with a defeated feeling. Westven wanted to see Mr. Huissoon, to whom he was recommended in Buffalo; and I had to deliver a letter to Mr. de Graaf, from his family in Holland. After a long search I knocked at his door at half past four. I gave him the letter and I was received in a friendly way. They lodged my wife and children. During the evening, a few more Hollanders came there. Snoeps and I slept that

37

night by a Mr. Post, formerly a baker of Middelburg. They encouraged us and were very friendly. Buffalo was a large and beautiful city. We saw here so many strange things that it would be difficult indeed to related even a small part of them. The waterworks attracted our attention above all things. But the paving of the streets in these American cities, which are yet young compared with those in Europe, have much to be improved upon.

On July 28th, at 12 o'clock, we were waiting for the train which was to bring our baggage, and it did arrive. There was not anything missing, but the boxes had been damaged very much by rough handling, though I had made them myself and extra strong. Snoeps and I had to drive a nail here and there. It often came to my mind in after years how we ever got along in this crowd of people. Here were Americans, Irish, Norwegians, Swedes, high and low Germans and English people and every one in that heterogeneous crowd tried to get his belongings on a wagon to be taken to the steamboat which was to convey us across Lake Erie. It was six o'clock in the evening that we got on board. W were sweating and covered with dust and also very tired. Snoeps and I got my wife and children, boarded the steamer and we left Buffalo at 9 o'clock in the night for Detroit, in the state of Michigan. This was one of those larger steamers which have the very best of accommodations and everything richly furnished. But alas, we poor emigrants had our places on top or around our baggage. There were far over 2000 passengers on board and we had hardly a space five feet square for sleeping quarters, which we had to be contented that night long. But, what was worse, a fearful storm was coming up that night. Thunder and lightning and such a tumultuous sea we were having now – like being on the Atlantic Ocean. But, during this dismal night, we experienced the Lord's saving hand. In the afternoon of July 29th, we arrived in Detroit. A large, yet an old, and well known city. She is situated on Lake Erie, but the other shore belongs to Canada. I cannot write anything about the city itself, for the deck on which we arrived is not far from the railway station. Our boat on account of the storm, we were late in docking. The train stood ready and waiting for us, and we were ever driven to incessant speed to get in the train. But how thankful were we that the fierce storm of the past night with God's benevolence had provided us with good bread and meat which lasted us till Milwaukee. The feat of the storm, and the seasickness on board, had been the cause that so few passengers had taken their supper. Hence, for a few Dutch ten cent coins we got as much as we could possibly pack and take along.

Again we were on the train, and the farther we traveled westward the poorer the equipment of the railway in regards to the emigrant trains. Because the cars we were in were nothing but freight cars in which benches were placed, and we suffered the most while traveling in these cars. During the last eight days we had slept but one night and it was almost unbearable to stand the jarring and shocking of the train while we were sitting on these rough benches, for the train, in order to arrive on schedule time, was speeding very fast. We had as fellow passengers a troupe or gang of mineworkers returning from California. We had a burning thirst, and only at the station where the train stopped could we get water. Then we had to hurry in order not to be left behind, for the train did not wait for us and our water jugs. Considering all we had to go through, it is a great wonder the courage did not fail us. We made a very short stop at Kalamazoo, 140 miles away from Detroit. Here a few Hollanders left us. They either went to Kalamazoo or in the vicinity where they had their places of employment. Towards evening a child fell from the car and landed under the wheels. The child belonged to a Norwegian family and was about six years old. At the next station the little corpse was taken off. It must have been a sad moment for its poor parents who thus had to lose one of the members of their family and even could not attend the funeral of their own child. For the train stopped only a short time, again to go ahead. The train went through high rocky promontories. All of a sudden the momentum of our train slacked up. We thought that a station was near, but the cry of Fire! Fire! brought about great consternation among us. And indeed, a baggage car was on fire, which, however was soon put out. A Swede had a box in which he had stored away a great quantity of matches. This must have been the cause of the fire because it was his box that was on fire. But, praise the Lord, no more harm was done. We were only terribly frightened.

Sunday morning of July 30th was beautiful, and our route west along enchanting regions alternately through extensive forests and on top of mountains from which we had a magnificent view, to be changed afterwards by valleys – wondrous and most beautiful to behold. Certainly, any traveler who is flush with money and can afford to travel in one of those luxurious trains could have gone on for days without every getting tired of the beautiful and changeable scenery. But, to be on an emigrant train night and day with small and sick children and not getting anything to eat but the common everyday necessities, and above all the unbearable heat, would it not make the most courageous among us become senseless and hardhearted? It was through Him, under whose guidance we were, and who continually protected us, that I was able to notice and observe so many things. We arrived in Chicago late in the afternoon. Our train went over a bridge standing on piles. I cannot say or tell the length of it. This bridge crossed a bay of Lake Michigan. Chicago counts already many thousands of people, albeit the city is still growing.

Throughout the whole states of Illinois and Wisconsin the cholera was raging. It was with a feeling of fear that we had to enter the city of Chicago. It was already getting quite dark before I found shelter for my wife and children. All my riches consisted of one dollar. Snoeps and I decided thus to walk around to rest here and there on a bench that night. We had been told that our baggage would arrive Monday morning, July 31st. We were afraid that something might be missing because it had happened more than once before that those boxes which contained the most valuable articles had never arrived at their destination. We were in a sorrowful mood that morning, for had not one of our fellow countrymen and traveler, a man who had become a tried and true friend of ours, been stricken with the cholera! Yes, he had contracted the cholera and already on the way to the hospital he died. His name was Goudewaard and came from the village of Dreischor, North Beverland, Holland. He was such an alert and clever man, and how we felt, and what sympathy we had for his poor young widow, his three children and his old father and mother. Just think of it – to be away only one more day's travel from their destination.

By the unloading of the cars, I found that all our baggage which was shipped from Buffalo was in good order. A son of the already mentioned baker Post, at Buffalo, had strongly advised me to get the accurate weight of our boxes, and make a list of it. Our baggage was loaded on handcars and brought to the steamer which was to bring us to Milwaukee. I convinced myself that everything was safe on board (and one can never be too careful about such a thing). All my fellow passengers from Antwerp have found out that I had the right system in marking my boxes with a red sign and having the address pained on them in black lettering. Not I could see right away which was my property. And now I went to get Mother and children, who had suffered so many hardships and privations. They had gotten weaker and had lost much weight. My wife and children had not occupied a bed – had spent the night on chairs near the table and had had nothing to eat, only something to drink. Well, when I got there that morning, this boarding house keeper demanded three dollars from me. I told him that all I had was two dollars – five trunks. But, no, he didn't believe me. He took me by the vest, tore it open to see whether I had any money hidden there. I was so consternated that this very day I do not know how I got out on the street. Neither do I know who got in between me and him. Someone, I suppose, who tried to quiet him down. But, I tell you, it was not before a few blocks divided my family and I from him that I felt free and started to breathe freely again. At last we were on the boat, at least not many emigrants. The day was sunny and nice. We were simply tired out and soon fell asleep. We hardly saw anything of Michigan Lake. These lakes – let me remark it here – do all contain sweet water. They are, however, not so easy for navigation, as at times ships run as much , if not more danger, to sail on them as on a body of salt water. Fearful storms will sweep these lakes and thousands of emigrants have found their graves in them. But the Lord was merciful to us and we arrived safely on the other shore.

At four o'clock in the afternoon of July 31st, we at last arrived at Milwaukee, our destination. Our boat landed alongside a very long pier, which is the landing place of all steamers. At last, here we were in Milwaukee. Our boxes were unloaded and there we stood next to them, not knowing where to go. Ere long a man who was decently dressed approached us. He addressed us in Holland and told us that he was running a boarding place. I let him know in as few works as possible my financial situation, also told him that we intended to go to Dom Klein, but that I had already found out in Buffalo that he had left for Michigan sometime ago. My own relatives, as I related to him, lived 18 miles from the city and mentioned the names of my brother-in-law and Mr. Lankester. So far he had listened attentively, but when I admitted to him that I had not any money left but that my baggage would be good security till I had written my brother-in-law, this complacent Dutchman had disappeared among the crowd. And this moment I shall never forget. I reflected upon all I had left behind, and what would the future offer us? And I admit it, though I am ashamed to say so, that at that moment I lost all courage.

The heat was terrible, unbearable for us who had had a nice breeze on board the steamer. We had a burning thirst which we tried to quench with a piece of ice. God's wisdom did not permit the water to enter our mouths. Still being in a brown study, a boy of about 15 years of age approached us and spoke to us in a low Zeeland dialect. He wanted to know if we had already a boarding place. I answered "No." He offered to bring us to his house which was not very far away from where we were. Of course, I did not mention my straightened financial condition to him. We placed our boxes as close together as possible and followed him. His parents came from Zierkzee and with several other families, whose occupation was fishing, they lived in a large house which must have been a museum because the lettering on

40

the building, though faded, was still readable the word "museum." I asked the lady if we could stay here a while at least, so long till our family was acquainted with our arrival. Without hesitating a moment she started to cook and bake for us. I spoke to the man as soon as he came home and related to him that my brother-in-law was a next door neighbor of Mr. Lankester. He ordered an express man to bring our baggage to his house. He himself went along and paid for everything. He advised us especially not to eat any vegetables and any other eatables on account of the cholera. I took dangerously sick during the night. I vomited and had diarrhea very bad. I had gotten so weak that I could hardly walk the next day. I wrote a letter to my sister and asked for the direction of the post office; also mailed a letter to Mr. Boda.

Most of the Hollanders did not work, and much business was at a standstill. He who had the means and could afford it had left the town and went into the country to escape the cholera. You can imagine that all this was depressing on our minds. On Wednesday morning, August 2nd, Snoeps went along with our host to catch fish. In the afternoon our brother-in-law, Slyster, had come with a wagon which belonged to Mr. Lankester, to take us along. Slyster paid these kind people who had been so friendly to us. We did not take our baggage along that same day; we left it in this place as we were assured that these people would well take care of it. Towards evening, after having traveled through forests and over many a hill, we got to Franklin Prairie. I hardly need to tell you that we received a warm welcome. Mother had suffered greatly through the long and arduous journey, and they hardly recognized here. Our youngest child was in a precarious condition, and it looked as if it was not going to live much longer. They did not know that we had buried our Mietzi shortly before we left Holland for the United States.

At eleven o'clock the following morning, I was working at the carpenter bench in the barn of Mr. Lankester. I got paid $1 a day. Then I also had to help in the field. Whether my brother-in-law saw that I would never be fit to become a farmer, or that I was not orthodox enough for these surroundings, or what reasons may have prompted him ever again to drive me to Milwaukee to look for a house and work, I do not know. Often I had to walk the many miles back and forth to Milwaukee. Sometimes I was fortunate to get a ride on a hay wagon, or on a grain wagon drawn by oxen. I personally suffered much. The more so because I did not know anybody in town and could neither talk English nor German, which otherwise would have greatly helped me to rent a house and get work. Now, you can imagine how I felt in the evening when coming home and not having found any work. But at last I was lucky, I had found a place to move into. It was the deserted parsonage (house of the minister). Our goods were washed and cleaned by my sister and on Tuesday, August 22, we left the prairie and came to town.

On August 28th I started to work for an English boss and made $1.12 ½ per day. Now I was a citizen of Milwaukee, yet young, but growing and expanding. Very beautiful and nicely situated for commerce, Milwaukee already counts 30,000 inhabitants.

Your Father, J. Remeeus

41

◆◆◆◆◆◆

[This memoir and travel journal was written by Gijsberta (Bertha Van de Ven) Vander Heyden. She was born 31 January 1910 in Schijndel, Noord Brabant to Willem and Christina (Van Kaathoven) Van de Ven. She died 30 January 1989 in Green Bay, WI. On 7 May 1940 she was married to Nicholas Bernardus Vander Heyden in Schijndel, Noord Brabant. Nicholas was born 14 April 1906 in Boxtel, Noord Brabant to Johannes and Maria (Verhoeven) Vander Heyden. He died 12 June 1967 in Sherwood, WI. The family arrived in Hoboken, New Jersey on 14 February 1949. These pictures and the story of Bertha Van de Ven and the Vander Heyden family is the property of the Vander Heyden family. Any use or copying without permission of the Vander Heyden family is not permitted.]

The Vander Heyden family shortly before leaving the Netherlands
Left to right front: Christine, Ida, William
Middle: Anthony, Maria
Back: Nicholas, Bertha holding Waltera (Teri)
Circle: Johannes who died in 1948 before the family emigrated
Photo courtesy of the Vander Heyden family

Dear Children,

It is now 25 years since we came to America, and the time is right for writing down some of my memories for the benefit of the ones who are interested in how and why we came here in the first place.

When we get married in 1940, May 7, the future looked not too good for farmers in Holland, but because we are getting of age, Daddy 34, and myself 30, we did get married anyway.

We rented a little farm, from an Aunt of Daddy's, about 25 acres, and started out with a couple of cows, some pigs and 80 chickens.

But we did not know how close we were to the Second World War, and even on our wedding day, a brother of Daddy's was called back to his regiment, and had to leave the party. That set off Daddy's mother crying, and left everyone in a more sober mood. We, Daddy and myself, took a walk to the farm fields, from my Dad, Willem Vande Ven, and my thoughts went far away. I told Daddy how I wish we could go away to America, and try it out to build a new life over there, because there was no future for farmers here. Never thought one day it would happen.

That night we take our bikes, and peddled from Schijndel, where I was living, to Boxtel, where we had our new farm rented and would live for 9 years to come. A honeymoon was not on the program for us, and some of our brothers-in-law were so nice to come after us, and reach the house on the same time, with the plans to keep us up all night. But lucky for us the house was strange to them and when we show them around and reached the back door, Daddy said, here is another room, and because it was dark they stepped out and Daddy locked the door from the inside, and we left them there. There was nothing they could do but go home, and we went to bed. Next morning, about 7 o'clock, after not much sleep, Daddy's mother came to our house and we got a scolding because we slept too late. And would we get poor, if we were trying to make it that way. We had wooden shutters for the windows on the outside, and she opened them all up. Boy was I mad. She was afraid the neighbors would see it, that we were still sleeping. They lived so close together, and it was a shame not to be up by 5 o'clock.

That was Wednesday morning, but by Friday morning May 10, 1940 we woke up hearing such strange noises and went outside about 4, at just about dawn, and we saw about 10 miles away above (De Bosch) planes striking at the city, over and over again. Was hard to believe, but all hell was to break loose for the next days.

We went home, to my father's house in Schijndel about ½ hours by bike, and on the way people were cutting the trees down, and let them fall criss cross over the roads because the forerunners told them the (Duitsers) Germans are coming. We had to turn back, and go back to our own home. We lived in unbelief for the next two days. But on May 12, 1940 we saw them coming, not with planes, but by motorcycle. We came from church, it was Sunday, and we just stepped down from our bikes on our house and they stopped too. We just stood there

43

not knowing what to do. They came to us, and try to talk, but we could not understand them. We did not know if it was German or French, but we found out they wanted food.

They went in the chicken coop for eggs and wanted to drink milk because water they did not trust, we found out. They had skulls on their helmets and were so dirty from riding for days on those motorcycles, that you could not see the color of their faces. But, after some hassling they drove off and for the next days to follow the streets were dark with thousands of Panzers (tanks), cannons, jeeps, big wagons and horses and thousands upon thousands of soldiers, riding or walking, all coming in Holland and pull farther to Belgium and France. Afterwards we found out how they over ran our defenses on the border and the thousands of our soldiers killed in the process. Daddy's brother, who had to leave our wedding party, was made prisoner of war and was for 2 months in Germany. He went over there nice and fat and came back so skinny as a bone, but no harm was done to them. Germany, or better, Hitler wanted to be friends with Holland. But when they ran into resistance, Holland paid dearly for it. Especially the Jewish people, who were taken away to the concentration camps and most of them murdered.

In Holland alone, 110,000 Jews died in those camps. A lot of Dutch people did hide the children of the Jews who did have a chance yet. But we had a camp right in our neighborhood (Vugt) and thinking how those Jews were treated there still runs shivers over my spine after 34 years.

That same Sunday, May 23, 1940 when we saw the Germans come in Holland, we went to grandfather's house that afternoon to help out over there. About 20 soldiers from the Dutch army who had deserted their regiments came to their house, thru woods and ditches, because they lived close to big woods and they avoided the big roads, otherwise they would have been captured by the Germans. They were hungry, and needed other clothes, because they were not safe in their uniforms. So grandma took all the clothes from Grandpa and 5 big boys, and we saw to it, they all were dressed like farmers so they could make their way home to their families. Daddy went to the neighbors for more clothes.

Grandma wanted me to peel potatoes for all those men, but I asked them to sit in a circle in the kitchen, gave each one a knife, and told them to peel their own. They were more than happy to help and get something to eat. We did not have meat, just some fried bacon to add to the taste of the potatoes and vegetables.

They buried all their uniforms and weapons and their possessions, even their blankets, before they take off. Later on Daddy take one of those blankets out of the ground. A big nice wool one of the Dutch Royal Army. I think Johnny take it to Madison. It is a dark green one, we use it for all those years. First we did hide it because we were afraid someone would search the house for Dutch soldiers. But afterwards we use it on our bed, and when in the last months of the war the German soldiers moved in our house, we have to leave everything on the bed including that blanket. So they slept under it too.

And when the Allied soldiers came in and the Germans had to run, I took the blanket outside on the wash line, hit it with a stick to get the bed bugs out. This didn't take me too long because the grenades were still flying over my head, to hit the Germans to make them move a little faster.

The next 5 years, from 1940-45, were filled with horror, excitements sometimes, sleepless nights from bomb attacks, falling planes, ground attacks to shoot them down at night with the help from search lights. One night I saw 5 planes downed from the place we live. In 1943, I remember one morning in early March, it was particularly busy with bombers coming back from Germany, and they had to fly over Holland to go back to their bases in England.

It was very foggy weather. Daddy was planting some early vegetables in the garden about 50 yards from the house. Our little John was playing by the kitchen window. I was sitting feeding Christine, beside the coal stove and was thinking it is may be the safest place in the house if a bomber should fall. And all of a sudden the awful noise came closer and closer, and it got so dark in the house it was like night. The chickens, which were in the yard, flew against the windows. I thought, this is it. One is going to fall on our house. I grabbed John and take him in the corner where I was sitting first and waited a couple of seconds. Then the dark lifted, and flames so big I never saw before or afterwards, spread over the house every over the trees but it didn't touch the house. It was more like an explosion. That's why the flames went so high.

It fell about 100 yards from where Dad and his little helper (John Troyer) were working. He was not hurt either. Every piece went far over their heads. When the fog cleared we found out the parts of the plane were spread for miles on the ground and so were the 10 personnel from the bomber. One only escaped with a parachute, really 2 jumped, but one pilot was shot down by a German fighter. The one who made it, we saw him coming down with his parachute, and Allied planes circled around him, until he was on the ground. Then they got after the German planes, who shot down No. 2 parachutist, and down that plane too. He came down in a swamp and they never got the plane out, so deep fell it in the ground. So far I know it is still in there. Just so good the motors from the bomber, there was just a pool of water left. But they found 8 bodies. I did not go and look at it, I just cry for those boys so far from home and family, to die in a war that they never wanted.

This kind of life went on until the invasion in Normandy. Then things started changing, but did not get any better. The gliders came in from England and landed sometimes in the middle of German troops. In Arnhem, 5,000 Allied troops were killed because they would not give themselves over to the Germans, and the help troops from the Allies were too far away to help them out. Just horrible. This happen over and over again until the Allied troops came closer and make better connections.

One afternoon, we were working on an underground shelter, when all of a sudden strange low flying planes, many and many of them came down on our fields and surroundings. Underground troops didn't know they were coming, but we didn't either, of course. And they came on the wrong place down, because Germans were all over the place. They stayed away for an hour or so, and the Allied soldiers, who came with those gliders, wanted to know where the Allied troops were. But only a neighbor boy, with a little bit of school English, try to help. We could not understand or read their maps which they had with them. They were thirsty, and I gave them cocoa milk to drink. They hide themselves for things to come. And when the Germans saw they could handle them, they set up position beside our house and start shooting at them. Those Americans shoot back, of course, but they ran fast out of ammunition. And in an hour or so it was all over. Two lay dead, and the rest were hustled off, their hands raised above their heads, to the nearby town of Boxtel. Those 2 dead soldiers lay there for 2 days before the Red Cross take them away.

These were awful days, and I prayed and cried a lot. So many nice young people had to die in some ditch or bushes. Afterward we hear some of them had made it to the Allied troops, about 5 miles further, with the help of underground resisters, but the Germans keep on looking for them if someone had hid them.

I was picking beans in our garden and some German soldiers came over asking if I did see any of those flyers. And they meant business because they had a loaded revolver in each hand pointed at me. I said, I saw some running, but did not know where they went, and that they were sitting in a deep ditch across from our house. How I prayed that they keep their heads down until it was night. But it was almost dark and they tried to look around, and a German watch soldier saw them and they too were made prisoner of war. I always hoped they made it back somehow to America.

The Vander Heyden farm in Schijndel, Noord Brabant, Netherlands
Photo courtesy of the Vander Heyden family

46

Then came October 1944 and we get in our house a first aid center for the Germans. A Red Cross flag was set on top of the house, and each morning Allied fighter planes came low over head to take a look, but they never fired on it. We had not a window broken in the house, and all the neighbor farms and houses was not a single window left from all the rain of grenades which came down every day for weeks and weeks.

Our house was full with German soldiers and we get a choice to live with them or get out. We decided to stay. A German, Feltweber, a doctor and 2 aides live in our house and bedrooms for 5 weeks. The living room was the place where they helped the sick and wounded, just on a mattress laying on the floor. They came in day and night brought in on a ladder or make shift litter. The walls of the house were full of bloody finger prints and after they were helped they were laid in the barn on straw. If it was bad they were picked up later for the hospital. If not serious, they were sent back to the front line.

I saw them going back, older people crying like children. They told me the war will be over for you soon now, but it is of no help to us. One night a shot down pilot (an American) was brought in. One side of his body was all ripped open. How did I ache for him and I could do nothing to help. I just could give him a little coffee was all that was permitted. They lay him on straw too, and was later brought to a hospital. I still see his eyes, staring at me, begging for some help, but was not able to say anything. How I hated that I could not speak English. I wish all your children could feel what it could mean, in a time of crisis like this war, to speak a language that you could help a human being. And what little it takes to learn an extra language. It would really pay off.

But to come back, on those daily bombardments of grenades at Daddy's father's house (John Vander Heyden) they were not so lucky. One afternoon we were talking to some neighbors about the safety of the shelter we made when a round of grenades came in again. We did not have the time to run in the shelter, and Daddy took Johnny and fell down on the ground, and I take Christine and fell down too. I was pregnant with William. Maria was inside in her bed. The pieces of the grenades came down all around us and we were not hurt. Daddy said there is something wrong at my Dad's house because we saw the smoke coming from it. So he was trying to go over there when some of the neighbors came running to our place telling us that Grandfather was killed and his brother Toon lost his right arm.

But Grandfather was badly wounded, not killed. A German soldier who was also running in their shelter was killed instantly. They heard the grenades coming too and tried to jump in the shelter, but a grenade hit the opening and Grandfather was just getting in. Toon, behind him, had his hand on the shelter opening when it struck and had his right arm cut off. Grandfather had his whole body full of slivers of metal, and the soldier who came after Toon had a big piece in his heart. The rest of the family was unhurt. One grenade came in the chicken coop on their place and flattened it, killing all their chickens.

Some soldiers brought Toon to the hospital and Grandpa was helped on our first aid post. They never went back to their house during the rest of the war. Some other families; the family of John Den Ouden, who lived in Schijndel where it was a lot worse, moved right in and stayed there for the rest of the war. Grandpa's family moved father up too, but we just stayed, because it was not safe anywhere.

We tried to live through it as good as we could. I cooked food for those Germans because they wanted to use the cook stove and we had only one. They brought the food in, because they steal everything, where they could lay hands on. Then we had at least to eat. We had still some cows. They had hoof and mouth disease and the milk had to be cooked, but the meat was not safe to eat. Lucky for us, so we had something left.

The Germans had a lot of vodka they brought back from Russia and they drank themselves drunk many times. We lived for those last 5 weeks in a kind of nobody land, each one trying to find food, just where it was, then stay inside and wait for things to come. But at the end of October the Allieds started to move up again and that was the final days for us in the south of Holland. They ran the Germans over the Meus, a river about 20 miles north of us, and there they stayed for the rest of that awful winter, when in the north part of Holland thousands of people died of hunger and nobody could do a thing about it. The Germans took everything out and the Allieds could bring nothing in yet. It took them more than 6 months to drive the Germans out of Holland.

I still remember the night when those Germans who were living in our house took off. They took all they could carry of food and medication from the aid post. There was some pudding left from the day before and that officer got mad that he did not know how to take that damn pudding along too. Too bad, we did eat it.

I can still see them go. So big they came in, with all their power and majesty. So small and humble they have to move out. They packed their stuff in wheelbarrows, baby buggies and all what could hold something, old bikes and so on. It was a miserable group. They were really defeated.

Next morning another chapter opened up for us. After a sleepless night spent mostly in the shelter, the Allieds drove in on big panzer wagons. About 10, maybe more, soldiers were sitting on top of it. Their fingers up in a V sign. We were told to greet them the same way, which we did of course. All people came from their holes in the ground and standing on the road, welcoming the Allieds. But an hour or so later, they came back on those big panzers, some of them dripping with blood. They ran into some resistance with dug in Germans farther up. It was an awful sight. The good hopes we had in the morning fell all in our shoes. We went in the shelter again and prayed that those Germans would not come back.

But a few hours alter the Allieds came in again, this time with so many panzers it was unbelievable. They did not drive over the road like the first ones did. They came through the fields, almost shoulder to shoulder. Ran over everything, except house, and this time I tell you, they did get through. But they had to build new bridges everywhere. They were all blown up, before they could move on.

The next night, we were glad to sleep in our bed again, but not much came of sleeping. The Allieds put up row upon row of cannons, about a hundred yards from our house. And those things were shooting all night through. I thought it was worse than when we slept in the barn on straw with the rest of those wounded and sick Germans. One of them snored so hard I still sometimes think I hear him.

But to come back on those cannons, we had an all brick house, and it was shuddering so hard we thought it will fall apart, every minute. We had to hold John, Christine and Maria all night , so scared were those kids. And that lasted for 3 days and nights to come. Then they moved up farther. And we had to give our living room again, but this time for American officers. They had their own food, nice white bread, we had not seen for years. Candy bars, cigarettes and all kinds of goodies. They ate beans for breakfast with tomato sauce, rolls and powdered eggs.

But they were very friendly and pleasant to have them in the house. The next weeks, we try to go from life again. So good we could. But it was difficult, short of almost everything.

But first of all we could be thankful. Daddy, Johnny, Christine, Maria and myself were healthy and that was more than a lot of people could say. Grandpa was feeling okay again and they moved back to their farm again. For Uncle Toon it was very difficult with the loss of his right arm, and he was not able to cope with it. Especially when the father of his girlfriend insisted that she drop him because he was not able to make a living. The rest of our close relatives came out okay too.

After a few days, when we could go visit our relatives again, we found out Uncle Chris had saved my father's homestead from disaster with the help from Sr. Gertrudis. They were both home yet, and some younger sisters and brothers too. They had to move too, but Uncle Chris and Gertrudis stayed on their own risk. Hide and milk all the cows even some from the neighbors who had fled. Slept at night in an underground shelter. In the morning they ran back to the farm and take care of their livestock and hide themselves when the grenades fell all around them.

And on that famous morning the Allieds moved in and because they shoot everything on fire, because of resistance here and there, Uncle Chris and his sisters lay flat on the barn floor against a wall, praying to be spared. They promised to give a lot of help and money to people who lost everything.

When the shooting stopped and they looked outside, the farm buildings were on fire, and they got out. Then the neighbor's farm started burning and try to do something too, but there was no help to it. It all burned down. And more and more farms started burning, because those Allieds shoot with phosphor and that start fire by itself. But the war itself was over for us in the South. In the North the war did go on until Germany fell on May 1945.

In those last months, however, we had to overcome another evil. Flying bombs, no pilots in them. That was Hitler's secret weapon, but he came too late with it. They fell on his own troops just so good than on us. They were mostly meant for the harbors and England. They were like missiles. Later on they had the V-2, and those were awful, when they hit a target. There was nothing left nor people or houses or trees.

On the morning of the 5th of March 1945, when William was a day old, we heard a flying bomb coming. But as long as the motor was heard they would go farther. But when it stopped, they would fall in a few seconds. And we heard that too. I took William and the 3 older ones in my bed and stuck them all under the blankets for protection from flying glass. And lucky again, no windows broke. That bomb fell about ½ mile from our place.

All over the village you saw graves from soldiers with a little cross on and their helmets hanging on top of the cross. They were Germans and Allied alike. Later on they were brought back to their own countries or buried in cemeteries all over the land. In 1969 and again in 1972 we visited such cemeteries and I can still cry. So many thousands of young boys killed in the bloom of their life.

But life had to go on, and America, Canada, Argentina and New Zealand, they open up their arms to take in all those people who lost everything and could not make a living anymore.

Aunt Petra's mother lost everything she had too, including her husband. He drove with his horse and wagon on a land mine, one of those evils left from the war.

And because Bertha's brothers and sisters were already living in America they told her, come over here, we help you make a new start again. And so they did make the move, too. And because Uncle Chris was engaged to Petra, he did go along too. Father did not like it, but he could not give Uncle Chris a future as a farmer neither, and that was all he wanted. And sure he make the most of it. Too bad Father could never see it.

Now I should tell you that we had our good days too, in spite of the war. Everyone was in the same boat, and you learn to live with it. Our first son John was born on February 20, 1941. And he was a great joy for us. Daddy was so proud of him; every minute he could make free, he was playing with him. The whole household is built around those first born, and we just enjoy it. He was very good looking and intelligent. And a very mild character, just like Daddy.

We had to buy most things we needed in the black market, but we were ourselves not holy beans either, and sold to the black market too. We had to in order to survive.

It was forbidden to make butter. You had to deliver the milk to the factory, but we did it anyway. We made the butter at night. Then we have to hide all the equipment plus the butter, because you could always expect controllers, and boy, when they found anything. They take you to city hall and once you are on the black list they never trust you again.

One time we hid for awhile our butter making stuff in a hole in the ground and cover it with straw and junk so it would not get any attention. Then some controllers came for a search party and one of those men was standing right on that spot. Was I afraid that he would fall through and discover the whole thing. But we had good luck and run never in serious trouble.

We had plenty of scares and sleepless nights because it was the same thing if you wanted meat for yourself. You could raise pigs, but you could not butcher for yourself. Maybe one, but the rest you have to bring away and was paid a fixed price for. But we worked at night and most of the time without light, otherwise you could betray yourself. We had some neighbors who were really good at it, to bring you on.

But I should say too, we did not turn away big families who had it hard and were hungry. We did sell on them too, but not black market prices. And the beggars who came to the house every day, there was no end to it. They had all big families and they just send the kids out to beg and the men stay in their camping place and lay around to play cards. If you asked the kids, what's your father doing, they answer he has the sickness. Sure they had!

Later years Hitler make an end to this, by placing those camp dwellers in big camps and they had to stay there and send the men to Germany to work in factories. That's at least one good thing he did. I believe in Holland they kept that law later on too.

I still remember the morning Christine was born, May 6, 1942. A gypsy woman was standing before the window of our bedroom. She wanted to come in. She could say the future for the baby, she said, but we did not let her in of course. I was so glad that it was over again, and every couple who has first a son, and then a beautiful daughter, feels so rich. They think they can feed the whole world.

And the world did go on in spite of night raids from bombers going to bomb Germany. You get used to that too. We were lucky to be a farmer. We had at least enough to eat.

Fifteen and a half months later, August 25, 1943, Maria was born and I had my hands full at the time. Help was hard to get, but Dad's mother was good to us and she came in now and then to take John and Christine along for a while, and helped out with household chores. We had to do the wash by hand, and later on by machines that you have to turn yourself. That was hard work.

So good as no soap was available, and what you got was through distribution and real bad quality. And the water we had to haul from a water hole to wash with. The drinking water came from a pit and was too hard to do the wash with. So work enough. Nowadays the farmers have running water, gas for heating, phones, light, everything we have here. A big difference from the time we started out. But all by all, the days went on. The children were healthy and did grow up fast. Maria walked already when she was 11 months old. Was kind of hard and we had to keep her a lot in the playpen. John and Christine did run outside and it was hard in the months when the war was getting worse, and those grenades came
 flying over, to catch the kids and run in the basement hoping to be a little safer over there. You could hear them coming. They made a high whistling sound before they struck. How

many times I run with those kids under my arms, in the kitchen table which was standing always in the way. The kitchen was small, myself big, because I was pregnant with William, and two kids to hold on to. I had blue spots all over my legs.

One time I remember a cold rainy fall day. The wood stove burning to keep the kitchen and the kids warm. Four soldiers (Germans) came in, dripping wet from sitting in those dug out trenches, and they wanted to warm themselves. They put their guns in the corner of the kitchen and threw the rest of their dangerous stuff, like live hand grenades, in the playpen where Maria was standing in. Boy did they scare me. And I could not say anything to them. Just take Maria out and sit and sweat it out until they left again. That was worse than working with a 3, a 2, and 1 year old, that they not touch anything.

No wonder I had thought later on when William had to go to Vietnam he hated it so, because fear of war and war material is born in him. From this date on I should on to the last months of the war, which I wrote earlier, and after Uncle Chris and Aunt Petras family left for America.

We still could not see at this time that we too should come to a point when there was no place to go. And that came in 1947 when a son of our landlord wanted to get married and we had to move out. We try on every place we could think of to buy or rent a farm, but no luck. Even Daddy's family and my father too, tried hard to find anything, but you could not buy a farm, you must inherit it, to get one. Daddy's family were still his parents and 3 brothers and a sister at home at that time. On my side, my father, a brother and 2 sisters were living on the old farm. So no room for us. Then Uncle Chris, who was living here in America a year already, wrote why try to come over here. There is room enough and we start thinking about it. We try to get information, and we found that it all was faster said than done.

We had six children by this time. Ida born March 16, 1946 and Tony born June 28, 1947. The year when Uncle Chris left for America. And the year it was so dry and hot that so good as no crops did grow. Everything was burned. We did not have a drop of rain all summer. And we had to sell all the livestock except 2 cows, was all we had left. And our horse, that we kept too. How we get through that next winter, I still don't know. But in October 1947 something happened that was even worse. Our oldest boy, John, got sick. He was for many weeks complained tired, but he looked good, eat good, was even getting too heavy. But we thought, blind as we were, he just don't like school. But one day he came home from school with a puffed up face and we saw really for the first time that something was worse. So we send for a doctor and he said that John had something wrong with his kidneys. And after a few days, doctor put him in a hospital in Boxtel where we lived. But it did get worse and he was transferred to a big hospital in De Bosch to stay there for the rest of his life.

Daddy and I drove up every day, one day Daddy, next day myself, with a bike a full hour to it and an hour back. Through most of the time, rain and wind, snow and cold to see him. And to see him grow worse and still could not believe that he never would get better. You see it happen to other people, but you kept on hoping it won't happen to us. But it did. After 7 months of real suffering, God take him back from us. He had so many injections he had spots as big as a hand on his thighs and arms. It did not even heal up any more. And he did get so heavy from water building up between his skin and flesh that he was just like a big lump. Then the day before he died, the doctor tried to drain some water off, and could not recognize him. The next day he died.

I am sure now that God did John and us a big favor, to take him out of his suffering, but I could not see it then and I did grow bitter and said, God, why us? We had such high hopes to take him along to America. He was always talking about it. He liked farm work and could, at the age of six, already milk a cow by hand, feed the chickens and help all, really, out around the house. He made his first communion in the hospital. The nurses brought him in the chapel from the sisters in his bed. They had his bed dressed all up with real flowers and put a big candle on each side of this bed. The priest came to him to give John the Bread of Life for the first time. It had to strengthen John and ourselves because he did not want to die. Some other children had told him what they had heard from the nurse that he never could get better and he cried. He understood even though he was just 7 years old.

I think this was the greatest sacrifice we ever had to bring. When I saw my mother die, I thought I cannot bear it, but this was worse. There is in my dresser a red box with little things in it which belonged to him. Some little pictures he get from the nurses with his first communion and some stones from his grave and a little booklet he wrote some words in and his name. He died on May 19, 1948. Life had to go on, however, because the time was growing short that we had to leave the farm.

We have to clear out by next spring. Uncle Chris found an uncle and aunt of Petra who would be our sponsors. Walter and Mary Van Eperen from Kimberly. Mary was a sister of Petra's mother, Bertha van Grinsven. Must be people with a big heart because they had 14 children of their own. We all should be grateful to them. Mary died, but Walter is still living on S. Wilson St. 222, Kimberly. He is 85 years old now.

When Terry was born on September 19, 1948, we named her Waltera Maria, after our sponsors. Later, she changed her name to Terry because Tera was an uncommon name here. But before Terry was born we had to go to Rotterdam with the family for a health check up and a lot of red tape in the American Embassy. But they all were very friendly and not snobbish. More than we could say from our own bureaucrats from which we were sometimes afraid to ask anything. Everything went out okay, but I had to come back when Terry was born to show the baby. They did not buy a cat in the sack, I tell you.

We went by train, the whole family. The neighbors take over the care of the farm for that day. We had good neighbors, except one that was a stinker. But he was a drinker and maybe he envied us that he could not keep up. I was so sorry for his family, they really suffered from him.

When Terry was 3 weeks old we went back to Rotterdam again. She needed a picture too for her passport. Sorry, I don't know where that picture went. But she is on the big picture we had made just before we left for America. That last winter in Holland we were really busy.

Had to visit all our relatives, sell our livestock, sold it most to relatives. It was just or it hurt not so much then. Our beautiful horse went to Grandpa Vander Heyden. That was the only thing I really, and Daddy even more, would have taken along if it was possible. That did really hurt. It was a mare and had the most darling colt you could think of. Then January came in sight and we must start to pack. We asked some rich guy if we could cut a little oak tree from his woods, to pay of course for it, to make a big crate, but he would not sell, so Daddy take it anyway, and did not pay for it. That wooden tray where we made bread in for all those years is made from that crate. That must be from oak wood, so it will not (sprintel), or better say sliver. We packed all what we could take along and sold the rest just to friends and neighbors. Was not easy, but had to be done too.

Then the first days of January all the kids get the measles, plus a bad cold. It takes almost 3 weeks before they all had it. And we have to get a check up from the doctor, and a certificate that all the kids were in good health, otherwise we could not get on the boat. When we make that last picture, we had to take Christine out of her bed, wrap her in a blanket, and take her to the photographer. You can see on the picture she was still sick. Then the last days come up soon, and we sent Christine and Maria to my father's house in Schijndel until the morning of January 31, we had to go.

Bill, Ida, Tony and Terry stayed at Grandfather Vander Heyden's place. We did go up and down there, because it was only a mile. We had to clean the house, and do all kinds of odd jobs yet before it was all finished. The last nights we slept at Grandpa's place too. We did not have a bed left to sleep in. Everything was packed or sold. The big crate was sent out by rail to Rotterdam and it cost plenty. The tickets for the boat I think we had to buy before too, but I am not sure of what. Terry has all those papers; I give them to her. Otherwise I could give more information. Maybe later on I can ask them back if anyone wants to know.

Then January 31 came and we had to say goodbye. My father would not go along to see us off in Rotterdam. We went to say goodbye to him the night before. Boy, did that hurt. I never saw him back again. He died on December 2, 1956. He was born August 13, 1878. (My mother died May 29, 1933 and was born April 16, 1884). Father died of age and a weak heart. Mother died of heart trouble and cirrhosis of the liver. She had gallstones but for some reason the doctor never take them out. Also a brother of mine died at the age of 19. He died of pleuritis; fluid in the lungs. I include this because John wanted to know our family health history. From Daddy's side: Grandfather was born February 4, 1880 and died of old age on August 15, 1969. Grandmother Vander Heyden was born on May 16, 1883 and died of a brain tumor on December 6, 1951.

So we better go in the bus, and travel to Rotterdam. A lot of relatives went along to see us off. On the way we passed the cemetery where our little John was laid to rest. I had to look for the last time and cried, of course. Christine who saw it, said, Momma don't cry. John is flying right along with us. Good advice. What could I do but take him along in my mind. I could not part with him neither.

When we reached Rotterdam harbor the boat was waiting for us. It was about 11:30 and by 12 o'clock the boat was to leave dock. So we had to hurry. The suitcases were brought to our huts, 2 we needed for 8 people. Daddy had a big hut with 5 of the oldest children and I had a small one with Terry in her basket. We had to say a hasty farewell, and before I had Terry in her basket, the boat was loose and sailed, or better was pulled out of the harbor in to the open sea. I tried yet or I could see our relatives standing on the harbor, but it was too late. We were off to the North Sea. We had to go right away to the dining room for our first lunch on board.

And because we did not have much of a breakfast that morning we eat good. But I was sorry for that pretty soon. The sea was so rough that the boat made such a motion that most people became seasick right away. And before it was 3 o'clock I was so sick that I wished the boat did go down and make an end to our misery. Daddy was lucky enough not that sick, but could not smoke. The kids had a ball. Mamma sick, could not go after them. Terry nothing to eat because I was feeding her myself. So we had to ask for a bottle and lucky on board they had everything. We give her all the way to America buttermilk cooked with a little flour and sugar. And for the rest some fruit juice. The food was really good and plenty. Too bad I could not eat, it came right out. So I laid down most of the day. If it was not too cold in a deck chair in my new fur coat.

The first morning we landed in England and the boat picked up some first class passengers. Vacationers going to Bermuda. When we sailed away from England, very soon we see the all white mountains of Scotland. They called it the slate I think. From then on it was just black water all we saw for the next week. I was getting sicker with the day because I could eat nothing. The stewardess told me you must be pregnant. I told her right off, because I thought it was not possible. But I found out later she was right. I was smuggling another baby along. I couldn't believe it. The first months I was thinking I was sick, because I was upset by all those troubles you had to get through, but another baby, that was my last thought. But after we settled down, there was no question about it. But when he was due, I did not know.

When we finally reached Bermuda, the sea was so rough that the loads who had to guide the big boat in could not come out from the island. So we drove around the island for about 24 hours. Now we saw Bermuda from one side and after a few hours from another side. The boat cannot even come close because of the riffs in the sea. When the sea calmed down a little the loads came out, followed by a bigger boat, to take on the passengers and off we went again, in the open sea. Another few days left of sea sickness. During our trip on the sea Tony was best known with our fellow passengers. He was just a holy terror. He was a year and a half old then. Could not walk, but run, from one end of the deck to the other and we constantly lost him. Other people with kids that age had them on a kind of leash or halter, but I did not think of it to take one along. He was all the time in danger and other people usual help keep an eye on him. But one time he crept under the ropes which were around the openings to lower decks and I could not reach him. He sat there just looking over the edge, and could have fallen over it, maybe 20 foot or more deep. Finally he came back, to my pleading and sweet talk to him.

On table he wanted always eggs and more eggs and after a week or so he broke out in a bad skin rash. So we had to feed him along, before our dinner, and put him in his bed and we could eat at least ourselves in peace.

Maria scared once the day lights of us by climbing on the rail of the ships in full speed and just sitting on those big knobs in the rail where they tied the ships up on the harbors. And the ship was doing 350 knots a day. How much that is, I don't know. But I think it means sea miles.

At night when the kids were sleeping, Daddy and I took walks over the decks if I was not too sick and the boat was a bit still. Looked in the ballroom where dancing, music and drinking was going on. A lot of people played cards or games too. Terry has still a ships newspaper. It said how many people were on the boat and who. Terry is called Mr. W.M. Vander Heyden. They could not figure out if it was a boy or girl and they never asked neither. But the Captain of the ship, who had no children of his own, said he wanted really badly to take Terry over, and he came back again and again. I started thinking that he meant it. For the rest the kids behaved good and finally the harbor of Hoboken, New Jersey came in sight. First I always thought how come I did not see the Statue of Liberty, but I found out later that we did not land in New York but New Jersey.

When the kids heard we were in America they just went wild. And I had a hard time keeping them together because Daddy had to go to the customs to fill paper, show our x-rays we had to take along from Holland, and on and on it went. I don't know for how many hours it take. You could not take any food or fruit along from the boat, and the kids were getting hungry and tired. But I did feel better since we had landed. The sea sickness just fell off like something you drop. And because it did go with the letter, and having a V, we were almost last in the line. Finally they opened up the big crate, and a lot of wooden shoes came rolling out, and they nailed it shut right away. Which was good because we had all the pork and hams from 2 fat pigs in it, and that was forbidden, but we just take a risk on. But we eat from it for months to come. Even Uncle Chris helped with it. He had missed it he said for 2 years.

When we finally were through, some people from the Salvation Army came to us. They were sent by Mrs. Walter Van Eperen, to help us with getting taxis to go the railroad station. We had a letter from Mrs. Van Eperen and they had our names to match. So we could trust them. They were very friendly and helped a lot. I was most afraid because we had to go with 2 taxis that we not stayed together. It is hard if you do not understand anybody, and it was kind of a long drive.

But we get there all right and they helped us with tickets and brought us in the train. Too bad I never saw those people back to thank them for everything they did. The big crate was sent out later. It takes more than 2 weeks before we finally did get it in Kimberly. We had another letter from Mrs. Van Eperen which we could show to the train personnel and order some food. That was 9 o'clock at night. The kids were over tired and Maria got sick and had to throw up. Boy what a mess. Then it was warm in the train and the kids throwed their clothes on all places and we could hardly keep track of them until they finally fell asleep just on the benches in the train. We did not have sleeping space. It was too costly.

That was February 14, 1949. The 15th we sat in the train until sometime afternoon when we had to take another train in Chicago. Uncle Chris and Aunt Petra met us over there and take care for the next train ride to Appleton. And that was not a pleasant ride either. Uncle Chris was not used to little kids yet, and sure they were unruly. Specially Bill and Tony. What did he expect from a 3 and 2 year old. That they sit nice hour after hour and smile? Boy, I am glad he had his share too from nice little kids.

But we made it to Appleton where Math Van Handel and sons and son-in-law from Bertha Van Grinsven were waiting for us with cars to pick us up and bring us to Math Van Handel. Everyone must have helped, because they had place to sleep even a big lunch ready and it was about 1 o'clock midnight, February 16, 1949.

When we lay in bed it was just of my bed was still moving ahead and all what I could think of was that I would do this never over again. I still hate to travel. I could not know by then, how close I had come to be sent back when 10 weeks later, Daddy got in a bad accident. Mr. and Mrs. Van Handel were really good to us, but it was still an ordeal to me because we lived upstairs and had to keep those kids down. It was winter and they could not much go outside. And it was so hot upstairs and those windows were frozen shut. I thought I die here.

Daddy try to find work, but he could not speak English, and it was faster said than done. Besides, it was winter and no need for unskilled workers neither. Uncle Chris worked at that time in Kimberly Clark mill in Kimberly and he worked part-time for room and board on the farm for Van Handel. So all Daddy could do, help in the barn and Math let us live for nothing in his house, even we did get free milk. This lasted for 6 weeks. I will be always grateful to Van Handel and Uncle Chris for pulling us through. Uncle Chris had bought a farm in Neenah, but could not move in before April 1st. He had not meant that farm, but he had to buy something to get us out over there. But, I think he is blessed royal that he bought that farm, if you know the money he had made from selling it later on.

Our biggest trouble was that Daddy could not get work and our little bit of money we had was going down fast We could only take along $90.00 for each grownup and $45.00 for each child. So $450.00 in all and we had to pay our train tickets from New York with it, and the freight for the big crate plus a smaller one with a bike in it. And besides this on the railroad they had let us pay $30.00 too much, but later on we did get it back. Then came April 1st along and we packed again for the move to the farm in Neenah. The night before we had a big snow storm and it brought all some troubles along. Besides that Tony had played with some old spark plugs and fell on one, right above his eye. Just what we needed. No time to see a doctor and no money either. A first aid band over it and away we had to go. What a ride.

Uncle Chris had bought a couple of horses from Art Van Handel, and those were loaded in an open trailer, and an old one beside it. Daddy was never so afraid he said later. Because he had to hold those horses with their halters, and just standing between those big horses. He was not scared of the horses but the floor was so bad he was afraid from falling through. Math Van Handel had a truck where all the stuff had to go on. Uncle Chris drove his car where we were all piled in. On the way a box fell off the truck. Maria saw it but because Uncle Chris had not seen it he would not believe it and we drove just on. I found out afterwards Maria was right but it was too late. We never had it back because there was no address on it. But we made it to the farm and how busy we were to get settled a little. Uncle Chris changed his work from Kimberly to Lake View in Neenah.

On the 10th of April Daddy found finally work in Menasha in a small factory where they made carton boxes. But our luck run once more out, after only 10 days working. Daddy did get in a bad accident. He was helping unload a box car with rolls of raw paper when a roll slipped off the front loader of a tractor and not knowing how heavy such a roll was (5000#), Daddy try to hold it but the roll catch him and Daddy came between the roll and the door frame of the box car with his head. Still wonder how he ever came out alive. Afterwards he said he heard his head crack and that was it. He passed out of course. They brought him by ambulance to the hospital in Neenah. He had all the skin from his ears and neck off, but must had not suffered serious in his head, because after 10 days he was back at work again. Lucky for us all, because Uncle told me that he had warned Daddy good to be careful and that in case he would die or was not able to work again, he was sending us back to Holland. But Dutchmen have hard heads it said in the newspaper that day, and Daddy came through nice and he never suffered from it later on. Later on Daddy had an accident. Someone hit him with the car when he rode his bike from work. He fell, but was not seriously hurt. After 1 ½ years of riding his bike, Daddy bought our first car and Ted Coppens learned Daddy to drive.

We had a lot of friendship with Mr. Arthur Nould, his wife and daughter, Celia. They lived across the road from Uncle Chris' farm. And since Daddy had regular work, things became easier for us. It was just $41.00 a week, but we made it. We did not have to pay much rent; I believe 10 dollars a week, plus light and heat. And Uncle Chris boarded with us until he did get married. Things worked out not the way we had expected, but we lived on hope once we made a go out of it. We could start out on our own.

We had good days, because we had a happy and healthy family and waited for the new baby to arrive. A happy day was also when we could afford an old radio. Then I get more used to the English language and picked up everyday new words. Also with Christine and Maria going to school helped all of us to learn. At night we take the little reading books, those with pictures in it, then we found out best what it means.

We had a garden that summer, but I found out that it was really hard to work the soil. It was all red clay. But a good summer passed, and the time must be there that the new baby was due. We were 8 months in America already and I was sure we brought him along from Holland. But because we did not have coverage from insurance (you have to be 9 month insurance first) and we could not afford to go to the hospital on our own cost. Uncle Chris found an old doctor in Little Chute who promised to come to the house when it was so far.

I met him once and he take my blood pressure. That was all the care I had before. But I felt so good as was possible, so I did not worry. Even the day before John was born, I worked all day, had a big wash done and all kinds of work. I even felt like doing a little dance with Terry in my arms because she loved music and I usually did this when the rest were all in bed. Then I give her a bath, fed her and she slept all night. So I did get through the same routine before I went to bed. I just loved little babies. But I woke up that night about 12 and told Daddy I think the baby will come tonight. But Daddy was tired and said you did not feel anything all day, you must be mistaken. Go to sleep. And so did he. But I could not sleep and went out of bed and did some odds and ends which should be done in case it was not a false alarm.

And it was not. So we woke Uncle Chris and he called that doctor in Little Chute, but to his horror, he heard a big argument going on in the doctor's house and he could not get an answer from the doctor. Because before Uncle Chris had a chance to explain, the doctor threw the horn from the phone down, and there Uncle Chris stood and time was pressing on. All what he could do was take the car and ride to Little Chute, which was a hour driving. But lucky he asked first Mrs. Nault, our neighbor, or she could come over. All help was better than nothing. She came over right away and lucky she did. We could not understand each other, but Johnny thought nothing about it. He found his way anyway. Poor soul Mrs. Nault, she prayed that no complications would happen. Daddy sweated and did what he could and my only wish was to get him out, doctor or no doctor. I couldn't care less. My only worry was that the other kids keep on sleeping and that we did not get an audience, which could have happened with 6 kids in the house. Then Uncle Chris came back with Petra, her mother and Mrs. Van Eperen, because that doctor was drunk and not able to come along. When we had called he had an argument with his wife, who was also drunk.

But 2 ½ hours later, the doctor had asked his neighbor to drive him to Neenah and finally there he was. But everything was settled already. He looked things over and left. He did not come back for 4 days and everything went just fine. I am sure that was the least complicated delivery I ever had. So you see, God is right there when you need Him most. Just ask for His help.

Aunt Petra did stay for 3 days, then she had to go back to work. Daddy could not stay home at all. He had only worked 7 months and no vacation coming. So I had to take over myself after 3 days. Promise to take it easy, don't climb steps and so on. But I was out of bed just a few hours and looked outside where the kids were playing and saw Tony hanging over a piece of netting which was around a big stinking mud puddle, which came from the kitchen sink. No sewer yet on that farm. He was not able to go back and would have fallen over it. So I had to run outside and grab him. He would have smothered in the pool.

When that doctor came back on the fourth day he did not have much to say. He came with his neighbor again and he kept the conversation on everything but me and Johnny. But he was so decent never to send a bill neither. Which was fine with us. Should include also that William was always begging in the first time we lived in America, Mom when will we finally get to America. And if I told him we are already in America he said, Oh that's nothing. We are just at Uncle Chris' place.

We were happy and our good times and anxious times. Special when Daddy came home sick from his work. He always thought it was just a cold on his stomach, but years later we found out that this were really gallstone attacks. He had them so now and then already when we get married. That he became greenish pale and had to sit down for awhile. But he did not want to go to the doctor. Real Dutchman! Can handle everything by himself.

First we thought if he had a car and did not suffer so much cold it would get better, but that was not true. But we had to wait buying a car that was 1 ½ years later. It cost $600.00. Until then Daddy did go to work by bike, winter and summer. In the winter he was sometimes almost frozen.

Next spring, April 1950, Uncle Chris and Aunt Petra got married and they take a honeymoon to Holland by boat. And afterwards they moved in the front part of the house and we upstairs and the kitchen and dining room. But later on, when Gary was born, and our Paul, the house became a little crowded and we had to look for a place of our own. Was faster said than done because we were still immigrants. You could not become a citizen before you are 5 years in America. So once again, we needed first down payment of our own. You cannot get credit on a bank if you are only an immigrant. So when we had saved $4,000.00 we finally could buy a small farm. How I ever scraped it together I still do not know. But everything count, and we really had to watch every penny.

Once in those winter days we did get in a car accident (wet sleet road) and we collected $90.00 from the car insurance. We just drove around with a big dent in the car and saved the money for a down payment on a farm. Later on in Sherwood we got it fixed. But then we lived on our farm we always wanted. It was just 40 acres, but that was all we could afford. We had by then $4,000.00 and borrowed $8,000.00 from the bank in Kaukauna. Borrowed $1,000.00 from Uncle Chris for the inventory of the farm, an old tractor and some more antique stuff But it worked and we felt the richest people in the world. Daddy had by then found better work at Kimberly Clark and earned about $70.00 a week. I always liked that place. Even in the years when we lived in Neenah and on Sundays we packed all the kids in the car and just drove around to look at farms. One Sunday we did get in Sherwood and how nice you could look away from that hill. Never thought by then some day we would live there. You can see if you wish hard enough for something you may get it too.

It started off the first days with finding out all about school for the kids, and I did not know what to do when I found out that next Sunday the kids did their first communion in Sherwood. And Maria was 8 years old already and had not much preparation because they attended public school in Neenah. So she had to go on Sunday morning to the Sister house and the Sister gave her some instructions. That was the third one to make the first communion on odd circumstances. First our little John on his sick bed in a hospital chapel. Then Christine at the age of 6 because our pastor thought it is the best way to do it before we left for America. Because he was afraid it would take a time before the kids could talk

60

English. But before this all happen, we get our youngest son Paul, and that was another reason that we should move on our own place.

Uncle Chris and Petra had already 3 children of their own and I am sure it was a welcome move for them too. They needed the house themselves. We looked around for a long time already, but it was hard to find something that fitted our pocket book. But finally we had luck and found the place in Sherwood where we lived for the next 18 years. And for your information, we paid Uncle Chris $1,000.00 back and the bank in Kaukauna just within 4 years. With God's blessings and a lot of hard work.

You know all what happen I think in those years we lived in Sherwood. I think it is reasonable to say, we live quite happy in those years. It brought its ups and downs along, but who doesn't have them. Life has to go on no matter what. We are all just people passing through the world and we try to make it so good we could. It doesn't make any difference if you live in Holland or in America if you live within God's commandments. God will be right there to help when the load gets too heavy. So I close with prayer that God may bless and guide you through all your life.

Will all my love, Mom

Interview for naturalization in 1957 before Charles Hayes, examiner for
the Immigration and Naturalization Service
Front: John, Paul, Waltera (Teri)
Middle: Nicholas, Anthony, Bertha, Ida
Back: Maria, Christine, William
Photo courtesy of the Vander Heyden family

Milwaukee County

[Arnoldus Hallerdyk (later known as Nelson Hollerdyk) was born 16 Jan 1821 in Zelhem, Gelderland, Netherlands and died 20 May 1906 in Waupun, WI. While living in Milwaukee he married Aleida Loomans on 12 April 1845. She was born 8 October 1823 in Winterswijk, Gelderland, Netherlands. This letter is from the Dutch Immigrant Letters Collection, Archives, Calvin College, Grand Rapids, MI, Box 27, Folder 28.]

Milwaukee 1845

To my dear father!
Dear and much beloved Father, Brothers and Sisters!

I cannot delay keeping my promise to you, since to my sincere regret I have heard this winter from those who came over to us, that the letter which I sent on February 1845 was not received by you.

You would very likely think that you had been forgotten, but that is not true. Although I am now far from you, no one is forgotten by me. So I let you know that we are, as a result of the Lord's blessing, still well, which we also heartily wish of you. If it was otherwise, it would be to our sorrow.

On July 1 we set out to sea from Hellevoetsluis, but the sea was stormy so that everyone became seasick. But I did not become sick at all and the sickness was not dangerous. After two or three days everyone was better. Then we went ahead slowly and had a contrary wind. The sea did not bother us. We did not encounter a threat to our lives on the way as we crossed the areas.

So we lay quietly on July 5 and 6. There were 155 of us passengers on the ship, and we had a surplus of fish. Then on July 25 we arrived in New York, where we remained for only one day. This is a very large city.

Then we left again by steamer for Albany; from there by canal boat to Buffalo. This was drawn by horses. From there we went to Westful, which is 565 miles from New York, where we made our first stay. We soon discovered that we were in a better land because the wages here are higher and there are no deductions. Everything is equally fertile here. One can raise all manner of crops on the same soil without fertilizing: wheat, potatoes, rye, peas, beans. There is little buckwheat here. Various kinds of crops which are unknown to you. The standard of living is very good also.

I have not seen rye bread in America. We have pork and beef three times a day. Living supplies are very cheap here. Wheat costs five shillings per bushel, a pound of pork costs seven cents, beef three to four cents, and everything else in proportion.

I got a job on August 12 (as a carpenter) and was there five months. J.W. Looman has also lived here with his family. On April 12 I became married to the daughter of Looman, by the name of A.L.B. Looman, born in Winterswijk. Then we moved to Milwaukee. This country is called Wisconsin, which is 146 miles farther, so that we are 2065 hours distant from Rotterdam. There are very good pastures. I do a lot of take in work and earn ten to twelve shillings a day. I have also hired two young men for two years, for 100 gulden per year, as apprentices.

Land is very cheap here. I have purchased sixty acres for 10 shillings per acre. The land is mostly wooded, but there is also much other land here. There is a good deal of woods on the land I bought, enough for fuel and lumber. We can cultivate and plow without clearing away the wood. I have sown with winter wheat.

In addition to this, things are favorable for everyone here. A day laborer earns as a rule six shillings at grass mowing time, at harvest time eight shillings and board. A farm hand earns ten to twelve dollars a month, but a person who first arrives here and does not know the English language does not earn as much. We learn English in six months so that we can converse with people very well and can understand in church.

There is freedom for all religions here, but there are many religions, and as far as we have discovered, the most important is that of the Seceders. We have also found that many are true worshipers, who leave behind what is past, and pursue what lies ahead, and true servants of Christ. No business is done here on Sunday. Then all stores are closed.

Dear friends and acquaintances, I do not wish to boast as I write, except as I have found things to be. Last May many have come over, among them a G.J. Meenk, from Winterswijk, whose son went with us last year. He found that it was so much better here that he felt obliged to ask his parents to come over. But when they were here, he had to hear a great deal of criticism because they thought that when they were here they would not have to work. But you people must not imagine this to be true: a person does not have to work as hard as in the Netherlands because one can earn as much in one day as in one week by you. So I think you can conclude yourselves that it is worthwhile to come over. I would also like to talk to you face to face. But I do not wish to be back in Holland if you think it is not worth while, so surely some will come over.

I with you would send a few letters since it is not certain that the letters sent here from Holland arrive. So I hope that you will send a letter. I hope with my whole heart that the blessing of the Lord may attend you. May He grant you His blessing spiritually and physically, either in your Fatherland or at sea.

I hope you will receive news from N.N. who has gone west. Please let me hear about it. I herewith break off with the pen. Receive the greetings from me and my wife. Let anyone who wishes read this. Dutch silver is not of value here but gold is. A franc is also accepted here and a dollar is forth f2.50, and a mile is 20 minutes.   A.Hallerdyk

◆◆◆◆◆◆

[Pieter Leenhouts was born 16 March 1780 in Biervliet, Zeeland to Isaak and Levina (Hendriks) Leenhouts. He died 14 February 1872 in Franklin, WI. On 13 November 1805 in Ijzendijke, Zeeland he married Janna Haartsen. She was born to Cornelis and Janneke (van der Meulen) Haartsen on 1 July 1786 in Schoondijke, Zeeland and died 3 February 1859 in Franklin, WI. 24 of the passengers on the ship *Elizabeth of England* which arrived in New York 24 July 1848 were the families of Pieter and Janna Leenhouts and Isaac de Mersseman who had married their oldest daughter, Janneke. This letter is from the Dutch Immigrant Letters Collection, Archives, Calvin College, Grand Rapids, MI, Box 40, Folder 22.]

Milwaukee   25 September 1848

Dear family,

It has pleased the Lord to provide for us a place to live here in America. We are planning to leave for Michigan on the 7th and we thought it best to take a few days rest. It pleased the Lord to arrange it so that when we left the boat we met some country folk with whom we became acquainted, and who provided a house for us, however without windows and doors. In this house we were permitted to live, eighteen of us, for $3 per week, and we have been there since then.

During this time we had the opportunity to inquire about transportation, because we were always planning to go to Michigan. We have become acquainted with J. de Vos, who formerly lived at Breskens, and who has a son who speaks good English, and of which fact we have made good use. He advised us to look around for wood land of which we might make use. However, we have changed our mind about that on account of the difficult and impassable roads, and we have definitely determined to go to Michigan.

Not long ago we received a visit of a countryman named Jacob Verdouw, who helped in America at harvest time. He told us that his boss was planning to see his farm consisting of 200 acres, of which 80 acres is wood land and 120 acres prairie and pasture, of which latter 40 acres are tillable and suitable for wheat, oats, corn, white beans and potatoes. The potatoes, however, have been spoiled by smut and so I have, as carefully as possible, investigated this land for the reason that it seemed to me that providing the price is right we would be able to make a very comfortable existence with the Lord's blessing. The price would average $14 per acre and that would include all his stock and tools, except his horses and wagon.

I have bought a lot in Milwaukee on Holland Hill for Izaak Mersseman consisting of 54 rods and a dwelling in which Levina Leenhouts is living. This is close by and she is planning to build a house separate for herself.

I could write you a good deal about the big journey we have made, but I will put it off to some time in the future, hoping that it may please the Lord to continue us in life and in health because we all have suffered much. Kornelis has been very sick, and Jannis, who still is in Michigan, has been deathly sick, of which fact we have received news on August 27th by Mr. Houtkamp, who told us he was in serious condition. However, the doctors have observed some change in his illness so that there may be some hope for his recovery. Thereupon, Susanna on September 3rd has left with Houtkamp and she promised that in the event he did not show signs of improvement to send us a message by express, and in the event we received no news we could hope for an improvement in his condition. Accordingly, we have some guarantee of improvement because we have received no message. My wife also is weak, and all of us are now and then suffering from colds and fevers, and everyone has to be very careful of himself on account of the change of air, food and drink. I also want to let you know that Abram came with Houtkamp and that Pieter remained with Jannis. I think I have given you a very short insight in the condition in which we are now living. We are very anxious to get some news from our dear relations and all good friends, and to learn how everything is going in our dear fatherland, because here in America we are receiving very unfavorable news that all commerce in America is idle except the immigrant who arrive shipload after shipload, so that many of them are unable to obtain work and are at a loss to know how to get through the winter. We are very anxious to receive news of our nearest relatives and of all of our good friends, in regard to their physical and spiritual well being, and whether or not some of them may not have exchanged the temporary for an eternal condition. It would indeed be very pleasing to us if the Lord would permit us to see each other face to face where we are, because the country around here is very good, and in this vicinity there is much land to be had which is just as good as that which I have. There is even a small house for sale here with one acre of ground; a good house for the sum of $500, which is the equivalent of 1350 guilders in Dutch money, and this is located but one-quarter hour's journey from our house. We also hear that around about here there is quite a lot of work to be had, and a fired man could find work and make a living because he earns quite a little in odds and ends and with horses. It costs only $1 to shoe a horse all around. If necessary you could keep two cows because my pasture is only 15 minutes away. However, I do not insist that you shall come, but I would like to have you think it over. I would also like to know how the harvest has come out and what the price was of the crops and also this and that about the estate of Luisleeren, whatever you know about that.

I must stop now. We send our greeting to you and yours, and remain in expectation to receive a letter from you dear ones. May the Lord give us health, peace, faith and charity through the Holy Spirit for the sake of His great name.

We have the honor to remain respectfully your servants,

Pieter Leenhouts and Janna Haartsen

◆◆◆◆◆◆

[Jacob de Priester was born ca. 1804 in Groede, Zeeland to Adriaan and Levina (de Munck) de Priester. On 9 May 1838 in Axel, Zeeland he married Antonina Labee. The first two letters were written to Adriaan de Priester by his brother Jacob and his wife upon arriving in the U.S in 1849. The third letter as written by Adriaan de Priester to his brother-in-law, Pieter Baden. Adriaan married Levina Hermina Baden on 17 December 1834 in Sluis. She was the daughter of Johannes and Susanna Jacoba (Bal) Baden. The following letters are part of the correspondence between Pieter Baden and Adriaan de Priester. These letters are from the Dutch Immigrant Letters Collection, Archives, Calvin College, Grand Rapids, MI, Box 18, Folder 15 and Box 4, Folder 7.]

Rotterdam, Zuid Holland – Buffalo, New York
J. de Priester to family   15 May 1849

Dear Brother and Sister,
Your last letter of March 29 I did receive and I read how all of you are doing.

For the last time I write from the Netherlands and want to say goodbye to you, my sister and brother van Kee, and also to all your children and the entire family, because tomorrow I and my dear one will sail for North America, together with 24 persons from Axel and Zaamslag. Please excuse me that I didn't come to say farewell in person, but I didn't have the money But, I am going with people who have it, and they will help me, because the last two years I hardly earned anything and at the end would have ended up in poverty. Don't be sad about this, I trust it will go well. I probably will find something. When I arrive at my place of destination I'll write to you about everything. I plan to go to Buffalo or to the Colonies. I hope you'll receive this in good health, just like my wife and I are. Greetings to the entire family and I think that within five months you'll receive another letter from me, and then you all will know how everything is going here. I don't doubt that you will receive that with much joy.

> Greetings to all of you.
> Your brother,
> J. de Priester

◆◆◆◆◆◆

Buffalo, New York – Sluis, Zeeland   4 September 1849
A. de Priester to A. de Priester

Mr. A. de Priester at Sluis
Dear Brother and Sister!

About eight weeks ago we arrive here safely and have made our residence here as my husband J. de Priester was placed as superintendent at a canal but it has pleased the Almighty, before he commenced his service, to take him from me by the present cholera epidemic after suffering a very short time. You will readily realize the position in which I find myself. My friend who is writing this letter has written Rev. Vermeulen as to whether he can take me under his care as there is here no prospect of earning my own living. If that is possible there is still a long journey awaiting me. Please notify the rest of the family about this and hoping that you will receive this letter in good health as I find myself. Together with the wish that you will be spared yet for long time such striking blows. Greetings and regards I remain your deeply grieved sister.

Wed. J. de Priester (Antonia)

♦♦♦♦♦♦

Sluis, Zeeland – Milwaukee, Wisconsin   12 June 1857
A. de Priester to P. Baden

Dear Brother,

Thanks be to God. We received your letter in good health in which you wrote to us the sad tiding that the Lord of life and death took unto Himself your wife. We all share your sadness, but on the other side we rejoice with you that you could yield her so joyfully to the Father in the blessed hope to meet again in eternity. It is only temporary here. We fully understand that you have a hard time making a decision about your two small children. Oh brother, we don't know it either. Talk with God. He will reveal it to you through Christ Jesus. And trust the promise, then you will not be mislead. Yes, brother, daily everything tells us that this is not a permanent city. Seek, pray, do not cease before you have formed that city that reaches into life eternal.

And where shall we start to let you know what is happening here. Sad tidings after sad tidings. You probably received notice of the passing of the wife of brother Kobus. But to understand his cross I only want to tell you that in a period of one year he lost his wife and four children, one of whom was his little son Isaak of about 7 years of age. He is being buried now, while I write this letter. Brother and sister Evers and children are in pretty good health, thanks be to God; also brother Zan, who lives quietly.

LeGrand, his wife and child are doing materially very well. But it is a very sad situation with their spiritual life. According to the last letter, everything is fine with brother Manus and his family. Myself, my wife and seven children, cannot thank the Lord enough for His unending love which He shows to us, unworthy people, from day to day. Though God took unto himself this past winter, our 10 year old son, He also gave us strength to submit to His will.

Does brother Willem not want to write any more? Does he carry so many grudges? Please tell him that I want to take everything on my shoulders, if he only writes, if it was only to make his sister happy. Tell your brother-in-law de Zwarte that Maas is still waiting for a letter that he promised to write.

The harvest on the field looks pretty good and up till now we didn't hear about potato disease. Brother, I may not leave this out and commit you and your children to God, and especially you brother, who will need it so badly because the flesh is weak. I pray that you take the work in your mind when you will be led into temptation and not sin against God.

Also greetings from cousin Kruger, Shaar, Johannes Wieke, cousin Leenhouts and aunt. Also from your brother N and sister and say hello to your family and acquaintances and especially to the brothers and sisters in Christ Jesus. And finally I let you know, with joy, that we shall have our Pastor Verhoef, who up until today preaches nothing else than Jesus Christ and Him crucified.

With kind regards, your brother in Christ Jesus,
A. de Priester

♦♦♦♦♦♦

[Pieter Baden was born ca. 1816 and died 8 February 1889 in Milwaukee, WI. He emigrated in 1844 from Cadzand, Zeeland and on 10 January 1849 married Maria de Swarte in Milwaukee. Maria was born 27 March 1820 in Nieuwvliet, Zeeland, the daughter of Pieter Bartholomeus and Jozina (Haartsen) de Swarte. She died 25 March 1847 in Milwaukee and on 16 July 1857 Pieter married Janna Geertruida Vruwink.]

Milwaukee, Wisconsin – Sluis, Zeeland   18 March 1849
Pieter Baden to A. de Priester

Dear brother and sister,

I have seen from the note enclosed in Schaap's letter that you are all fit and in good health which gives me great pleasure. At present I am also fit and well but last summer it was not so. Last summer I was stricken twice with serious ailments. Last year, March 16, I arrived here in the city and had to remain in bed for 12 weeks due to pleuritis from which I fortunately recovered. But then the schoolmaster came and I had to go out there again and I caught another severe disease keeping me in bed for six weeks before I made good recovery. Then I sold all my land to the schoolmaster and bought 50 acres here near the city as that sold land was too far from the city. I was 45 miles away. Even though this land costs more, at least I can go back and forth to the city in one day now. Thus, I and the schoolmaster are not near each other, as I live near the city and he 45 miles north of it. You have read in Schaap's letter that I intended to marry. I am curious to hear your reactions. Yes, I was married on January 11 to M. de Swarte, daughter of the old de Swarte of Nieuwvliet. Now I have become a farmer and am a carpenter no longer. My farm consists of two oxen, which I use for work, and 2 cows, chickens and pigs. Sometimes I wish you could see us at work. We live here in a beautiful country and a nice neighborhood. Jan Baas was the first one to come here and Schaap is here also. He bought 20 acres of land. Nil Zee lives here too and also purchased 20 acres of land, as did J. de Swarte and P. Fullien. My wife's father is my nearest neighbor. This winter has been rather severe. Snow was on the ground for 14 weeks.

We lead an easy life here. This year I only had to pay 2 dollars and 75 cents tax which is for a whole year. And they have to come and collect it themselves because a revenues service is unheard of here. Every year a different person is appointed as collector of taxes during certain designated days. Once collected, the revenue goes to Milwaukee. Milwaukee is a new city. Twelve years ago the area was a complete desert. But then the first white man came to trade fur with the Indians. Now it has become a city of 25,000 inhabitants. A river goes through the city, and a large section along this river houses grain mills and factories which are all made to operate by the stream. Houses along the boulevards look so great and are built so neat, three and four stories high. There are many amazingly large stores, as I just saw. The state of Michigan lies directly above us. That is where the van Raalte colony is. Many Hollanders are there but it is to be pitied that these people have settled down where ministers rule even more relentlessly than the pastors by us. They make laws upon laws, for the purpose of taking money out of the people's pockets. American law is more than sufficient for us. We came here to be free, not to let these men rule over us. All that these ministers come here for is to become rich and to rule these simple Hollanders. Further, it is such an unhealthy land that every year many people die. But common sense is unheard of. Bouwers is there too. He has written that in the spring, once there is open water, he intends to come to us. But then he must first sell his land bought there. And that is not easy as they may not buy from anyone but the ministers. In case they do not sell to the minister then the profit derived from the sale must be given to the ministers; such is the law. It is not American law, but law made by the ministers themselves. I have been waiting a long time _____ finally came to us. It all began to annoy us. It is now five years ago when I left Holland. Since then I have done almost nothing than wandering and traveling around. Those two sicknesses I suffered last year compelled me to decide to take a wife, and now to my great pleasure I have found a wife, even one from my native country. All the Hollanders that know me, and I too, expected that I would take an American wife because I associated mostly with Americans. I hope you all will take delight in this. You all must have the compliments of Jan Baas, his wife, and his daughter Bettje who is also married. And Jan Baas requests a letter from van Melle. Further, give the compliments to J. Hekane and tell him that the reason for me not writing him is that I did not yet have a fixed location and could therefore hardly expect a letter from him. But assure him of my continuing friendship. Also, greet all friends and acquaintances. Warm greetings from me and my wife, who calls himself your brother.

P. Baden
Your sister, Maria de Swarte
Milwaukee, Wisconsin

◆◆◆◆◆◆

Milwaukee, Wisconsin – Sluis, Zeeland   28 November 1850
Pieter Baden to A. de Priester

Dear brother and sister,

As we write Mother Fars, we would like to take the opportunity to enclose this little writing note hoping that you may receive this in health. Currently we enjoy a great health. Hereby I would like to announce that my wife gave birth to a daughter Jaziena Susanna on the 27th of February. Brother Willem arrived here on April…and stayed with us for four days. Then I brought him to the city where he found work that same day. He made about 6 shillings daily. Would he have been able to speak a little better then he would have earned more a day. Nevertheless, he did fine this summer, so there is not much to comment on for me. Other people knew him better than I did. Hollevaar and de Loop was in the city this summer, but outside the city, and I did not hear anything about this. We had a dry summer, but a wet autumn. The harvest was rather good. We have 3 ½ acres of great wheat, but how much wheat I do not know since it has not been threshed yet. Grain is very cheap. The best flour is sold here for 3 ½ dollars per two hundred pounds. All grained grain is put in storage right away and is sold only. I shall also write a little about the household here. Soap, vinegar, salt and syrup we make ourselves. Butchering we also do ourselves. This all we do without paying any taxes. We have two cows and sold some cattle this summer. Butter has been rather expensive this summer. And I have three oxen and two pigs. We all lead a satisfactory life. I have to give the compliments to brother Evers from J. de Swarte. He also would like to extend them to dear ones from me and to brother H. Schaap who is doing well at the moment. Be also greeted by my wife.

We call ourselves your brother and sister, P. Baden

◆◆◆◆◆◆

Milwaukee, Wisconsin   1 May 1859
Pieter Baden to A. de Priester

Dear brother and sister,

Peace and mercy from Him who is, was and who is coming. This is my honest wish brother and sister. The news I hereby send you is sad but at the same token also joyful. It pleased the Lord to bring home my beloved wife on March 25 after a long period of pain. Her end was great and inspiring for all of God's people. Her bed had become a pulpit. It took six long days before she, and we with her, could rejoice in that strong illuminating light. Her life was a great example for those who knew her, and she was friendly to all who knew her. Just as she was loved by all Christians who knew her. But she was, she believed, not easy on herself and when she was ill stricken, whenever I or the doctor or minister asked her how things were, she answered that she wished the Lord would be as gracious and good to let her soul rise up; and it did please the Lord to clear up all darkness. She was weak and speechless when the Lord came to her and she started to speak so loudly and with such a clear voice that everybody looked at her. First she knelt down for the Lord in guilt and testified that the Lord had worked in her for such a long time. It was hard for her to believe. She cried it out sweet Lord Jesus. That is believing! It was as if all God's people knew the hour had come. Our house was crowded, as the doctor arrived at that time. She told me, to tell the doctor I do not need anything from him," that she expected Christ, her soul doctor, anytime. He would relieve her from a sinful body. Two days before she gave birth to a little son, stillborn. It only lived 15 hours, and when she found out that the child was dead, out of need and desire, she indicated that we should not bury the child but put it with her in her coffin. The good people simply could not bring themselves to leave her bed. The house was full of people day and night. Everybody came to see her and she spoke to both young and old, to everyone his or her share. Not hasty but calm, pointing all to Jesus as deserving savior. O brother and sister, it was a feast for my soul and for the people's souls. She was free from me and from two children. She recommended us to God and his mercy and hoped that when my time had come that we would come together in Jesus, in the Father's home, not to separate again and to be without struggle and free from sin. Her cry was often, "Come sweet Lord Jesus, come soon. Not my will but your will shall be done." She said goodbye to all with gladness and her desire was that everyone would be as glad as she to go to Jesus. She spoke rejoicing about her dying as well as her faith. And the Lord was to me, especially in those days, a great source of strength. We all gained strength as the cross came nearer. It sometimes renewed my soul so powerfully that I was strong in death. But now everything has healed and my dear wife is no longer. And I remain behind with two small children. The oldest one is 6 and the youngest is 2 years old. And then I have those never-ending thoughts about what I should do, about what I want to do. I have 10 acres land and two cows. Sometimes I think about going to the city and establish my children at a boarding home. But that has no future. Then I have to pay 5 dollars weekly for my children. Now, I can afford this well but then I have to leave my children with strangers and that is what I do not like. But the Lord will provide somehow. I do not know what to do, and further, righteous people in the city and the minister pray for me, and that I should go there, but the people here advise against it. So this is the struggle; what can I do best for me and my children. Great is the struggle, great is the loss, and great is my fear. But she is free from struggle and cross and the worldly things and sings before the throne. She was 36 years old and was buried on March 28, her birthday. We were married 8 years, two months and 10 days. Mother ten Hout came to see her two days before her death. "O," she said. "Mom, I am happy to see you," because she thought she could not die without having seen her. And the old woman was so glad to be with her. She wished she could have gone with her. She asked me constantly whether I could let her go to the Lord. But I could do this better than I thought. And if you would like to know how I am doing at the moment then read the 102nd Psalm. There you will find it. That is my situation. Yes brother and sister, if I did not have the assurance, I would succumb to the fight. But thanks be to the Lord who lets His light shine upon me and He will now provide. I will be through his power more than a victor. The church here is in a sadly state. She is full of strangers and changes shockingly fast. But let us honor the old and not depart from God's word. Then we will be fine. Reverend Klein has also seceded from the church and is alone now. Once removed cousin Belloo, and uncle and aunt Leemshoud are doing fine. But they are getting at an age now and do not got out as much anymore. Greet from me Maas and his wife, and Kruger, and Johan van de Waal and the whole family, and brother and sister. With best wishes, I call myself your loving brother in Christ

P. Baden

Brother…for me. I expect a reply soon.

♦♦♦♦♦♦

Milwaukee, Wisconsin – Sluis, Zeeland   1 May 1860
Pieter Baden to A. de Priester

Dear brother and sister,

Dear brother, your letter of September 1, 1859 reached us, thanks to the Lord, in health and
we hope and wish that it may pleasc the Lord to have you receive this one in health likewise.
Brother, you write me that the morals and values of life in general decay due to the worldly
trends and carelessness of people. But brother, Jesus teaches us a great lesson. He says
nobody plowing while looking at that which he leaves behind is competent to enter the
kingdom of heaven. We cannot serve God and the world simultaneously. But that it all is
about the two-fold struggle of flesh, world, and the devil is something only those realize
whom God has redeemed. The flesh always goes against the Lord, and those two are always
the opposite of each other. And it is such a small thing for people to serve with everything
one has the Lord God, or to sacrifice everything God gives us in nature and through His
mercy, like Adam before the fall, living for God with all his belongings. So now we also
have to be faithful to the covenant of amazing mercy which blesses our soul, and to live with
all we have for the Lord. So, brother, let us proceed with the fight of mercy; after all, if God
is with us, who will be against us. And let there be no idle person to lead us on the wrong
track. The Father knows what the need is of His children, be it physical or spiritual. Brother,
let us read many psalms that will be a good lesson in forgetting all idle sons and to rely solely
on free mercy to become righteous through Christ's blood. And brother, as far as your wife
is concerned, my sister, it would be highly desirable for her if she would break through more.
Since God is not honored by being quiet but by honoring him, as David said "when I
remained silent my bones decayed." He prayed throughout the whole day, so sister, we
should honor the King publicly and openly and not feel ashamed. Thus, sister, we have to be
noticed and heard. One has to be able to distinguish our banner. With regard to cousin's
situation, it is sad. Unbelievable that somebody, at such an age, is able to do such a step.
Amazing that she has so little insight in the truth, and so little knowledge of the covenant for
children, and, contrary to God's will, and against the covenant, entered this marriage even
though the Lord pays so much attention to His children. It was the sins of the first world that
the children of God considered the people's children as clean. And Paul says one really takes
on a heavy ballast of heathens; and what bond can light possibly have with darkness? So she
has entered marriage, against the will of God and she, thus, cannot expect anything else than
only cross. And if Christ and body cannot live together, than she can only acknowledge her
guilt and confess it before God and the people. Only then, there will be hope for recovery.
As far as the living situation is concerned here, it seems to worsen over time. The decay of
church and country occurs rapidly. With regard to the church, it no longer looks like a

church. The pastors and most of the people lead a worldly life. Most of them follow the heathens readily. The fear for the Lord has ceased to exist. The majority of those in Holland who seceded from the main church have sunken even deeper than the main church itself. The ministers have high salaries and do not work vigorously. They are afraid too, and hence they succumb. Even though God visits this country and its people by way of witnesses, it is to no avail. It is now May and it still freezes every night. In the behind laying year, it froze every month. The money circulation is tight and work not enough. About me and my household; I, once again, caught a flu and ear infection. I am still recovering. But the Lord made it all right with me. May it all free me more than worrying and disbelief. My wife and children are, thanks be to the Lord, healthy. And the name of my wife is Johanna Josiena te Sligte, born in the municipality of Aalten, Gelderland. Father de Swarte died on March 20 and went to heaven with gladness. But he did not go in a regular way. His horse hit him and the wagon rode over his chest. Fatally wounded, he died two days later. As far as brother Willem is concerned, he visited J. Ooievaar four weeks ago. However, I have not seen or spoken to him in four years. But he still is the same, his wife too. Beloved brother and sister, let us serve the Lord more and more each day, and that we walk with Him like a child. And that we may be more surrounded with the truth, and that the candle of love may burn because the time in which we live is bad. The devil rages through the world like a roaring lion. Let the Lord always follow us closely. That He may guide and protect us since we live in days of darkness. Yes, I believe we live again in the days that the wise have fallen asleep with the foolish virgins, and that we will hear the cry of "see the bridegroom comes" soon. Brother, I have heard that you extended calls on ministers, and that the congregation has parted in two. When you write, write then who you called and whom the seceded called or currently have as minister, and whether you yourself have seceded or not? If you have, then I hope and wish that you have done this with the Lord's will in mind, and have not simply followed a trend. So that you may be able to defend your deed adequately because many secede while not knowing why, and after a while they return back again. But if God lead you out of the church, do not follow Him because of the people since that is only harmful. Brother and sister, let everything we do be directed by the Lord. That we may know His will in everything, and follow it consequently while denying our own will and lust, as flesh and blood will not inherit the kingdom of heaven. Greet all friends and acquaintances and all brothers and sisters from us in the Lord. Also greet Johannes de Waal and all those whom I will not see again on this side of the grave. Those I wish and hope to meet again there where no separation will take place. After warm greetings from me and my wife.

Your loving brother and sister in the Lord,
P. Baden

My address is:
P. Baden
Milwaukee
State of Wisconsin
Care of P. Leenhaas (Pieter Leenhouts)
Box 375
North America   P.S. Write again soon!

◆◆◆◆◆

Milwaukee, Wisconsin – Sluis, Zeeland   20 March 1862
Pieter Baden to A. de Priester

Dear brothers and sisters,

Your last letter found us, thanks be to God, in health and we hope and wish that you will also receive this letter in health. I should have written sooner but due to circumstances and most because there is much discord in the church which at times is the reason for delay in writing. But I will not write at length about the quarrels except that liberalism is entering the church as well as the spirit of the age to which the law is opposed and that results in much dissent and separation and shunning and everyone feels that he is right, but the real evil is the loss of fear of God. You will be hearing much about the war here in America. The nation is undergoing a wretched experience. God is visiting this land with many judgments and that because of its sin of departing from God's law and terrible wastefulness and pride. The southern states want to separate from the northern states. The southern states are slave states and the northern states are not and that's what the war is about. An army of a million soldiers are opposing each other and there is bloody fighting. The northern troops have captured a southern fort. In that battle ten thousand southern men perished. The number of northern men that died is unknown although it is reported that twenty thousand perished. The men are falling like sheep for the slaughter. (At this point a few lines have been omitted due to translation difficulties.) The provisions which must be left behind are forgotten and cities and villages are set afire; everything is destroyed. It is apparent that the nation is destroying itself. Its luxury could be borne no longer. Now it will fall under God's judgment as thousands of human lives are being offered up and the nation is sinking into debt. Money is losing its value but the printing of paper money goes on. The sun or prosperity has set for this country. I would also inform you that brother Willem has also volunteered to be a soldier. As soon as I heard about it I went to see him in the camp and conversed with him but he was equally hard and indifferent. I described to him his own present position for time and eternity but it did no good. (A few words here which were not translatable). But the last time when I visited him as we were parting I again reminded him how in many ways we differed of religion at which he burst into tears. I told him that on this instant I was bearing witness against him and that I hoped and wished that in the great day of days it would not be necessary for me to testify against him. His wife is remaining here and has no children.

The harvest of the past year was meager. It looked very promising at first but when the wheat was in the ear and the oats in the bell the Lord showed His power by sending caterpillars so that in two days nothing but straw remained of the oats. The potatoes are poor also and many are rotting. As to my household, I and my wife and five children are all very well. On March 16 of last year my wife gave birth to a son and his name is Benjamin. He is a dear boy, fat and chubby. He is now a year old. The beginning of the winter was mild but the latter part of it was severe and cold with much snow. There is still snow on the ground and today is the 20th of March. Dear brother and sister, the situation of America and of the church and of the commonwealth has caved in. One hears little of spiritual life among the people. However, I believe that there are many pious folk but it seems as if they have fallen asleep with the foolish virgins. The leaders are making friends with the unrighteous mammon. That is the condition of the nation and people. There, brother and sister, you have a short description of country and people and I hope and wish that it is better with you and that the God of peace make you all of one mind to serve him in spirit and in truth for to serve God is a loving service where there is peace and salvation and although the world is destroyed, God doesn't change. Thus, brother and sister, let us be much at throne of grace to implore the Lord to make us more and more holy and that we may become more and more purified by the blood of Christ and that Jesus may be our only good and that He may be our mediator and that we seek only in His blood the forgiveness of our sinful nature.

Now with hearty greetings from me and my wife and children to you all. Your brother in Christ.

P. Baden

◆◆◆◆◆◆

Milwaukee, Wisconsin – Sluis, Zeeland   20 March 1863
Pieter Baden to A. de Priester

Dear brother and sister,

On September 22 we received in good health your letter of August 26, 1862 and we hope that it may please the Lord to have you receive this letter in good health as well. As far as my household is concerned, at present, thanks to God, we all are doing reasonably well; apart from the toothache which has been bothering me for the last eight days. With regard to church life, that is dead and boring. There is virtually no development of spiritual knowledge. In general, it is dry and deadening. All congregations fall apart as a result of quarrels and bickering. This is the fruit of worldliness as God and mammon are both worshiped here. In so far as the state of civil life is concerned, from day to day it becomes more sinful. Everything is expensive, especially clothing materials. Yellow cotton, costing 9 cents in the old days, costs now about 42 cents, which is 21 stuivers (nickels) in Dutch money. Coffee 25 stuivers Dutch money. As far as brother Willem is concerned, at present I do not know anything. He promised to write me but has not done so. But this I know, that his regiment has suffered severe losses. However, I am not aware of any deaths or injuries, as these are reported in the newspaper. As far as the well being of this nation is concerned, there will be a draft this coming spring another six times hundred thousand men, and that means that all men between 18 and 45 years will be under compulsory military service, without distinction of whether they have many or few children, and whether they are fathers or sons. See, brother, liberalism does not know of mercy. Last fall already four out of our midst were drafted. Among those drafted was a man with 5 children and a pregnant wife at home. The country is being flooded with paper money from the state which does not guarantee the money's value. At the end this all will result in state bankruptcy. And there with the debt will be paid. I am enclosing a bank note worth 10 cents so that you can see what kind of money the government is issuing. See, brother and sister, such is the situation in this country. So the Lord is shaking this country but does not abandon it completely. And what is America when abandoned? It will not survive. But, brother and sister, since nature is so wavering, we must cling more firmly to the throne of grace to be more and more secure in Christ because the days are so grim and because earth will be lost eventually anyway. Brothers and sister, I still have one desire. I still would like to speak to you all people from mouth to mouth. But whether this will happen on this side of the grave, I am not sure about. In case this will not happen then I hope to meet you there where no separation shall occur. This winter has been rather mild. However, today it is March 20 and we are having a severe snow storm. Last season's harvest was weak and with little result. And so, brothers and sister, you are informed a little about the situation here. Now I wish to you who worship the Lord yourself that you may grow more in knowledge and in mercy of our Lord and Redeemer Jesus Christ. For the others, I pray that they may realize their death sentence through Adam, and that they may seek refuge in Christ, the second Adam, in order to be cleansed of their sin. That is my wish. Now it is time for me to end and after greeting you on behalf of my wife and children, I call myself your brother in Christ.

Pieter Baden

This summer a man from Michigan, Frans van der Reneet, will come to the country. You can give him a letter to take with him.

I kept this letter in my possession until the 8th May. During the time in-between I was ill-stricken, and on May 5th everything was covered with snow. It all seems more like a winter than summer. And as far as the situation of this country is concerned, this worsens from day to day. On April 30 we had a national day of fasting and prayer. But the government has nothing to say about that, so many people disregarded the day as the partisan spirit increased. I fear this will only bring about more confrontation. After heartily greetings from me, my wife and children,

P. Baden

◆◆◆◆◆

[Pieter Lankester was born in Veere, Zeeland, Netherlands and arrived in New York on 15 August 1849 on the ship Leila with his wife and four children. His first marriage was to Pieternella Hendrina Kuiler. After her death he married her sister, Anna Sijbilla Kuiler, the mother of David. After her death he married Christina Braam, the mother of Maria and Cornelia who immigrated with him. After Christina's death he married Francina Goossen, who immigrated with Pieter and their daughter Petronella. The letters of Pieter and David were written to Johannes Marinus Kuiler, the brother of Pieternella Hendrina and Anna Sijbilla. This letter is from the Dutch Immigrant Letters Collection, Archives, Calvin College, Grand Rapids, MI, Box 40, Folder 15.]

Franklin County, Wisconsin   31 January 1850

Dear Brother and Sister,

I hope you will receive this letter in good health. We all are in good health. Some time ago I wrote a letter to Mr. Minderhout telling him about our situation and I asked him to show this letter to you and other people, thus saving costs of postage. And now again I send a letter to Rev. Snijder, again with the same request. I hope you have read them both so I need not repeat the same I requested in those letters for your reply. Please do me a favor of an answer as soon as possible because I am in want of information about you.

From my letters you certainly read about Milwaukee, a big and busy city. However, there is no starch factory, so starch is very costly over here, namely 30 cents Dutch money per American pound and this is only 4 ½ Dutch ounces. The best flour costs 5 Dutch cents, so, after my thoughts, one could make some very good profit out of it. So I am requested to establish such a factory. In this country one can act freely, therefore I am thinking to start this business in behalf of David, to set him on the track, but my knowledge of these affairs is not satisfactory. So my kindly request is, as soon as possible, to forward the exact processing rules. It would be an excellent business for David and even when I should stay outside the town I could daily visit and teach him, using my horse cart. One sees no flour here. Wheat is brought to the mills, is grinded and unbranned, and the flour is put into barrels. The waste is kept at the mill, but when you have your wheat grinded you can keep the waste yourself. A barrel with flour weighs 196 American pounds (88 kilograms) and costs at the moment 9 ½ to 10 guilders. It is the very best quality, which enables you to calculate the possibility of a big profit. In Buffalo was a person coming from Arnemuiden. This was a Brabander (Sic! Because Arnemuiden is located in Zeeland), who had been a starch maker at Arnemuiden. In order that he should not make starch his principals offered him a job as a foreman earning 50 dollars a month just for looking around.

I must finish now. My address I have to the Rev. Snijder and to Minderhout.

My sincere greetings and name me your affectionate,

                                                                        P. Lankester

                                    ◆◆◆◆◆◆

P. Lankester to J.M. Kuiler in Veere   10 October 1850
Franklin., Milwaukee County, Wisc.

Dear Brother, Sister, and Children:

In the hope that you will receive these words in good health, which great privilege we have also enjoyed up to this moment, so that we are as healthy as we ever were in the Netherlands. We enjoy great beneficence, because here we are released from earthly difficulties and tyranny. We live without the burden of suffering, and we are not tormented or oppressed by anyone, and these are great privileges in life. Thus we live more freely and restfully here, just as the richest people in the Netherlands. And anyone who has a little money here can live so pleasantly that he will lack nothing. I have (aside from my farm, which you know I have rented) for my families use 4 or 5 milk cows which give so much milk and butter that we can hardly use it all. All kinds of garden products, much more than we can use, the same kinds of spice. (Pot herbs) as you have, potatoes and all winter vegetables from the cabbage family we have in over supply. People eat bacon and meat three times daily – so much as a person wishes. Bread is made from the purest wheat flour, the finest kind which you can buy at $4 (or 10 f) for 196#. I bake my own bread from this flour and anything else I wish to make such as my necessary biscuits and sweet breads. For that purpose I have set up a brick oven with two openings so I can bake whatever I desire. I have also learned to make good yeast which I make every week. It is as good as that which they have in the Netherlands. So my biscuits are as good as those in Middelburg. For the rest, I have nothing to do with the farm. This summer I had a nice house built for the farmer next to my own farm yard. There is also a new farm yard built next to my farm for a man from Velp, near Arnhem. This man is a painter and is married to F. Remeeus, a daughter of Karel Remeeus – they lived at the end of city hall street. This man was in America two years before I was here and lived 80 miles north of here. When I heard of that I wrote to him and he came to visit me, and he liked it so well here that he sold his property and bought land next to mine. At this moment he is busy building his house. We enjoy each other's company, and that is true of all the Zeelanders who live here. I also have one of the finest horses and two small wagons for traveling, with these we drive everywhere we please. In good weather I drive to Milwaukee two times per week – where it is so busy there that you hardly know how to get around in the streets. Milwaukee is about 15 miles away . We have plank roads here and on such roads I can ride 10 miles in one hour. Generally, people here have horses and carriages especially in the cities, nearly every shopkeeper has a horse and wagon because the distances are so great. And you don't have to pay to use the street, except the plank roads which you pay 1 cent per mile for the upkeep of the roads. There is still so much that I could write but I'm not sure what value it would have because I don't want to provoke anyone. Everyone must know for himself what he does. I only want to give you a change – we at last have no remorse over our choice. All this pertains to our external life, that you may know from us our good circumstances.

But above all the materials given us the privilege to worship Him without obstruction according to His word – so that no one here is misjudged as a result of his confession or religious convictions. Thus, people have freedom of worship here. In fact, the state itself encourages the people to worship and pray on the day of the Lord – for that purpose there are sign boards on houses indicating where worship is available. We, along with the congregation in the city of Milwaukee, have called Rev. Klijn as our pastor and preacher, who, we trust, will come over to serve our church. The Americans offer us everything presently – a parcel of land, and more in order to build a parsonage for him. So it is very different in the Netherlands: where they do such things as a form of coercion, and if it were possible, such people should be banned from the earth, yet there they are the religious leaders for a sinful land and church. Dear brother, I esteem it is a privilege to be down so low and

78

humble myself by writing to you. Truly I have no hate for you, but you seem to manifest hatred to me. I wish always to pray for you while I have breath, now broken read Psalm 37 time and again. It is often a soul food for me – really it is so glorious to be connected with the Lord. Now I will write a little more about the foregoing matter.

It is a quotation from my will which was prepared by a lawyer from Steenwijk who now lives in Milwaukee. The quotation concerns specifically the money that David has coming to him from his Grandmother, and about which you were so restless because of my emigration. From this you can see that I have taken care of him and he is protected by the law. Also, I have asked my neighbor and friend to serve as an executor, and have established an upright and wise man as the guardian of the children. Our children are doing especially well. They are growing, and especially David who is as tall as I am. He has great pleasure in his work here, and when he is finished with his apprenticeship he will be very capable. He is doing well with the language, both with understanding and speaking – also he handles the horses well, just like the Americans. The farmers here are all gentlemen – all dressed in wool with pleated white shirts, and they live like gentlemen

I would like to have Poppe and Adamse come here. There are still good opportunities in my neighborhood. Thousands of acres still lie uncultivated. The whole of the Netherlands could be transported within this one state of Wisconsin.

Now, the Lord reigns, and He does what is good in His eyes.
You are heartily greeted by all of us.

Your brother,
P. Lankester

◆◆◆◆◆◆

Franklin, Milwaukee County, Wisconsin   26 December 1855

Highly Esteemed Brother and Sister and Children!

Your letter of June 1855 found us in good health through the goodness of the Lord. Kooman has sent it by mail. He has also written to me and asked for some advice. He lives about 60 miles from us. I wrote him that if he intended to live among us he should let me know and then come to Milwaukee and that I would pick him up there with my horses and wagon, but at this moment I haven't heard any more from him. Very likely he was working. That is usual, for people in all the trades are so busy that I can't describe it. In a word, all tradesmen are so busy here in the West that carpenters who do good work earn two dollars per day. Masons also easily that much, and that's the way it is with everyone who can work. I had long intended to write you but was constantly prevented partly because I knew that our son David was to be married, which occurred on Tuesday, the 18th of December 1855. He married a Dutch girl from Zeist, near Utrecht, by the name of Margrieta Smidt, 21 years of age. They live near us, in fact, in a house that I had newly built two or three rods from my own house. David and his wife speak English as well as their native language, and the other children are also beginning to speak the language pretty well for their age. This is an absolute necessity in America. Whoever knows the language well can succeed in all trades. I really can't explain to you how everything goes here. This past summer we received many blessings from the Lord. We had a temperate summer, not as hot as other years, and we had a very good harvest. There were no setbacks, except perhaps the potatoes, among which there was some spoilage. Because of the European war all grain is very expensive. As long as the Western states have existed, grain has never been so high. Hay also is very expensive. The price of hay at this time is from 14 to 20 dollars per ton depending on the quality. This year we have laid in about 100 ton. A ton here weighs 2,000 pounds and a pound is as large as the old Netherlands pound used to be. All foodstuffs are almost once again as expensive as when we came here, and all other necessities are also much more expensive, but since that time earnings and profits are also once again as high. When we were first here the price of a bushel of wheat was 50 cents, and at the moment it is $1.50 to almost two dollars for the best kind. The same with hay. It used to be 3 and 4 dollars and now it is three or four times as expensive, and there are no complaints about that because earnings and profits are so great. It is impossible for you folks to believe the rapid progress in this country. It progresses with giant strides. When we first came, the first railroad was being built, and now there are already, as far as I can tell, more than six, so that goods can be sent from all sections of the country. Railroads are the key to progress in this country. The price of farms is rising in our area. Some land is once again as expensive as it was six years ago.

Our children are all very glad that they are here. When we speak of Holland they all say that they would not like to go back. This is not because there is so much so-called joy and pleasure here for the young people to enjoy, such as young and undisciplined people seek. No, there is nothing of that kind here – no celebrations or so-called holidays. On all holidays we hold religious services and then all who can, come to church, and the rest are all busy at their jobs.

Brother, you write that you have used the baking powder but that it didn't satisfy you. That's your fault. Thousands of people here use it and it is sold as a main article in all the best stores in packages of one-half pound. But I never bought any that was as good as what I make myself. I bake all kinds of tasty little snacks with it whenever we want something delicious and fresh to eat. It can be done quickly. As far as yeast goes, I bake everything with it just as well as I ever did in Holland. If I had known about it when I still had my bakery, I would have saved hundreds of guilders by using it. All the bakers in America use such yeast, which they make themselves, although there are many breweries here. And so they don't bother to make dry yeast. I haven't seen that here yet. They consider it to unimportant a commodity. Sometimes they sell liquid yeast to private people, but not to bakers. They make it themselves. They would laugh and jeer at such an unimportant thing here. No, brother, you can't imagine on what an unusually large scale everything is here. In Buffalo I was in a hardware store that was three stories high and each story was a store of at least a hundred feet long, and in each store there were more goods than in three stores in Middelburg. On every floor there was an office with three or four clerks, and so it is with the other employees, and those store employees earn easily as much as twenty to forty dollars per month. It's this way in all the trades. This is an enterprising people who do gigantic deeds.

It's the same with farming. The invention of all kinds of machinery is a great thing. Even our crops are harvested by machinery, fourteen acres per day and much more neatly than when mowed by hand. Hay is mowed in the same way.

I would be able to end now except that I noticed that I have made a mistake. I saw that the ship of which I spoke on page two is really a steamship. It is an unusually large steamship. The keel is 700 feet long and the deck 500 feet long. The beam is 80 feet wide and the height 60 feet. The first class cabin will be 200 feet long with conveniences for three thousand passengers. There will be sixteen steam engines with 14 thousand horsepower, and in the state of Ohio they are busy building such vessels that will be driven by heat. They also have the invention of central heating in the houses of the rich and in churches which are being newly built. The furnace is in the basement and it heats the entire house or church, and you can see nothing of pipes or that sort of thing. Only in the floor or the walls of the rooms there is a ventilating turning damper. The same is true of the newly developed vessels. If I have a chance to send Weems a portrait or drawing or a fine steamship, I will be happy to do so. They are very nice for framing. And they are such gigantic vessels that you can't believe it, everything equally beautiful. If our niece Betje comes over to us, she will necessarily come on such a ship. Have Betje write us a note sometime, or Kornelis. That would please us very much. And I also expect a letter from you, brother, when you have a chance to write. Just put it in the mail and it will get here fine. I have written you a pretty long letter which I very likely won't do again. This was because I was sick and could not leave my room. When I am healthy I don't have so much patience and I have my work to do. I mean I shall not write so much.

What you have written me about F.F. M. I can't change at the moment because Mr. van Steenwijk is presently in New York since his honor has a temporary appointment there for a year or two as Commissioner of immigration for the state of Wisconsin with an income of thirty eight hundred dollars per year. When he returns I will speak to him about this matter. Don't worry about it. He has exactly the same character as Mr. Snijder over there with you. Greet the latter heartily for us. Now I must end because I am constantly thinking of new things to write. I would rather be able to tell you these things by word of mouth because I would be able to relate many unusual things, for example, how the large cities here are supplied with constant fresh water. Here in Milwaukee they are also busy with such a project. They are building a large masonry reservoir, four or five acres in size, outside the city beside the lake. Water from the lake (which is especially good) is brought into the reservoir by a machine. There it is purified and filtered. The same machine forces the water through pipes into the city. Then on all the street corners there are hydrants which one merely turns open to get the most delicious water without any trouble. If you don't hold on tight to the glass or whatever else you want to catch the water in, you will lose it because of the great force behind the water. I was scared by that kind of hydrant when I was in New York.

In our country we also have springs which produce water summer and winter and which never freeze over. In the summer they are always cold and healthful. Even though you are in a sweat when you drink of it, it does no harm, and no matter how dry it is, they constantly run over. In the same way there are different kinds of springs, such as sulphur springs and silver springs which are very healthful. Not long ago I spoke with one of our countrymen who was reliable. He told me that he came from the state of Virginia (spelled Versiene in the original. Tr) and that he had seen a fountain or spring of oil. The oil was scooped into barrels and sent all over. From that oil many other kinds of oil were made for druggists. It was green in color and had to be purified. While I was writing this a neighbor of mine dropped in who said that he had received a letter from the Netherlands which said that they were told in the Netherlands that we suffered a great deal from wild animals and Indians. How do they get a hold of these lies? It's true that there are bears in our state, but certainly not where we are. We would be willing to walk a good piece to see one. There are a few wolves. Once by chance when I was observing our cattle in the pasture which my binoculars I saw one walking among the cows. That wolf killed a number of sheep of mine and my neighbors, but a few days later he was killed too. I saw him fall. And those Indians, we see them very seldom and those unlucky people do no one any harm, except perhaps in the wild country. But here with us, as in the Netherlands: very peaceful. We are having very cold weather presently. Conditions are such that one must be careful that his nose or ears don't freeze. During the winter we have two months, sometimes three, when everything is done with sleighs which are very useful here. Dear brother, in accordance with the promise made me when I left, namely, that when my son David arrived at his majority or came to marry, that his grandmother's inheritance would be settled on him, the enclosed receipt will serve as evidence and I hope with all my heart that it will be satisfactory to you. You can rest assured that you will never be asked about it again. We heartily hope that you will receive this letter in good health and that the Lord's blessing may rest upon you and your children, and above all that you may all be the Lord's, to be bound to him, soul and body, for time and eternity. Although the times in which we live may be sorrowful and the Lord's benefits and afflictions, for the sake of our sins, many and great, we will have no fear, having Jesus as our portion. Then finally we will carry our souls out of this world like a treasure, for the world passes away and all its attractiveness, but those who do God's will live forever.

Cordial greetings from all of us to your wife and children, and it will always please us to receive letters from you. I hope that you will write me soon about the receipt of this letter. Greet everyone who asks after us.

Your ever affectionate brother,
P. Lankester

Town Franklin, County Milwaukee   15 February 1855

Dear Brother and Sister and Children!

We have had the privilege of receiving your valued letter brought to us by Westveer and Remeeus in good health. We hope that you and your dear family also share in this very high privilege. We and our children enjoy great benefactions from the Lord. This past summer I had an attack of cholera which was quickly quelled by the indirect intervention of the unusual blessing of the Lord. Our children all look very healthy. David is taller than I. We hope that the Lord will make things pleasant for you and your wife and children, and above all, give you grace to be properly prepared for eternity, for Death beckons every hour, and wouldn't it be tragic to enter eternity without a portion in Christ. And we do not receive a portion of Christ except through a new creation, but once that is granted we can understand something of the Apostle Paul when he says in the entire fifth chapter of Corinthians, but especially in the application of verse 15. If you have not learned to understand that in relation to the covenant you will make a wrong application of it. O brother, it is a blessed privilege to be able to testify with Joshua, "As for me and my house, we will serve the Lord." Joshua 14:15.

I will leave it at that because I have so many letters to answer, but very likely you already know that Westveer, by peculiar circumstances, didn't get here but stayed in Buffalo so that he is more than nine hundred miles distant (3 miles per hour), but Remeeus got here with his family. His brother-in-law is my neighbor. I myself picked up Remeeus in the city of Milwaukee for a few days of rest from travel and after fourteen days he departed for the city and immediately got a job. He did his first work in America with me. You cannot imagine how much work there is here especially for carpenters and masons. If masons are skillful in their trade they can sometimes make two dollars per day, more or less. The same with blacksmiths, yes, with almost all the trades. Conditions are also good here for farm hands. If they can do their work well in this country they can earn up to two hundred dollars per year, including board and laundry. If they go out to work by the month in the busiest part of the summer, they can get from 20 to 30 dollars, but that is only for a few months.

Brother, you ask me to tell you about means for leavening, as you call it. This is not as much to be used in the baking of bread as for other things. For example, the best kind of sponge cake or prime pigs in the blanket such as I baked so many of in Middelburg. Doughnuts or pancakes baked with it are unusually good, but it can also be used for bread, but I think that would turn out to be too expensive. I will tell you that I make my own yeast, for here there is no yeast except in places where many Europeans are living. In those places there are many beer breweries and thus also yeast, but it is always liquid. I have not yet seen dry yeast. So everyone makes his own yeast, and I do too, and the bread I bake is much nicer than when I was in Middelburg. The wheat which I grow on my farm is of the same quality as the Polish wheat which I used in Middelburg, and of that wheat we can use only the best flour. I have baked bread as good as the best with this flour, very light when divided into loaves. While I was in the Netherlands I would have been able to make a lot of money. The flour is ground unusually fine. If you saw the whole process of how the milling of flour is done here you would be astonished. Sometimes we bring a load of unsorted wheat to the mill (they are all water or steam mills here). When we arrive it is dumped into a bin and seems to fall into the cellar. From there it is conveyed upward by machinery and there it is separated, so that all the bad wheat falls out by means of an iron [grate]. Then it runs through an iron drum to crush the hard pellets which are sometimes there and to get rid of the dust and chaff, so that the wheat in a few minutes runs down very pure and clean into the bin that stands on the millstones. Then it is ground, and the meal is again conveyed upward, by machinery, where it is cooled and then dumped into the sifter, all by machine. Then the miller attaches bags to three separate places, the one for flour, another for very fine middling (as it is called here) and the third for bran, and that all goes so rapidly that if we come to the mill with a load of wheat and there is no one ahead of us, we can be served in two or three hours. And the flour is so choice and the bran and middling so clean that it is unbelievable. The millers are not paid in money. They pay themselves and they do that according to the market price of the grain this way: an eighth part for the miller, but that is merely according to average market price. The more expensive, the less he takes. And the millers haven't anything to do. Sometimes the mill is operated by one man. Wheat meal is hardly known here because everyone from the President to the day laborer eats the same kind of bread. Coming here is a great change for indigent people although presently because of the war everything is more expensive than before. Pork remains cheap. Since autumn I have butchered as many as twenty-four hogs of which I brought five to the city, among them two for T. Remeeus who couldn't believe that one could buy a hog for so little money. Hogs come to the city daily by the thousands. They are all butchered by the farmers and brought to the city by the wagon load. They are sold with the head on. The present price was four dollars per hundred pounds for the best. The hogs are bought by anyone in the city who has money. They are salted down and sold by the barrel. It is a country with great emphasis on trade. From the least to the greatest, all are intent only on making money. The Western states are developing with incredible rapidity, and that is caused by the railroads of which many are being laid so that the farmers who live two or three hundred miles from Milwaukee and for some time could not get to market with their produce, now can, and in the future will be able to get to the market of their choice with all they have to sell, vegetables or cattle of whatever sort. It is possible to get from here to New York by train with the exception of one small ford which can be crossed by steamboat, so that everything is being connected. I must close; my paper is almost full. If I have time I will prepare another letter to enclose with this. Then you can pay the postage on the two together.

Now, brother, greet all your relatives and children from us as well as Cornelis and his wife and our friends in Veere, and when you can, write to let us know how you are getting along. That is always very pleasant for us. Now, brother, kindly give my regards to those who know me and accept our cordial greetings and the Lord be good and gracious to you and bless you with temporal and above all spiritual blessings in Christ Jesus.

Your well meaning brother,
P. Lankester

◆◆◆◆◆◆

David Lankester to J.M. Kuiler family
Franklin   1 March 1863

Dear Uncle, Aunt, and family,

We would love to visit you some time in Holland and speak face to face with you. I would
like to travel with my friend, and am a little jealous of him, but it is best that I don't think
about that too much because there is no possibility for me to go with him. Not only because
of family obligations, but rather because of the war being waged at this moment makes travel
by ocean more dangerous every day due to the piracy that lies in wait for us. Yes, beloved, I
can understand that you desire to do something about his affair, and I will gladly say as much
as my (limited) ability permits. Still, I don't know when to begin or end because this war is
so big, bloody and destructive that no pen exists to adequately describe it. If God does not
intervene and is pleased to give a salvation, we are afraid that the suffering will go on until
there is total destruction and ruin on both sides, because both sides seemed determined to
hold out to the very last, and both sides fight on hopelessly. Whenever a new report comes
about another battle, then the question is not how many hundreds, but how many thousands
remain dead on the field of battle. Thus, as you can well imagine, the death rate passes a
human capacity for grief. I don't know if you know how this war started, but I will write
about that as briefly as possible. It begins actually in connection with the election of a new
President in November 1860. Now that is usually a significant matter here as there are
always two and sometimes more striving for the office. In the last election the striving
parties consisted of Democrats and Republicans, and the Republicans won. As soon as the
South understood, since they are all Democrats there, that this choice of a new President
would work against slavery, they began a rebellion and separated themselves. The U.S. had,
at that time, the old President (Buchanan) who continued to be entrusted with power from
November – March, and that gave the South a chance to be prepared (for war) because he
(Buchanan) did not interfere. Thus, when Lincoln became President on March 4, the
rebellion was already strong. He had to begin with the preparation of troops from the ground
up. He began this then, with volunteers, and they came by the thousands, so that an army of
about 600,000 was organized. Then people thought the rebellion would quickly be put down.
I thought so too. But the opposite view quickly became apparent, because very quickly we
experienced a defeat. But people still took hope (comfort) from the fact that the army was
not yet well organized, and people hoped that things would go better as the military (art)
training improved. Well, it did actually go a little better shortly thereafter, however, our
army was diminished quickly due to sickness, death, and causalities in battle, that the
President was forced to call for man troops up to 600,000. Thus, in total, over 100,000. This
last draft occurred last summer in July and that didn't go so easily as the first call. At first
they got many volunteers by offering large premiums which were promised by both the
government and leading citizens because every city and town know how many had to be
delivered (the greatest number went because of the promise). Still no matter how much they
tried the total number required could not be acquired in this state, so that our governor finally
had to resort to the lottery because Wisconsin was still 4000 short of the total required. Our
town was required to provide 53. Fifty-three from a total of 330 eligible men. On that day I
was in Milwaukee; it was for me and thousands of other men a more fearful day than I can

describe. I will never forget to praise the Lord for allowing me to escape (He alone was responsible). Perhaps you are thinking that I was more frightened than I should have been, but you must reflect a bit and remember that at the present it is quite different to be a soldier in time of war. It took a lot of effort to carry out this lottery, because when they first attempted to apply it in Milwaukee the people chased the lottery commissioners and their helpers out of town and for ten days they were not able to operate (i.e., until November 10).

The governor threatened (the people) that the first person who claimed to resist would immediately be transported to the army to serve for the duration of the war. Yet in another place the people chased the officials away and dragged some of them through the mud and set a few of their houses on fire. Then the governor sent a regiment of soldiers there.

They positioned a few cannons where they could sink an oncoming steamboat, but the soldiers outsmarted the people and came unexpectedly over land, and so from that side they caught the troublemaker. So now they have a lottery here as they do in Holland. For here the papers with names on them are put in a box which is turned often. Then another blindfolded person takes the papers out until they have the needed number. Then the chosen persons are given notice to appear before the commissar within five days and they bring you directly to the camp. Thus, you can easily imagine how anyone with a wife and child feels; he must leave everything in a few days and present himself at the camp to be trained and then sent immediately to the battlefield with hardly any hope of returning. I don't want to write too much about this, but I know of several regiments that were sent out with 1000 men in September, which now have less than 300 strong men. We have a Dutch helper who lived with us a few years and he volunteered with the 263 Wisc. Regiment and he writes to us saying that of the 100 men in his company only 40 remained and that without any battle losses and all this occurred since last October (6 months). The loss of so many people came from fatigue and privation which these are so great that you would hardly believe it (without the evidence from those who experience it). Many times they have to march for weeks and even months through the woods, the wilderness and impassable roads, and then sleep unprotected in the open air. In addition, they don't get half enough to eat, and what they get is most often a kind of dry biscuit and some poor excuse for coffee, and that is all that they get. Except when they are regularly garrisoned, then it is a little better. Although in general, they are treated like animals. Thus, it's no wonder that people have begun to oppose this situation. And still more of the 4000 who were conscripted by lottery, there remain only 300 or 400 in actual military service. Most did not appear at the required time, and many deserted from the camp (and the balance that remained were sent to the South without their knowledge and without an opportunity to say goodbye to their relatives.

We have a neighbor here, a poor man and the father of 6 children, who was also caught in the lottery. He had a few days home leave with his wife a short time ago. Then he became sick and was too weak to travel back to camp, it seemed to be a blessing in retrospect, because if he had gone back to camp, they would have sent him off to battle without any opportunity to say farewell to his wife and family.

Now I will tell you about the financial effects of this war in America. In short, there is no gold or silver coin in circulation – not even a copper cent – nothing but paper money. First people tried to use postage stamps for small change and then the government came up with the plan to place paper money in circulation for small change also, so that presently all our money consists of these paper notes and bank bills; just as it was earlier in the Netherlands. Whenever you wish to change this paper money for hard currency you must at present pay from 40-60 percent to the banks. This as you will rightly imagine increases enormously the cost of all goods from foreign trade because the (purchaser) businessman must pay in hard currency, and in return get paper money of far less value. Many items presently are 200 times more expensive, as, for example, cotton cloth.

Yes, dear Uncle, only the Lord knows what will happen to this land. From our viewpoint, the future looks very dark, for recently the Congress passed another law, a so-called conscription law under which almost no one will be free from military service. The Congress has also given the President authority to call up to another 800,000 men. The general feelings is that he will act on this quickly if the war does not end, and there is not the least hope of that. In America, they carry on war as they do all other things. That is, Americans like things in giant sizes. At first people say that such enormous plans are impossible but they know how to carry it out. If I should write about the growth of trade and other affairs, and about the way this is done here, many people in Holland would not believe me, but this time I will not expand on that because the paper will quickly be full.

I prefer to end with information about our family. The most important news that I know at this moment concerns our intentions, if the Lord wills and we live, to give up our farm and to move to Milwaukee in the fall. We have already bought property there and we intend to build a house on it this summer before moving. From this you will understand that I have totally changed the operation of my business, but, that is rather common here in America. People who are farmers one day become shopkeepers the following day, still something else, because if one thing doesn't work, people quickly run to something else. Here, there is not the least difference between farmers, city dwellers, or gentlemen. People are addressed Mr. from the poorest day laborer to the President. It is the same with respect to clothing. House maids, if they can afford it, wear clothes as good as their employers. Thus, on the street you can't distinguish one from the other. And this is true among most Hollanders in America. Also, for people in general are inclined (to jump, to rush to consumption). And that is the reason that so few from this servant class make much progress. I would write more of this, but for this time I'll stop.

Hearty greetings from all of us and also from father and his household.

D. Lankester

♦♦♦♦♦♦

Town Franklin, County Milwaukee   2 April 1863
Our leaving this place causes much sorrow [moving from Franklin to Milwaukee].

Dear Brother and Sister, Children and Children's Children!

That the God and Father of our Lord Jesus Christ may be a saving and redeeming God for
you in Christ Jesus for now and above all for an approaching eternity is our heart's desire and
prayer.

Dear brother, it made us deeply happy that we and all our family might receive your letter of
March 6 in good health on the first of April and be informed of your physical well-being,
although it also told us of the loss of your son, concerning which we had yet heard nothing.
Yes, brother, thus the Lord constantly knocks at our door and wishes to make us constantly
aware of that word, "It is appointed unto man once to die, and after death the judgment." For
it is the great purpose of God to place us under the Gospel here on earth so that we might be
prepared for eternity. O, what a happy privilege if, by regenerating grace, we can witness to
the truth and that the fruits are immediately evident in being able to say with Paul, "For me to
live in Christ, to die is gain." Then it need not be difficult to endure for a time in this vale of
tears, but we can be assured that when we put off this earthly tabernacle we shall receive a
building made by God in heaven. Dear brother, let us examine ourselves narrowly before the
Lord that we may never be found among those builders of whom we read in Matt. 7: 26, 27.
Brother, we must learn to understand that dear chapter especially from the thirteenth to and
including the twenty third verse, for we live only once in the time of preparation. As the tree
falls, so will it lie. O brother, I can't tell you with what sympathy my soul is touched at
times when on Sundays I preach the beloved gospel of salvation from the pulpit and see so
many before me who by eloquent deeds say, "Depart from us, for we have no desire to know
your ways." O, what has man become through sin! Through grace it is my heartfelt desire
constantly to make my fellow travelers to eternity aware of the great purpose of God for poor
sinners. Presently God's judgment has come to rest on this nation. There is much religion,
also many pious and godly people as well as many godly ministers among the Americans.
The result is that times of prayer are held daily in many places at which various private
persons are invited to pray. Some years ago I was the representative of the great many
American and pious Dutch ministers. I was nominated as delegate from our Classis to attend
the General Synod that is held annually. It was 500 hours, or 1600 miles from my home, in
the state of New Jersey, in the beautiful city of Newark. It was a pleasant trip. We traveled
through New York. I was gone four weeks, all at the expense of the Synod. There also were
daily hours of prayer. In New York there are daily prayer meetings at noon. It is a place
where great events often occur. It is an exceptional commercial city. There is one street
where 700 omnibuses per hour pass regularly to transport passengers from one end to the
other. You will have been aware from the newspapers of the sad circumstances related to the
all-destructive war. It is a war that has no equal in world history. Two of my hired men have
volunteered. They are both in the South fighting the enemy, or rebels. I get letters from
them daily. There are three young men of our congregation who have been drafted. They
are also in the South. There is much talk of a second conscription, which may include our
David because married men are not exempt. It is a dreadful judgment on this nation. A few

years ago we talked here as though no war was possible in the United States, but the Lord knows how to visit a people when the measure of iniquity is full. In this war, too, the Lord has a definite purpose. It is a wonderful country and people. However wicked, they always have impressions of religion, although mostly on mistaken principles. With almost every regiment there is a chaplain. The soldiers are supplied with religious newspapers and tracts which are very good and moral, especially emphasizing preparation for eternity. They have sent us a few of them. In some regiments no work may be done on Sunday if it is not absolutely necessary. Others are completely religious. In these papers we often read of unusual deaths in the hospitals and how the Lord converts many sinners there. These hospitals are often visited by important ladies who help there. Even the wife of the President of the United States goes there. No one here is too important to offer services of this kind. They even send crates with all sorts of refreshments from the North to hospitals in the South, hundreds of miles away, and these are distributed by those women. We have also read in these religious papers of the depraved condition of the Reformed Church in the Netherlands. A certain minister from Leyden, while serving holy communion, expressed his astonishment saying that he could not understand that after 1800 years that ceremony still existed, since it was merely the memorial of the death of a friend. We read in this paper that at a later celebration he expressed his astonishment again concerning the mystical ideas that people in the church held regarding it. A second matter came to our attention of a certain minister at Tiel who compared the Lord Jesus with Santa Claus in that the good deeds of both are remembered long after their deaths. O brother, who will not shudder and shake in the face of such wickedness. And that which is tolerated without punishment causes us to shake and fear that the Lord, when his long-suffering and firm patience come to an end, will visit such a country and people with his fearful judgments. Is that defending the faith for which our forefathers offered their blood and property against its enemies? On the other hand, we also hear that the Lord has converted many and set several on the right path in that same church, I mean ministers, and the Lord has continued to save many and to cast out those wolves in sheep's clothing or turn them to him. O Brother, it has appeared at all times that a country and people or a person that does not recognize God, but mocks him and tramples on his truth and lives and conducts himself according to the desires of his heart – such a country or people or person, when the measure of iniquity is full, will be visited by the Lord in a most fearful way. We have at hand too many examples of this to enumerate, in sacred and profane writings, given for our admonition. Brother! Because of the war and resulting scarcity of workmen and farmhands I have decided, the Lord willing and we live, to move from our farm to the city of Milwaukee next autumn after the harvest is in. David and his family too. To that end we have bought property in the city. I bought two lots next to each other. On one of those lots there is a house for David. On the second lot I shall have a house built this summer. So, you see, we are facing a great change. I myself and my wife desire a little more leisure at our time of life, and David and his wife would not be happy living away from us. For that reason we decided to stick with each other in the city. And I have no greater pleasure than to be with my family. The farm on which we ourselves lived we will lease out, which is easy to do here. It touches my heart somewhat because both David and I have nice and convenient houses. Closely considered, it is best to lease because the war makes it impossible to get laborers or farm hands. Here a farm hand is paid two hundred dollars per year and in the summer months twenty dollars or more per month. We have recently sold our second farm of 70 acres, and if times improve, I will also sell the large one of 180 acres since David is more inclined toward trade or business by which one can earn a great deal here. You will remember Elias Braam, the brother of my former wife, who lived near me in Veere and in Middelburg. He lives near me here and owns a store of all kinds of goods and he is doing so well that you would be surprised. He has more than thirty acres of land, a good house and barn, all free and clear, and besides that a lot of money out at interest. Shop keeping here and there with you differs like night and day. It is incredible how much shopkeepers make on everything. For example, more than two Dutch cents on a pound of butter, and everything else in proportion. I must stop. Last evening I received your letter and I hasten to write you immediately because David has written you a letter in which he lets you know that the portraits you asked for are on the way to you with a friend of ours. His name is Frans van Driele, son of CC. van Driele and Pieternella Sonius. I suppose he will drop off the pictures with our family in Goes and they will take care of them from there. It is possible that he will get to Middelburg. I have sent my picture along too. If you happen to have something that he can carry along, he will be glad to take it for me. When you write me, tell me something of the deceased saint (?). How is Gebuct (?) How is your son getting along in the bakery? Say a special hello to Betje and all the children from all of us. There is also a picture for Betje. We all send you hearty greetings.

Your ever loving brother,
P. Lankester

Greet all who know me or ask about me.

◆◆◆◆◆◆

Milwaukee   27 May 1865

Dearly Beloved Brother, Sister, and Children,

I have long intended to write you, but I heard that you were going to write me and so I was waiting for that letter. But up until this moment I have found nothing from you, so I thought, I won't quibble about that, and decided to write my brother-in-law anyway. It could well be the last time as my days are hardening to their end. We are all, through God's unending goodness, enjoying good health. Our oldest daughter was married on May 13 to a widower from Madison where he is the foreman of a printing shop which prints the book of the state, because Madison is the capitol of the state and the seat of the government. The man's name is Johannes Willem Corscot (Korschot), and he is the foreman for that works, and earns from 75-80 dollars per month. He was born in Winterswijk in Gelderland. They moved to Madison on the 22nd of May, a busy day for us. Madison is one hundred miles away and can be reached in four hours by (train).

We have had exceptional events here in America. First, with the Civil War, which as everyone expected, ended with the defeat of the Southerners and Richmond, the capitol of the South, was captured with thousands of troops, and because it was the capitol city, the South lost everything. A few of the Southern generals resisted with their followers, but they have also been defeated and many were able to flee, but were caught by the cavalry. He was dressed in women's clothing to escape identification. We have also caught many of his cabinet. I think that they will hang all of them, but you have probably read all of this in the newspapers.

The second great event was the murder of our brave President, Abraham Lincoln. It was a dreadful event. And everyone was so surprised that the murderer was able to flee, but they hunted him up and finally found him in another state hiding in a barn where he resisted wholeheartedly. He had broken a leg in his flight and was shooting out of the barn. Then, in order to save lives, the authorities set the barn on fire and shot at him – and so they got him. There was a $100,000 reward placed on his head. I've heard that the murderer was supported by 300 people. There are a lot of such people in Washington and they will all be hanged. Our new President, although a Southerner, will not be so long-suffering as Lincoln. Our murdered President had his own grave in Springfield, Ill, but the body was also on view in Washington. But following his wishes it was transported the following day and it stopped in Chicago. People streamed there by the thousands, and the train did not move for one whole day. The thousands that saw him passed by the casket all night long. Our minister, who happened to be there, saw him that night too. His casket cost $2000. I have never seen such a procession. They have burial ceremonies all over, just as if his body was present - including a burial coach and a funeral procession. The procession in our city was so large that it took the official mourners one hour to walk by. All the shops were closed, and everything stood still, all the houses were decked with black, all the churches were in deep mourning, and all the ministers were asked to give a suitable address and to hold prayers on the day of the funeral, which was on Easter Sunday.

We hear that drafted soldiers are all coming home. A half year ago we bought a substitute for our son David for $600. The war power of America became so great in the last years that almost all powers in the world should take hope. England's sea power is no longer equal to ours.

Wonderful and awesome things occur here in all matters. They have put up a trade building here which people say is the largest of its kind in the whole world. It stands alongside the train station, the cars ride through the building in order to load grain. The top part is for grain and the bottom is for all other trading goods. One and a half million bushels of wheat (2 ½ bushels = a mud in Zeeland)

Things are similar in church affairs. A few weeks ago a preacher arrived here who was chosen by the Synod to be a means in God's hand for the conversion and quickening of his people, to enlarge the Lord's kingdom, and to give witness to the Christian life. There are an enormous number of churches here, and each church has its own minister, but all these have helped the visiting minister in his work. This visiting minister is Mr. Potter and he's been with us for fourteen days, preaching three times each day. The regular minister does most of the praying. I have never heard a man with such gifts before. He preaches in the largest church in the mornings and afternoons where about 3000 people attend. In the evening at 7:30 he preaches in a rented hall which can easily hold 6000 people. I have never seen so many people at one time. They have a prayer service before every worship service. Mr. Potter invites all the people to bring to him whatever problems they may have with respect to their own or their families situation, and to offer prayers for these. I have seen and heard many kinds of people; men, women, sons, boys, and daughters standing in line in order to make their wishes known to him. I have been there several times with our minister. Sometimes it was very moving to hear. Some people had husbands and children in the war or on the battlefield who were unconverted, and their families sought prayer for these people. It brought tears to my eyes. This minister would accept no money and they took no collection. The American churches seldom take up collections. Everything here is like a wonderland.

Just today I had another surprising occurrence. You know that much oil has been found here, so that some people have earned thousands and millions. The oil comes out of the ground. People bore into the ground in places where they expect oil to be located – sometimes 50, 100, and up to 600 feet deep. And then the oil rushes out of the ground in amounts from 20-300 barrels or vats per day. Then it is refined. You know that I have some property here and on that land are 8 or 9 springs. These are places from which, as they say here, living water springs. You can't run out of water. They run day and night and when you dig a hole around the spring it never freezes. This is also mineral water; good for your health.

A few days ago we read in the paper that people can almost predict where they will find oil – when certain conditions exist – and that is in locations where there are springs. So we thought about our land and wondered if there might be oil there since we have conditions needed for finding oil. I didn't mention this to anyone. But then I didn't know that there was a commission to look for oil. Someone told this group about my land. Without my knowledge three of the men rode to my land and took samples of my water away to study it. The next day they came to me and asked if I would come to their offices on the following day. They wish to make an agreement allowing them to bore for oil and also an agreement for buying oil if they find it. But we don't yet know, since this has just happened today. In a few days we will go to my property with them and an expert to make a further study. I don't know what will come of that. But you see brother, wonderful things occur here. Just as I was writing, David took some men from the oil company and an expert from the city to our land to do further research. I don't know if anything will come of this. The oil is called kerosene out here. It gives an excellent light and is also used as paint for some kinds of work.

Your loving brother,
P. Lankester

♦♦♦♦♦♦

Milwaukee   20 February 1867

Cordially beloved Brother and Sister and family,

We received your letter on January 8 in good health as we hope you will receive this. We were dreadfully shocked by the death of your son Henderik since we had not received that letter. Yes, Brother, our life is like a vapor, and everyone must experience the trouble and the adversity of sin in this world, and we have a blessed privilege if we have a firm foundation for expecting a better life in eternity. By God's goodness we all still live under His present grace. Our daughter, the widow Putz, was very successfully delivered of a healthy daughter on December 10, 1866. She is again living with us. Our youngest daughter, Pieternella, is also still with us. Maria is still in Madison. They are very prosperous there. Presently her husband makes about thirty dollars per week or a hundred and twenty per month. Everything is also well with David. His wife expects any day to be delivered of her sixth child, all alive and excellently handsome, healthy children. It is because of David's request that I write you so soon, since he has no time at the moment to write you. He had heard from his housemaid who lives with him and has just come from the Netherlands that in Amsterdam a machine for peeling potatoes has been invented and is for sale, which would be very useful here. Although here one can get a terrible lot of machines of all kinds and descriptions, we have noticed that that kind isn't here yet, and for that sort of thing one pays a large patent right here. David wants very much to get such a thing here since that might have unusual results. So David's request is that you should write immediately to your son in Amsterdam to investigate thoroughly whether or not such a thing is to be found, successful and efficient, and if so, if it should cost somewhere between 20 and 40 guilders, to pack it well in a small crate and send it over. That is very easy to do by steamship. I will enclose an address so that everything will go right. In New York there is a commission of Hollanders that looks out for their property. Among them is a good friend of mine, Rev. H. Uiterwyk. I will write to him, he will see that it gets on the express train and then it will get to me. There are people here who have made large fortunes with such things. Recently there was a man here who invented a machine for making curved metal spouts which could be made by the thousands per day and shipped by the millions. That man sold his patent rights for just the state of New York for twenty thousand dollars and still retained the rights in other states. It was a very simple device. I saw them being made because a friend of mine was working with them. So David would very much like to investigate the matter, not to manufacture the thing, but to get the patent rights. I think it likely that David would be able to get that because the husband of our Maria, who lives in Madison, the capitol, and is well acquainted with some important people, could speak with them.

Now Brother, if you can, do it quickly. He will send you the money as soon as possible. You don't have to be worried about that. I hope to write you again later. Greet my friends and family for us and receive cordial greetings from us all.

Your ever loving brother,
P. Lankester

P.S. In the meantime I will write to Rev. Uiterwijk, my good friend, and everything will go fine.

◆◆◆◆◆◆

Milwaukee   21 February 1867

Dearly beloved Brother and Sister and Children!

Yesterday I sent you a letter which very likely you don't have yet. The reason for this letter is that I forgot one thing and another in my letter. In my earlier letter I asked you for a machine for peeling potatoes which is manufactured in Amsterdam. As I wrote in my earlier letter, it was Daniel's request, who at the moment has no time to do such things. He hopes to write you afterwards. David has a house maid and she told him that it might be a very good business for him to apply for what people here call the patent rights as is done very much here and many make large fortunes in this way. As I informed you earlier, after I had sent the letter of February 20, it occurred to me that I could have some other things sent over in the box. I would very much like to have some pure Haarlem oil for me and my family because we are not sure that what we get here is pure. And also some artist brushes, which are very expensive here. All kinds of brushes are very expensive here because brushes and everything connected with them are imported from other countries. Here the bristles or hair, are not removed from the hogs although they are butchered by the thousands. But the hair is mostly thrown out or hauled away by wagons for other purposes. So you would please send me a great deal if you would send over in my box with the machine fifty bottles of Haarlem oil and two dozen artist brushes in three sizes, the one somewhat larger than the other.

Now I must close, and I hope that you will be able to send it. In this letter I will also indicate what you must put on the box. There is in New York a Dutch minister with whom I am particularly acquainted, who is a member of the commission to help the Hollanders along.

Be so good as to address the box with paint:
> Rev. H. Uiterwijk
> No. 41 Hammon Street New York

As soon as David has time he will write you and send some photographs.
Farewell

In my previous letter you will find something more. We send our cordial greetings. Please put the bill in the box or in a letter.

Your ever loving brother,
P. Lankester

P.S. Our hearty greetings to our family and friends. Meanwhile, I will write to New York. If you send what I asked for before that time, write me the name of the ship and captain together with the bill.

The reason why such a machine could be such a good thing here is that handwork is very expensive here and people are generally too lazy to peel potatoes and so potatoes are served unpeeled. Also, there are such large hotels here. There is one that has 365 rooms or sleeping accommodations. People here like anything that is new. Maids earn three dollars per week.

The Lord bless all of you. May it be so!
It is not necessary to send your letters with someone else. We have heard that your son, Gerrit Jan is married with a school comrade of mine. This way we receive more nieces.

◆◆◆◆◆◆

Winterswijk, Gelderland, Netherlands
Photo courtesy of Mary Risseeuw

[Jan Derk Droppers was born 21 July 1832 in Winterswijk, Gelderland to Gerrit Jan and Janna Geertruid (Vardink) Droppers. He died 21 April 1906 in Milwaukee, WI. On 23 July 1853 in Milwaukee he married Geertruida Boeijink. She was born 22 September 1835 in Lichtenvoorde, Gelderland and died 17 February 1878 in Milwaukee, WI. These letters are from the Dutch Immigrant Letters Collection, Archives, Calvin College, Grand Rapids, MI, Box 21, Folder 15.]

Milwaukee, Wisconsin – Kotten, Gelderland
                                            May 1873
J.D. Droppers to relatives

Dear Uncle and Aunt and those who are yours:

We have received your letter in health with joy. Never was a letter more desirable than yours. I have thought continually at times and wished that we might receive a letter from Holland. Continually we think of and speak of Holland and the friends that are there, with great pleasure.

I would like to be by you for a while and see those places where I lived in my childhood days, the land of our birth, the land where our dear parents have lived so long and provided and where I lived in my school and youthful years.

95

I was visiting Brockmilen and her husband over a year ago. The railroad goes now from Milwaukee through the Holland settlement. Milwaukee is now a large city…….or so necessary now we have insurance. There are now over a hundred trains that come and go every day out and in Milwaukee. Then there are still steamboats and ships which sail on the lake to various towns and places. That fire that we heard about in Holland (Michigan) was certainly bad. The Hollanders in Wisconsin haven't had any loss from it. In the state of Michigan there the Hollanders have had much loss. A small town by the name of Holland was almost completely burned up. A great deal was given for these people. The crops last year were very good….

Hoping that you will receive this letter in health. With regards, greetings from all of us and the blessings of the Lord and His many deeds be yours as well, is our wish.

With regards,
J.D. Droppers

♦♦♦♦♦♦

Milwaukee, Wisconsin – Kotten, Gelderland   25 January 1881

My dear friends the Vardinks,

I received your letter last summer. We were happy to read a letter from Holland once and to hear of your condition and how it goes with you all. I had intended to write you quickly in return but because of the bustle it was set aside and forgotten by time. Now in the beginning of the year it isn't so busy. Also, I received the letter about the death of the elderly father. And I have written the letter over and sent it to the family because we do live far from each other. Except my youngest sister; she was married in Milwaukee and lives on the……….. for the most part English. I get an English paper every day, a Holland one every week. My wife's mother is still living. Her first husband's name was Boijink. She came from near Aalten. They did live long here in America. The man she now has is an American. They live 70 miles from here and they came here from Holland a year before us. A brother of my wife, Jan Boijink, was married to my sister Janna. He passed away twelve years ago. She is now married to F. Westendorp. One or two months ago he was back to Holland and was also at your house and met you. They live 250 miles from here and yesterday I received a letter from them and they are well. And in your letter you ask for a picture and so I will send you one of me and my wife. This is not new, this was taken about six years ago. Now hearty greetings. How I hope you won't wait as long as I did with writing.

J.D. Droppers

♦♦♦♦♦♦

96

[Jan Berend Hijink was born in January 1831 in Winterswijk, Gelderland to Steven Jan and Arnold Hendrika (Blekkink) Hijink. He emigrated with his parents in 1847 to Sheboygan County, WI. He relocated to Milwaukee for the first time in 1848 and on 28 July 1853 married Wilhelmina Rademaker in Milwaukee. This letter is included because this family was so instrumental in the establishment of the settlements in Milwaukee and Sheboygan County and gives a vivid account of the early history of the Reformed Church in Milwaukee. Wilhelmina died in 1861 and on 19 September 1881 in Franklin Township, Milwaukee County, Jan married Tannetje Nieuwenhuis. In 1883 the family moved to Newkirk, IA. This letter is from the Dutch Immigrant Letters Collection, Archives, Calvin College, Grand Rapids, MI, Box 33, Folder 16.]

Newkirk, Iowa – Milwaukee, Wisconsin   30 March 1899
J.B. Hyink to Rev. Wm. Moerdyk

My dear old friend and brother,
Your postal of the 16th is at hand, and contents noticed. It pleased me very much to see your familiar handwriting. It reminded me of the good old times we had together in years gone by. (This paragraph was written in English). Since writing Dutch is easier for me than the English, so I will write to you according to your request. I have also just taken a pencil on account of convenience.

Well let's go! Bringing back as many reminiscences to my mind as possible. I came in the spring of 1848 to Milwaukee, while my dear brother (the father of Lydia ter Horst who died in 1854) a week or so before me had come to Milwaukee. Our intentions were to look for work and earn something so that we could help our parents who were established in a large grove at Sheboygan County in '47. I write this down because of the story told by my brother about the events which took place in '49 in the congregation of Sheboygan Cty. and I had for that year rented myself (hired out) by a certain Jacob Kiesel.

Then, in regard to the congregation of our Dutch people in Milwaukee, the situation in '48 when I came there, one could hardly say, that there was a regular organized congregation, also there was no church building. But they had on West Water Street an upper room rented from a certain jeweler with the name of Pieters, an Amsterdammer by birth. (They were Roman Catholics). That is where we on Sundays had our divine worship. A.J. Brusse was a sort of lay minister in those days, and lead the congregation in such a manner. He also held catechism (so as that is called) and my brother and I went also by him to catechism, because we were both already upon that path of life where of Christ the Leader is, and were edified by his instruction. He was earnest and well-meaning in order to spread the good seed. Well, in name J.W. Dunnewoold (afterward Dominee) was an Elder, and Beernink was Deacon, although their activities were hardly noticed because basically there was much confusion and this was brought about by Reverend P. Zonne. He arrived in Milwaukee in the fall of '47 and stayed there during the winter. And he took over the entire leadership of the congregation as it was then established in his hand. The Elders were L. Rademaker and J.W. Dunnewoold, Deacons Beernink and Veldhorst. While Dominee Zonne in the winter served the

97

congregation, he found fault with Elder L. Rademaker and deposed him, and after a short time cut him off entirely from the congregation. L. Rademaker came to them no longer under his hearing, nor even went any longer to church, but stayed alone by himself.

In the spring Dominee Zonne moved to Sheboygan Co. and appointed A.J. Brusse as the leader, and that is the situation in the spring of '48 through the summer until harvest. However, the people were sorely dissatisfied in regard to the handling by Dominee Zonne of Elder Rademaker because they desired to have him returned to their midst, because he was loved by all. He also had been an elder in the Netherlands by the "Afgescheiden," and had suffered through all the persecutions by the government. These activities were set in motion against the "Afgescheiden," and through that he was no stranger to the regulations and order in congregational government. So he was awaiting an opportunity that a pastor from Michigan might come to place the congregation on a good and orderly base.

I moved in the beginning of '49 again to Sheboygan and while living by Kiesel, Keemink (namely that Keemink the second man of Mrs. Stouthamer) came also by Kiesel and people asked him how the situation was in Milwaukee and the congregation. Whereupon he gave this account. Well, we have had Dominee van der Meulen by us and he has properly organized the congregation. He has held a congregational meeting, and Rademaker is again chosen as elder, and the others also are retained, namely Dunnewoold, elder; Deacons Veldhorst and Beernink. Also a third and new elder, namely E. Jansen, a man who with Dominee Zonne had settled on the Zoutspring, but since he had no chance to establish himself, he moved to Milwaukee and being a good carpenter he found a better livelihood. So then this faithful and well-meaning man came to be elder, and has served the congregation of Milwaukee until a very high age.

From this point onward you have, according to our thinking, a well established congregation, Reformed, in Milwaukee. Also in '49 the first church building was erected. It was an inexpensive building, because the work was done for nothing to a great extent. Here was opportunity for volunteers. If you remember correctly, according to the saying of my brother, Elder Jansen must have been the supervisor of project.

Permit me also briefly, hereby, to interweave something special or interesting. According to the way my brother told, there was at that time a large tamarack swamp north of the dwelling of Sam Brouwn, and Mr. Brouwn was good natured towards the Hollanders and gave them freedom to cut tamarack trees, just as many as they could use for the building. That was good! All right then – now to cutting wood. Elder Rademaker was to cut down the trees and Dunnewoold and Keemink were to carry the trees out of the swamp. Ged Soulen (the father of Hendrik) was then a teamster and he was to bring them to the appointed place. However, Keemink started to complain to Rademaker that the trees which he cut were too heavy, so that he and Dunnewoold could not carry them. Because they carried them out of the swamp, both of them, either at an end, and so they were working. Until Keemink said, "But that can't go that way, Rademaker! You cut 'em much too heavy, we cannot carry them, we already have had to let some of them laying." And what was the answer of Rademaker? "Well now, if they are too heavy you better leave them where they lay." Quite a few were left which they could not carry. When by estimation enough were cut, he laid down his ax, and went and took hold of those trees and carried them out alone; those that Keemink and Dunnewoold with the two of them could not carry. And so you can imagine the strength of that man.

And what became of A.J. Brusse, you ask. I'll let his own brother answer that, who also that same winter came by Kiesel, and the above account was shared with us. And adding to it, my brother A.J. has gotten it into his head to permit himself to be baptized in the lake, but it was very cold, that I can tell you.

In 1850 I returned again to Milwaukee. The congregation was flowering and growing, and a call was made to Dominee H.G. Klyn of Graafschaap, Michigan. He came over in '51 and he served the Milwaukee congregation for several years and then moved to Grand Rapids, MI. While there he promoted the first "afgescheiden" or secession as I call it, but enough about that!

See there! My brother, something of this and something of that out of that particular time. If you want to know more regarding these things in connection with the celebration this coming summer, let me know of such. Very likely through my memory being sharpened, I could be yet of more service to you, which I would gladly do.

Were it not so far removed from us, and the high cost connected with it, very likely I would try, the Lord willing, also to be there with my wife; but the outlook regarding that remains dark. For this time I must put down the pencil once again in the hope that you may receive these lines in good well-being, and that the good hand of the Lord may be over you and yours.

What a great deal has happened in Milwaukee since we moved from there. Many of my old friends have passed away. That is why I begin to think that also my time begins to draw near, because I have lived already for 68 years.

Well, Dominee, can I also expect a letter back from you? If you have time, as you please, and let me know the growth of the congregation under your hand. The Lord strengthen you in all your matters of work, is the wish of your old friend and brother, J.B. Hyink

Greetings also from my wife to Mrs. Moerdyk.
(Translated by H.J. TenClay May 18, 1968)

◆◆◆◆◆◆

Milwaukee & Sheboygan Counties

[Gerardus Brandt was born 6 May 1800 in Kapelle, Zeeland to Jan and Jannetje (Bosman) Brandt. He died 29 December 1859 in Fox Point, WI. Gerardus, his second wife Leena Vendvijlle and four of his children from his first wife (Cornelia de Wilde) arrived in New York on 27 September 1848 on the ship *Garrone*. His daughters, Catherine and Jannetje found work in Milwaukee while the rest of the family settled in Oostburg, WI. Gerard was an early leader in the First Reformed Church in Oostburg, but by 1854 was persuaded to join the settlement at Fox Point. These letters are from the Dutch Immigrant Letters Collection, Archives, Calvin College, Grand Rapids, MI, Box 10, Folder 14 and 16.]

Town Holland   21 January 1850
(Delivered to J. de Jonge on the hill in Milwaukee and further to Catarina and Jannetje Brandt)

Dear children,

When I looked at your letter yesterday at R. Traas', I felt there was verified what read in Solomon's book of Proverbs that good tidings from far lands are as cold water to a weary soul. I was privileged to rejoice in this that you are both well, although Kaatje does not make mention of it. But we may believe this much then because we find nothing said to the contrary. Up to the present we've been in good health. We thank you for wishing us a blessed new year and hope the Lord will grant it to you, is the wish of all of us. Kaatje asks about my trip home. This was as follows: On that same Friday I was still in the city of Milwaukee at noon at half after twelve, and in the evening at six I was back at Amburg again in the old lodging, having walked the whole time. On Saturday I set out in the morning at half past seven, and in the evening at six I was home all tired out. At Port Washington I was so tired that I had to take a rest. That day I thought about you; on the one hand I was happy that you had struck it so much better and could now rest, and on the other hand downhearted on arriving home. Frequently I thought, would they now really be thinking of me. I don't know of a time when I had such a journey. I was mistaken regarding what Kaatje wrote. Looking at the letter now I find in the last line that she is very well. We are glad that you are happy in your service. The English language will, perhaps in time, become familiar. Do make use, if you can, of the catechism. What you have learned heretofore will come back to you the more, and in your latter life you will be glad about it. We cannot make out what you mean about the cloths you write about. We have put eight in the package and a piece of Jannetje's dress. For the present, do not send any money. I understood when I received the letter from de Jong, in which I read that you had been only a short time in your service yet, and that of course you had up to that time been at said de Jong's, my wish would be that before you send anything you might make things right with those folks, for it might prove to be disappointing to them, and too you might be able to help Jannetje, for she might perhaps feel bad that she is not earning now, and possible she might need something. Do come to each other's assistance in whatever way you can, take counsel together where it is needed,

Jannetje dear, you ask my advice in this. I should think it is good to be with those folks in such a way that it is most advantageous for you, and that you will be free every day, if at least you have nothing more than your board. But, could you get more. People sometimes say, better half an egg than an empty shell. In the meantime, look about for something better; be it by looking yourself or by another person. Because of your health you can't come home now. I hope that when you receive this your outlook will already be better. You write that it is granted you, indeed, to pray. Ah, yes, that is the best way you can enter. With Him is strength and readiness to help if one asks in faith. What I have written Kaatje I am writing to you, in regard to church and catechism. When you get to see each other, I hope you two will not be too anxious about us. If anything serious happens we will write and send it by post. We are still living in the same old way. The buckwheat is threshed and partly cleaned. We eat many pancakes. We have the flour fresh from the mill daily. The new mill grinds better than the old one. Our potatoes are all spoilt, except the heads. And so it goes, too, with our pork – that is too spoiling day by day. The cow that we brought home last is still the same in the matter of giving milk as when you left, although we know she is with calf. The cattle are keeping fairly well. James asked to tell you that our black hen is dead, we believe from the cold. It was been so cold that we found it good to lay five blankets on each bed, and to that the boys did not object. We hope that with you there was been no lack even if it was a case of one or two fewer. We have received a letter from William de Jong from Goes. We must conclude from it that such a rumor about me is in circulation in Goes as Traas has told me, for he writes of bringing his mother to them and reports that cousin Sluiters also was willing to contribute to it. The letter bears the direction, to G. Brandt and further to the Widow Lauwerisse. He reports the death of their smallest child fourteen days after our departure; also the death of the Widow C. de Jong, former bookbinder; and that William Vleugel's wife drowned herself in the well and that Lauweris the tailor was in the east. Near us a man was found dead in the woods on the Sheboygan road. He had been shot in the chest. It is presumed by his father-in-law. They are Norwegians. He had been married only three weeks. They say the inhabitants here are busy wanting to build a pier or bridge at the lake. For that purpose a directorate has already been named to promote the enterprise. If this goes through it will become easy to come from Milwaukee here and return. I know of no more special news from here, also nothing special about our family. We are still chopping daily. This the boys enjoy doing to my delight. Do the people where Kaatje lives have children? If yes, are they large or small? Greet Smit from me and from all of us to J. de Jonge and wife and the whole family. I am not promising to write you so much each time I write. Greetings for us all and we are your loving parents and brothers,

G. Brandt L. VendeVijle
Izaak Brandt Jacobus Brandt

P.S. You make no mention of what you sent along with Traas. Now it is true that they are reliable people, but on another occasion you must send writing along. Then I can see it at once. About that watch and that ring of your mothers. I left them with Pieters the watchmaker. I could not get more than a dollar and eighty one cents for them. I made believe it was for someone else. He said that if that amount was too little that in two months it could still be gotten back. He valued the ring at 52 cents, so that the watch then comes to a dollar and 29 cents. If now you could get that, you could keep the ring for yourself, if you wish.

See what you can do. My name was not mentioned. If you do that, merely ask whether some man did not bring that there and that you would like it back. Paying interest he did not mention. You will be able to recognize both pieces.

♦♦♦♦♦♦

Town Holland   8 January 1851

Dear Brothers and Sisters,

When I was still in Zeeland, I would never have thought that I would wait so long before writing to you. Being here I have often had the intention but have sometimes been hindered by work; then again, I did not have the desire. I often think about you and wonder whether you are still in the land of the living, and then I am convinced that I must write in order to find out. So, that causes me to take up the pen. Sometimes I think that some of you have longed also for a letter; but when I recall the heartless farewell from some of you, I just cannot believe that there is a longing. Yes, brothers, it is being experienced that temporal affairs can break heart cords. After being here I have at times thought of some of you when I read God's word in Solomon's Proverb 27:10, the middle part: "neither go into thy brother's house in the day of thy calamity." I thought to myself, "Ah, if I could have learned that lesson, maybe love would not have cooled so much." That matter has been settled, even though we wish to be of service to one another. Now, that is most likely closed on this side and in eternity we will not need each other's help, for their relatives will not be needing each other. When a tree in the chilly north falls separated from the Lord it falls forever, and if it falls in the warm south of God's loving nearness, it will be in eternal fullness of joy, according to His own witness in His holy word.

In this matter, I cannot avoid asking you in writing, "How do matters stand when each one of you comes before the Lord and in your heart ask, "What is dominant: hope or fear?" I do not write this because you are obliged to reveal this. Oh, no, but should the nature of His grace have become manifest to any of you since I left Zeeland, where it was then hidden, it would be a joy to my soul. For I can in this regard openly confess that I feel, though we are far apart, that I am not separated from you in spirit, as my wife and two children sometimes can observe. It is something which we always owe one another: to bring each other's needs before the throne of grace, for we are dealing with an omnipresent God who can grant our requests as if we were in each other's presence. I may also reveal that you are sometimes the objects of my thoughts in our public worship when we pray with the congregation. I pray that the kingdom of Christ may prosper in the land of our birth and among our kindred and all who are dear to us. Most likely the same ideas will come to your mind because I am writing this.

Surely the news has reached you that there is a dominee in our midst, and that is true. His name is Peter Zonne, although he does not shine according to his last name. To the contrary, he is an example of unfruitful labors. I shall not say more about this now. But in 1849, in July, Rev. Budding was here and then a Reformed congregation was organized. I was elected as an elder with two others from Gelderland, but they resigned; in their place two

Zeelanders were elected, originally from Cadzand. Also at that time two deacons from the same island and one from Groningen were elected.

We live far apart. One week I have to go three miles east from my home and next week three miles south. The places where we meet are school buildings, and also where we have catechisms for children; this has been assigned to me. I do that on Saturday afternoons. The Lord still grants me the necessary grace to do this with pleasure. The attendance at the worship services is quite favorable. The congregation has more than sixty members. I have herewith given a short account of our public worship.

Brother and sister, I have written especially because there have been matters made public which are not good for everyone to know, but they are all inquisitive. I hope you will understand. I have heard that a rumor has been circulated among you that I am the heir of the estate of cousin G. Kopmels. I will not say what you can make of this now.

On May 23, 1849 Kopmels came here with J. Kastele and C. Bliek, his girl, A. van Boven, and J. Kleinepiet and his wife. On May 29 cousin bought 80 acres of woodland from Zonne of which three acres were cleared and cleaned up and upon which there was a house costing 1700 guilders. This cousin paid and then all the persons named above went to live in that house. In June cousin became ill; I do not know the day, because I lived three miles away. On June 23 cousin died. But I received no tidings of his death.

Now I must inform you that Zonne, during the time of cousin's illness, made a trip of 200 miles. About two hours after cousin had died, he came home. (I found out about all of this later.) Now there were people in my neighborhood who I had told that my cousin had a son in Holland. Those people knew more about the law than I, and they urged me to do something about this. Then on June 27 I went with an interpreter to the Justice of the Peace to administer this matter. Then with that document I went to the mayor in city hall on the 29th to list the personal property. We were referred to Zonne but those people. When he read the paper he laughed about it and said that he had another document. He read it to us and that was a testament written by him on June 27, four days after cousin's death. The contents of that testament stated that the named C. Bliek and J. Kastele were to be life-long tenants and that Zonne was to be executor. The balance of the estate after the death of those two individuals was to be assigned to the son. I answer that if he would furnish me with a lawful discharge, I would withdraw. Then J. Kleinepiet showed that document to the judge and it was declared to be of no effect; it was written in Dutch and not by a mayor as it should have been by law, and witnessed by two disinterested individuals. I immediately got the impression that it was false, because A. van Boven said that he did not want to be a witness to this and he was just the one who knew all about the case. Then Zonne kept back the letter of ownership. Unfortunately it was not yet registered, otherwise he could not have done any harm with it. But now he has investigated everything. He later wrote a purchase contract that he had sold that land for the above sum, but to three men: G. Komels, C. Bliek and J. Kastele. It is with life-long tenancy, and that after their death it would be his land again without being obliged to pay anyone anything. This I have received back from him and now he has given a letter of ownership for another 80 acres of woodland, which is worthless by a half. What will now come of all this I do not know. The rights are strange here and bothersome, if one does not know the language. I have to do a lot of travelling to take care of this. I have already made eight trips to the capital and this is as far a ways as Bartsbad is from Gors. I have written three letters to Frederick in Friesland. I have received one back from him with a power of attorney to do business for him. He wrote that he thought his father was still in Zeeland, so cousin Kopmels left without his son knowing about it. He wrote that his father did plan that after his mother's death, but that he had then advised him against it; he promised to allow him to keep his mother's property until his death. But that did not seem to help, and now he had silently left. This surprised me, because Zonne told me that his son was so bad that he did not deserve to get anything belonging to his father. If I was to write all the dirty tricks of that man, I would need at least four sheets of paper. But enough of that. I must tell you that I fear Frederick will not receive much of his father's estate.

I have also been told that a rumor is circulating where you are that I am living in adultery, or in other words, the life of a divorcee. At least it is being questioned whether this is true. I could write a great deal about this to prove its untruth. This I do not wish to do but advise you to inquire from Cornelis Pot and his wife, nee Hoefsmit, of Kloetinge. They have heard this from their brother Traas, who lives in this place. Then my wife will sign her name to this letter, and also my two sons; the girls are not able for they both live in Milwaukee and that is 45 miles from here. Kaatje earns a guilder and fifty cents in Dutch money per week. Jannetje was even with Kaatje last summer, but she is now sickly and must be careful. If they were to come to your house you would not know them.

I am not at peace about everything but what shall I say. My prayer is often that the Lord will protect them. In August they were at home for fourteen days. They already speak pretty good English. They would now be able to help us find our way if we had to travel around in America. Here the boys are way ahead; at present they take lessons every evening in English from a Peter Souffrouw from Oostburg in Cadzand.

Be so kind as to allow G. den Herder, our former neighbor in Goes, tailor in Wyngaardstraat, to read this and then I ask that he pay the compliments to W. ten Kate Smit on the Scheerkendrick inner port from that Souffrouw and all his relatives. I enjoy a great deal of friendship from these people. He and his mother and his brother live near us and his three sisters live 15 miles from us in the city of Sheboygan. One is married to Quintus who publishes the Dutch newspaper and the other two to German men.

These last lines will not be of much interest to you, but I do this at the request of Souffrouw. That slander I wrote about earlier in the letter surely originated with those good Kees and Jaus with whom I made the trip. My above mentioned neighbor has told me only a very little about those good individuals. You could find out from him who I mean.

You will very likely find errors here and there, but I hope you will understand what I mean. Having pressed you people to my heart in my thoughts.

Your loving brother,
G. Brandt

◆◆◆◆◆◆

Town Holland   10 January 1851

Dear Brother and Sister,

"As cold water to a thirsty soul, so is good news from a far country," says Solomon in Proverbs 25:25. Now I wish to tell you this and that about myself and about my family and also things in general, but want to write the truth and then you can judge yourselves.

We set sail from Ellevoet on August 12, 1842, and after we had been at sea for nine days, there was a heavy wind at night, so that the trunks began to be thrown about. Some people cried, others were busy collecting their goods, others prayed, and others sang - of which our minister was one, but he was alone. He was at peace in his soul as he later told me. On the contrary, I was very much afraid that we would perish.

Kapelle, Zeeland, Netherlands

The second night after that I was lying in quiet meditation on my bed and then I was reminded of the words which we read in the prophecy of Isaiah 63:9, "The angel of His presence saved them." This made me feel especially strong in my soul but I could not remember where these words were to be found. In the morning when the minister had finished the devotions, as he had conducted them on the mornings and evenings during the entire trip, I asked where the words were found. He told me immediately and he explained that chapter each day which I could consider as being of the greatest blessings I enjoyed, and so though I had before been filled with fear that we would all perish, I could later believe and feel assured that we would complete the trip so that fear disappeared.

I was very weak during the entire 45 days of the voyage. My wife was very strong on the contrary, as also our two smallest sons. The others felt better than I, but not much. Having arrived in New York after the 45th day, we remained there three days with A. Benjamin. If I were to tell you about all we saw and heard there, it would fill my letter. But I do want to tell you some things. First of all, we sailed around in a river. The banks were almost entirely filled with large ships and steamboats. That is an especially beautiful sight. On the other side of the river there are hills and valleys and all inhabited. The streets in the city are fifty meters wide and there are houses on both sides.

In many stores one finds a faucet along the counter, and if you turn on the faucet, clear water spouts out. They are found also on street corners from which water flows continually. On one side of the street we say a flowing fountain which was a granite pool thirty meters in diameter in which the water is always bubbling, but it is hard to explain. As we went through the city, I said to Benjamin that I had not seen such large stores in Rotterdam. He said (and his wife also) what was in them and that there were even several which were as long as the Wandel church in Goes. I said I did not believe it and then he took me to one and I was convinced. The meat market on the west side of the city is four acres in extent. I will stop telling about New York.

After our layover we traveled by steamboat to Albany. We arrived there the following morning, and there we immediately transferred to a canal boat. There a doctor from Zeeland came to us. He told us our children had American croup. He gave us medicine. On that boat we had many Irish fellow passengers. Now I must also say incidentally that there was a family of Amsterdamers I had met at sea and the man could speak a little English. We made a great deal of use of that! They were respectable people. We have associated with them up to this time. Our farms are adjacent to each other. This is a little digression. The Irish people who were on the canal boat gave us lice.

We traveled eleven days on that boat, and were drawn day and night by two horses. With such a boat there are four horses: two in the boat and two pulling the boat along, and they were changed from time to time. That canal is 500 miles, or 167 hours long. This goes on day and night. There are day after day at least four thousand horses in the business. Those boats are all numbered and we have seen some with a number over 500. Of a hundred horses there are at least 70 with black and white hair and of 100 cows, 99 with red hair. This is in passing.

This is a downstream waterway from Buffalo to Albany. We were raised possibly 60 times and sometimes as much as eight feet. At Buffalo we transferred to a steamboat, on which we traveled over the lake, so that we had gone higher on the downstream stream to Buffalo. Then we came to Sheboygan which is now our seat of government of the county (not of the state). There we live at a distance of five hours, five minutes from the main road which runs from Milwaukee. This city lies at the left as you come from Sheboygan. And there we have forty acres of woodland. On July 2 we will have lived on our farm for two years. For the past eight months we have lived in the house of that Amsterdamer. He had two houses on his farm. In that house Jan, on November 11, had a stroke and became lame on one side, and on December 14 he unexpectedly passed away. Oh, terrible time about which I cannot think back without emotion.

After that I chopped down trees with my other two sons all winter. Then the snow lay 2 and ½ feet deep until the 14th of April, so that it was difficult work. During that winter we cut down and burned six acres of trees. An acre is a square of 160 American rods. A rod is 16 and ½ feet long and wide. The underground is cut off level with the ground. That is done first that this is piled up. Then the small trees are cut down, the thickness of a wagon tongue or a bit thicker, a little above the ground, and then the branches are cut off and thrown on those piles. Next, the large ones are cut down 2 to 2 and ½ feet above the ground. The branches are often cut up so that they can be pulled by two oxen and they are then brought together, and 10, 12 to 20 or more are burned, and when it is all burned up the ashes are gathered if one wishes to sell them, and a person can get six cents per bushel, and 2 and ½ bushels equal one Dutch mud (?) And one cent is 2 and ½ Dutch cents. So a person has 40 cents in Dutch money for a week of ashes. You probably think that to chop through those tree branches is hard work, but I believe that two men would have to work just as hard to saw as much wood as two choppers. They stand on the tree and chop from opposite sides toward the middle, with short handles on the axes.

It is a pleasure to see how handily this is done. Then when the wood is all burned from the ground, people begin to force split oak logs, usually 10 to 12 feet long, and pile them 7 or 8 feet high and the bottom openings are so narrow that no small pig can get through, and that is necessary because they run around in the woods wherever they please. They are coaxed to the house with a little food and this is done also with oxen and cows which are coaxed to the house with salt which they like exceptionally well. That is not like it is in Zeeland. The animals roam in the winter as well as in the summer. In the winter when we chop wood they come to us and eat the tips from the branches. Now I have wandered away from the track.

In this way we cleared six acres the first winter and on this we had summer wheat and oats and Indian corn, called Spanish wheat by you. This crop grows well here and also other crops, except the tick-beans, as it is too warm for them. The summer here is short and hot. When the crops are growing they develop fast. We did not have enough potatoes the first year to provide for our needs but now we have a lot of them left. They were not entirely free from disease so that they were also affected in the cellar.

The house we live in is 30 feet long and 20 feet wide, constructed from 48 logs and very sturdy in times of storm. Here we also find that beginnings are difficult but we have coped with them and now once more live on our own land.

I have written before about matters to date, and now it is March 30, 1853, as we have learned more about America since that time, and are more used to it here than we were then. We are more accustomed to the climate. It is very healthful here, which is surprising since there is a great deal of variation between cold and heat, which is very remarkable in the spring and fall. It has happened since we have lived here that on one day we had a pleasant rain with a heavy storm, and at night a hard frost with snow the following day. For example, in late April and the first of May we sometimes had frost at night. In July we have had frost and then again at the end of August, but this is not the case very year. But we must sow the wheat early between September 5 and 12, which is considered the best time by Americans. For rye this is not so important, and in the spring one cannot sow or plant much before May with good results, but still it is harvest time in July and August.

We are well adjusted here now and would not want to return. We have now cleared 16 acres. Wheat has been sown on four acres, and rye on 2 or 3 acres and the rest is partly pasture land, and in some of it we will plant peas, white beans, barley, oats, buckwheat, Indian corn, potatoes and horse carrots, yes, everything one could want.

Then we have two oxen with which to do our work, two cows with calves, one young ox, a bull, 16 ducks and 6 hogs which we give a little good to in the evening, and during the day they roam in the woods where they are well off, and then when in September we fatten them and feed them Indian corn, they are nice and fat by November. In things temporal we are living well because everything one makes here is for one's self. What tax on our 40 acres we have had to raise so far has been at most 5 guilders 40 cents a year. And for that the children go to school till their 20th year during the 4 winter months if one wishes it. To get our grain ground is indeed somewhat difficult because we live 2 ½ hours from where it has to be ground. Yet, on the average one takes to the mill not less than three or four hectoliters at a time. Then one gets that ground and at the same time bolted into three kinds: first flour, then shorts, then bran. Whether it is due to that or not, I do not know, but I believe it is due to the way it is separated that it does not become moldy. We do not find this to be the case even after it is six months old. The potatoes are good. We still have 8 or 10 hectolitres to sell. They are now very cheap. One cannot get more than thirty three or four pennies (Dutch money) for a hectoliter. Wheat is 16 shillings, rye 11, barley 9, buckwheat 9, coffee beans 8 pennies. The sugar syrup and vinegar we make ourselves if we wish. Clothing prices differ little from yours. Our children are all now at home. The girls have learned sewing so that they are now working for themselves and are done with being maids. Last summer they became members of the church with Rev. Klein in Milwaukee and have brought their certificates with them. The boys have all this time been at home. They have grown quite a great deal. We are all still very well and are especially curious whether you are still all alive. Write back at once.

G. Brandt

Town Holland   30 August 1852

Dear Children,

Experience teaches that to postpone a matter seldom comes out right, as is the case now with writing you. We have received your letter dated the 17th of July – on time, at any rate inside of four days. It came to me by M.H. Muller. He had advanced five cents on it, which seemed strange to me and upon inquiry at the post office they told me it had been wrongly sent and therefore the five cents additional. But I think it was because that paper was in it. So I advise you not to send me paper in such a way anymore and a clear address on the letter and that you tell me whether you received the former letters, for I regularly paid three cents. Your letter was a joy to us. Still on reading it, it proved distressing and that was because Jannetje continues to ail. We all long for you to be home and in the hope that you might be healthier. I would advise you not to postpone this too long for the nearer to winter the less pleasant travelling is, and especially if you are weak. We are longingly looking forward to your coming and are ready to welcome you, yet would naturally long for word beforehand how you are thinking to make the journey; whether with bag and baggage as people say you are expecting to come. If you should come by boat you must at any rate find out whether it touches at the pier of our town, for if we must go to Port Washington it ought to be at full moon since parts of the night will have to be added to the day. Or if you wish that I should come for you in Milwaukee and we should board the boat there together, I will do that if you will set the time beforehand. All that is your choice. We are curious what result your new doctoring is having. I don't expect much from it, but shall hope the outcome will be otherwise. You must experience what we read in Mark 5 verse 26 and Luke 8 verse 43. I hope that you both may have found that chief physician or may find for your souls and that your membership and bond to His church may lead you to what you write us about and that the symbols in remembrance of His suffering partaken of by you may have enabled you to look upon the significant reality. Namely, to have discovered through faith that your sins too have cost Him that suffering and at the same time that out of love for you He was to do that. It is at times my prayer when I think of you. I hope it will be answered. I think of you often, yet not always in prayer, for that is a work of the spirit if understood correctly. But in this respect we are growing far apart and estranged. While in the Netherlands I had not imagined anything of the kind. I cannot always feel at rest about it, although I must surrender to it. You write of bringing store goods, but that again is difficult. Although we are becoming interested in wearing apparel, I haven't bought anything for myself yet, but I will have to shed the Zeeland farmer costume. Your mother has need of chemises, but what on the whole is scarce are woolen socks. Still, such things I cannot expect from you, for I must pity you when I think how much they take from you for a piece of goods when I consider what those costs are for the boys. The most important other need in the family is snuff and tobacco for your mother and for the boys, coffee, tea and soap. I can give little advice in this and we are under the impression that you maybe need these for your own. You ask about our crops and cattle. In regard to the former, we may be thankful and have abundant reason to be so because they are reasonably good for the number we have. But we do not have as many acres as some have. As for the cattle, we still have the same oxen and two milk cows: one fat cow, one pregnant heifer, two calves of each gender, four big hogs (we believe for they do not come home, and four smaller sized hogs. Then we also have a sow with seven pigs. Eight or nine ducks, 2 cats, 2 dogs. We can live from the eggs of our chickens. We are hoping for something better and have a hog in the pen. We are all well now. Isaac has suffered for six weeks with rheumatism. He was so stiff at times that only with great effort could he bend over. For three or four weeks he wore that rope wrapped flag cloth around his abdomen and under it his abdomen developed little sores and now he is better. Sometimes he didn't know what he was ailing from and sometimes he thought it was because he had no pork. James has grown less than Isaac. He is becoming rather engaging. He says he is beginning to think of girls. This summer, on a Sunday evening, he approached a daughter of Wolfert and offered to see her home from Souffrouw's, but she was ashamed to accept because she thought he was such a small boy. Sometimes we get a great deal of news from the paper from the island Goes. There they are very busy digging a canal from Amszwest to Wemeldingen so that it (the island) will now be in halves. Of the uncles and aunts we know nothing. Things here are going quite their old way. I know of no special news except that Traas has rented his farm so that he is giving up farming. Two weeks from next Monday I have to appear again in court in Sheboygan for Mr. Zonne. That case is not yet disposed of. What now is to happen is unclear to me. Jannetje, in the beginning of my letter I was somewhat brusque of expression, but I am really convinced that you did it with the best of intentions. You will notice, no doubt, that my sentences are beginning to be broken. We hope this may find you in good health. Greet from us all our good friends.

Your loving father
G. Brandt

♦♦♦♦♦♦

Town Holland   29 November 1852

Dear children,

We did not strike on our way back in regards to the weather. Lucky we did not need to walk. On Monday at noon we rode off and I got home Wednesday noon. My legs pained me a great deal so that last week I did not walk far at all. Today I have been to the Falls, according to my promise, and spoke with the tailor about your work. He said that he had work for you right away if you come, provided your work well. It had to be such, as he had an instance only last week in the case of a woman who had made a vest and put the collar on wrong, and such he cannot employ. But, he is anxious to have help for he says that there is a sort of competition between him and another and that in six months he had won around twenty clients from the other tailor. He does not work for himself, but for a store and is busy most of the tie cutting. Everything is made from orders and he said he would give you a pair of vests to make and then he would, of course, know. He let me see a vest that had also been made by a woman. He said that she was even one of the most noted in the Falls. I said that I thought your work was not second to hers. I didn't want to say it, but the work didn't seem to me like the work that I have seen you do. I believe sewing is well paid there. At least in the same store is a Holland clerk with whom I first spoke about it and he spoke of vests costing ten shillings to make. He said too that during the past summer they had had a girl there to help a few days and they had given her six shillings a day. We spoke about how it could be arranged for you to do the work at home. Possibly that could be done if you should wish it. This we would arrange then as you wished. Now another matter regarding the trip home. We had agreed that I should come for you. But that trip will cost 4 dollars if I can make it in 2 days and that will be impossible. So then it will cost all of 6 dollars and then we would be away three days at that. I asked deNooijer's wife what she had to give this spring and she said 2 dollars. I think you will have to pay that too to make an agreement first and if you then leave in the morning you are with us by 4 or 4:30 in the afternoon and need not wait if there is snow. Should you be prevented so that you don't come, then write as soon as you have this letter. Otherwise, we shall be expecting you. Our compliments to Rev. Klein and in case you come, ask for your church letter. Tell him that Rev. Verschuure wishes to pay him a visit. Although I really believe nothing will come of it. Greet J.H. Hyink and his wife for his father and mother. Tell him that they moved today into their new house and that Jan Willem is coming next week. Thank them for the trouble they went to for me. Greet J. de Jong and family and Smit and tell them that I still know they said I should go to the woods.

Now I hope that you will understand me in everything. We are still all well and hope that for you too.

Your loving father,
G. Brandt

♦♦♦♦♦♦

Milwaukee Wisconsin – Goes, Zeeland, NL   12 June 1859
Catharina Johanna Brandt to relatives

Dearly beloved Uncles, Aunts and little cousins!

Since a long time I have felt like writing a few lines to you. I can no longer delay. I have often asked father to write to you but it seems he cannot get to it. So I will, in as far as I am able, direct a few lines to you people. We are very eager to hear from you. I had probably written sooner if my health had permitted, and hope you will accept this in love. Since father's last letter we have received three letters from you folks, two from Uncle Jan Schipper and one from cousin Jan Lindenberg, which pleased us very much. It is a shame that these were not answered sooner.

From your letters we learned that Uncle Jacobus and Mother Sara have exchanged the temporal for the eternal. May it be that they have entered into the land of everlasting rest and are freed from all misery. The loss is always sad but there are good memories, and we have a living hope of seeing them again sometime. We have also learned that Aunt Martina has been ailing for quite a while but had recovered and that the others were in good health. From Cousin Jan's letter we learned that at that time things were going on as usual. His mother did say when we left for America that even if she could come to America in her slippers she would not want to. But I think they would be better off coming here especially he and his sisters, but perhaps there is no occasion for it. We have often longed to see some of our relatives. There is opportunity here for anyone who is willing to work to get ahead, although times have not been as good here this year nor last year as it was a few years ago. But still the wages are higher compared to Holland. They would have to be, otherwise we could not expect anyone to come here and we would not dare to advise it either!

As far as our situation is concerned, that has changed. In 1854 we moved from Holland where we lived previously, about 40 miles south to 8 miles from Milwaukee. This is a large city. Father was called here to be active as leader in the worship services, for which they paid him an annual salary of $100 and a free home, so that he cultivated only a small piece of ground. (There are about thirty Dutch families living here). But this leadership lasted only three years. In the year 1856, on May 15, Mother died. She had a stroke and was bed-ridden only seven days. She had been quite well.

We then found ourselves in a difficult situation for Jannetje was married and I had become ill in late March. Then we had no one who could do our work and we struggled along until June. Then Willemina Meeuwsen came to live with us from the Town of Holland. You undoubtedly have heard this from her sister. She lived with us about five months and then became married. We were very happy to have her with us. From her we heard some news about you.

Then on May 29, 1857, father was married to a woman living here and who was a widow. She is a native of Gelderland. She has no children and is 17 years younger than father. She also has 20 acres of land. When father had married this woman trouble broke out in the congregation because she could not prove, according to some, that it was not to back out of making payments.

Now that is how things came to an end. There is still a lot of difference of opinion among the Hollanders, mostly about public worship. The Dutch ministers still want to rule here, but this is free America. So father is a farmer again. He first bought 100 acres of land for $1,500, but he sold part of it again, so he had about 40 acres left, of which a large part is hay land, which is under water most of the winter. During the past winter he has been quite busy. He has eight animals to take care of: one horse, four cows and three calves, and besides he has to prepare wood for two stoves, and now he has to work hard again. In the Town of Holland he had the boys at home, but that is not the case now, but mother helps a good deal. She always did this, and she likes to do it. She is a healthy woman. Sometimes she has a headache, but otherwise she is quite well.

Father is also very well in America, which sometimes surprises me. He has not yet been ill here. He has had colds and fevers but not really sick. Last year he was so fat I do not think you would have recognized him.

112

As far as my condition is concerned, that is not good. As I have told you I became ill in 1856, due to nerve problems and bad colds so that I was completely bed ridden. During this illness I have already had four doctors which has cost us a great deal. To one we had to pay $81 and still no improvement. Some doctors here charge a scandalous amount. And in the case the one I mentioned he was also only after the money, and a Hollander at that. But one cannot rely on that. The first time that I had those nerve attacks it was just when three people died suddenly of cholera. The man was in the course of five hours well and dead, and the wife lay from Sunday noon until Monday evening, and that entire night I spent with her in the company of another girl of my age. I did not wish to do this, but many people were so afraid that they stayed away. It is usually the case that they think only of themselves. Then this girl also died two days later, which moved me greatly, Not it is the custom here that women also go to the grave, and it is still customary among Americans to bring the body into the church to a place in front of the pulpit (when there has been no contagious sickness). Then the casket is opened and anyone who still wishes to view the body can see it. Then the minister preaches a funeral sermon and speaks to the family. This having been concluded, the body is buried.

When our dear brother died some Americans also came to see the body. Now I was also to the grave of the girl and was very sad but could not cry. When I came home it became still worse. Then I suddenly began to cry and some people thought I also had the cholera but one man who knew about it said that it was a case of nerves, and since that time whenever something happened it often reoccurred.

Last summer I visited Jannetje a couple of times, I had not been there for two years, and she is no farther away than we call each other. At present I am still weak and must spend part of the day in bed but am better than formerly. I am sometimes despondent but at other times I can submit to the Lord and say, "May it be to His honor and my commitment to His service!"

Jannetje, as I have already stated, was married on May 5, 1855, to a boy from the land of Cadzand. His name is Jacob de Swarte. They have two children, but the first one, a girl, died at the age of seven months. Now they have a darling little boy, twenty months old, who looks a lot like his grandfather, and is also named after him. They have a good living.

They bought four acres of land from Father and he also works for somebody else as well once in a while. They also have a cow. Jannetje is not doing well at the moment. She is bothered by the same thing as I am. Her husband and child are fine. Izaak and Jacobus both live in Michigan for three years already. They work at a lumber mill and earn twelve to twenty dollars each month and enjoy free boarding. Four weeks ago Jacobus came home. We get to see him every year. Izaak came home last autumn. We had not seen him for two years.

Izaak also got married on March first of this year. He married a girl from Noord Holland named Tryntje Wagenaar. Izaak intends to become a farmer in the Town of Zeeland in the near future. Together they purchased forty acres of land from Father. Further, he plans on taking over Jacobus' property since they worked hard there. Besides the land is of good quality. The harvest last year was rather poor. There was enough straw, but no grain and at some places there was nothing at all. Last spring was too wet and during the summer disease victimized the wheat. It was rather special that the potatoes, beans, and peas fared well. Until so far, the crops prosper well this year. One believes here that the chance of war causes the prices here to rise. The flour (meat is unheard of here) costs nine dollars per two hundred pounds. It is ground of winter wheat and costs four dollars more than last winter. However, where Izaak and Jacobus live it costs twelve dollars. The oats and potatoes are a dollar a bushel. According to Father, two and three quarters bushel is one mud. Probably you know that one dollar is worth two and a half guilders. As stated before, groceries are rather expensive, but in Dutch currency converted, the coffee costs between fifteen and eighteen cents a pound, sugar between six and seven, and butter between twelve and twenty. And the materials for clothing as well. One cannot buy more here with an American dollar than with a guilder at your place. But we still do not regret our coming to America. One has to work hard here as well, but the freedom is quite pleasant. The air of this region is clear and fresh. Father once in a while longs to see his friends back, but apart from that he feels at home here. Izaak and Jacobus are both convinced that they could never have advanced so much as they do here. This land they bought from Father, as stated earlier, cost them five hundred dollars. Now it is their property. And they rent it out for five years for forty dollars per year. I also want to mention that they both are taller in height than Father. Jacobus hopes to see Holland again in the future. He is a remarkable fellow with an inquiring mind. I believe he will not become a farmer. We pay five guilders and forty cents each year in taxes and for that the children go to school until they reach the age of twenty; only during the four winter months if they so desire.

It is quite a problem for us to get our grain ground because we live two and a half hours from the place where it is done. But a person does not go, as a rule, with less than three or four bushels at a time and then one gets three kinds of things: flour, then cracked wheat and then bran. Whether that is the reason I do not know for sure, but I believe it is due to the separation that it does not spoil. Even when it is six months old it is still good. Potatoes are fine here. We still have eighty to one hundred bushels to sell. They are cheap here now. It is not possible to get more than thirty four or thirty five nickels for a bushel. Wheat costs sixteen shillings, rye eleven, barley nine, buckwheat nine, oats seven and butter one. Eggs cost ten to twelve stuiver for twenty five. Pork costs three and a half per pound, beef two and a half per pound, and coffee beans are eight stuiver. We make sugar, syrup and vinegar ourselves if needed. Cloth is rather scarce and of poor quality. Our children are not all at home. The girls have learned to sew so that they now work for themselves and are now no longer ironing as servants. Last summer they became confessing members of Rev. Klein's church in Milwaukee. They took their membership certificate with them. The boys are still at home. They have grown a great deal. We are all well and are very eager to know if you are all alive. Write back soon.

But dear ones, I still have something to add. I hope this will not offend you in any way. When Uncle Jan Schipper sent us his first letter he wrote about the many changes which took place over there. But he goes on, if only we were able to announce that a change of heart, namely the conversion, this would be even more desirable. It would have been dear to him to see this. Nevertheless, he writes, the Lord has decided already who will be saved and who will not. And this is true, but as we can read in Lev. 29:29, the hidden things are for the Lord and the open things are for us, as is according to His will. But we cannot for a moment assume that we know what the Lord has decided. He orders you to sow on your land so that He may be glorified with bread. Now you would not say I will not sow and thus I will harvest because this would go against reason. Now the Lord offers you His gospel and calls sinners. In Ezekiel 33:11 we read that the Lord does not desire the death of sinners, but seeks for conversion and life. Oh, I would like you to be able to write to us about people being born in Zion. Oh what great news this would be. Do not delay any further, but work while it is day time so that the night fall will not surprise you by disabling you to work. Do not be fooled by the enemy that the Lord Jesus died for everybody, or, things are not as bad as it seems, as many have come to believe. What this all does is it creates then everything Jesus said to Nicodemus will have no avail. As we can read in John 5, God is gracious. Yes, He will do so before Jesus, His son. But he is also righteous and made us perfectly according to His image. However, we lost His image through the fall. And so, there is no other way than through Jesus Christ, his son, who himself says, "Nobody is able to come to the Father but through me." Oh seek life there where it only can be found. Since He himself says my yoke is soft and my burden is light. As far as we are concerned, I believe to be able to say, that we follow the path of our ancestors, as far as I can see, even though it is accompanied by constant lamentation. We say this may be the truth. But the inherent sin in our lives away from Christ, that makes it often so strangling and dark. We have to say that sin is a heavy burden to us. Sometimes it is in control, but then a feeling of guilt reveals itself, a feeling of having sinned against the holy and gracious God whom is so worthy to be served and worshipped. Oh to serve the Lord is not hard. Even though the world thinks and assumes it to be a demanding and arduous life. But one cannot judge the food one has not prepared. And when one has the opportunity to get a taste of what it is like to serve the Lord then one has found that which one cannot find anywhere in the entire universe. Izaak and Jacobus a year ago publicly professed not to be able to live in sin any longer. In the former days, whenever we exposed them, they remained in silence and preferred rather to speak about something else. However, now they will have to testify that they are serious about it in life. Jacobus himself is quite vigorous in detecting and punishing sins. Yes, his is an example to us. Since a while back he has the desire to preach God's word, even among the heathens. But in case the Lord who calls him, then He will provide for a way. And so to his great joy, Father comes to see that the prayers so often prayed in private and in public have been heard which is a great privilege to be able to say. See Lord here I and the children you gave me. Yes, how would this be for our dear great grandparents who, as we may believe, together with their eldest son, entered the land of eternal rest. Could they say this too? Only the Lord knows how many prayers they sent to the Lord, and we and you. O that eternity, which never ends, is a tremendous relief for God's people to be with the Lord forever. I have to admit that during this hardship I had a desire to be dissolved as well, sometimes to be liberated of my body, but sometimes to be with the Lord too. During that time I could have said that I did not care for anything in this world. Oh, if only this was the case. But that would be against the Lord's honor. But now I must end. I am able to say a whole lot more about this, but oh, come to your senses before it is too late. This is my wish and prayer. In case we will not meet again at this side of the grave, then may it be so on the other side.

115

Now I would like to make a request. If you have the opportunity once to let us know something regarding Mother's family; who is still alive? We would be grateful if you could do so. The oldest sister lived in Ellewoudsdyk. Her husband's name was Jan ten Velde. We also found out that Uncle Willem is a school teacher in Hulst. Hereby we send you a little seeds of nice flowers. It is not quite the uniqueness of the flowers themselves, but rather the fact that so many little flowers develop is special. Each flower blooms only one day. Whether you will like these flowers I do not know. Receive it as a memory. If you have a chance to send me a little seed, I would greatly appreciate it since flowers are of great interest to me. Receive now warm greetings from all of us: from me, Jannetje and her husband, Izaak and Jacobus. Give my greetings to Mother Willemynte. Mina told us that they thought to come to America. In that case I would like to see her. Once again, be greeted often I am with you all in thought. I call myself your loving niece. Write back soon if you can.

Catharina J. Brandt

♦♦♦♦♦♦

[This letter was written to his son James who was a student at the Holland Academy in Holland, MI. It was probably written in December 1859, but was not mailed by Gerard, because the appended note was written by Catherine on 29 December 1859.]

Dear son,

Looking into the letter you sent us I can rejoice that it is granted you to heed so carefully the utterance of your heart and to the deeds of the Lord regarding you. My wish is that you may continually find that in your experience and to that end. I want, too, to wish for the lesson that Paul gives in 2 Timothy, verse 22, of which you already gave hint in your letter. It if should please the Lord to grant you that continuously in large measure, you would be able to say as C. Deminicus, never to have felt regret for having served the Lord so early. I must be short and so come to your remark regarding what I wrote in a P.S. in my letter. I would be able to be of service to you even with no money. As for instance, two weeks ago Cornelis (van) Zante was here and asked minutely about A. B. Eernisse; how the matter of payment was and although I did not tell him, he then began to say for what reason he was going to Town Holland (Sheboygan County). That he had 307 dollars on the farm of the brother of P. Eernisse and had yet seen no interest in three years and that there was still one ahead of him with 175 dollars, so that he was thereby mislead. Then the idea came to me that Bram had said to Isaac that he had so much money in that farm that he could not pay his own debt now and that seems to me now untruthful. So it would perhaps be good for you to be curt in going after it (the payment for the farm). However, you must decide. Greet all the friends.

Your loving father,
G. Brandt

Oh brother, hurry, hurry, our beloved father is dead. What shall I say. Come home as soon as possible for I don't know what to do. He has been in a runaway with the horse. Let Isaac

116

know. Do come. I beg you. Oh, brother, do come, Father is dead and do think of me, your miserable sister.

♦♦♦♦♦♦

Town of Milwaukee   9 May 1860

Dearly beloved uncles, aunts, and little cousins:

Up to the present time we have been disappointed in our expectations of receiving an answer from you people to the letter I wrote last year in May. We thought you did not receive it, so we decided once more to write to you, especially since so many things have happened here. We hope you accept this in love.

In my former letter I wrote you that we left Holland (Town of Holland in Sheboygan Cty) in 1854 and that now we live eight miles from Milwaukee, which is a large city.   The reason why we moved was that Father was then called here for religious service, to be a leader here and carry on catechetical work, yet this lasted but three years because then trouble arose between him and the congregation partly also because of the domineering and partisan spirit of the Holland ministers here. To tell it all would easily make my story too long drawn out, and it would do you little good.

I have also told you in my former letter about the death of mother. We were surprised to receive a short letter from Mina Meeuwsen. She had written nothing to you about our situation, as mother had died in May 1856, and I had been ill all summer and was still sick when she left us. She lived with us five months, and this would not have been necessary if I had been well. Then, we did not receive the note from you until February this year, what the reason was for that we do not know. Father too would have been gladdened to have seen it since he was frequently desirous of hearing from, and yet so negligent about writing. What the reasons were I cannot say. We often requested him to, but it seems he could not get to it. We still have a portion of a letter which he began but did not complete. The two previous letters of Uncle Jan Schipper we received one from Uncle Adriaan, and one from Cousin Jan Lindenberg, and from it we learned about the death of Uncle Jacobus and Aunt Sara. Do pardon their not being answered sooner. We are very sorry that you did not receive our letter of last year since we were frequently desirous of a word from you.

Now you will perhaps notice from my story what sad tidings we have to tell you (or you may have been apprised of it from rumor or from someone else) it is then this that our beloved Father too is no more among the living, but on the 29th of December in an unfortunate and heart moving manner exchanged time for Eternity, by the running away of the horse he had driven to the city that morning. Because he had quite a lot of work at home, it was quite often his wont to leave late, and so it was too that day (because our horse is quite lively for it was only seven years old, a big brown white-faced), so it was bound to be late before he was back. Then too, it would not have been so late had he not had to visit some of his friends that he had to see. On his way back the horse must have frequently tried to dash away, as others

117

say, and since it was a good sleigh road and there was no load in the sleigh, he made good time. Then too, our horse can't stand anything at his heels or he starts to run, so we think that this was the case here too. Not too far from our house there is a ditch through which water washes out and from there on the horse must have started to run away, for from there on the sleigh had left tracks. Father had written to you that trees here are chopped two feet more or less above the ground and the stumps are left standing, so it was here too along the road through which Father must go and right between two big stumps, as big perhaps as there are nowhere two to be found, on each side of the road. Now the sleigh had run up against the one and on the other Father seems to have struck his head. He must have been there in the evening around seven o'clock already. And strange it was that that evening not a person came down that road. Mother and I were indeed restless that evening, thinking that all that time Father had stayed with one of his friends, so no one went out to look for him. Too, Mother and I were alone in the house. At eleven o'clock I had gone to bed but was very restless, but Mother not at all the whole night long. In the morning at daybreak she went outdoors, not expecting to see anything there. Not far from the house she saw a horse standing yet did not think that this could be ours, but still she was not easy. She went there and named the horse by name and when it turned its head she saw that it was ours, then went a bit farther and say there our dear Father lying in the middle of the road partly frozen too. O my Dear, what a circumstance. This you can somewhat comprehend, but yet not exactly what it was. Left home sound and well and carried in dead. Oh how I was affected I cannot express to you. Sick as I was I ran from my bed in a skirt when my father was being carried into the house. My dear Father, who had in my condition in which I had lingered four years, had carried me to and from bed hundreds of times, was dead. Oh what a circumstance. Cry, I could not. Everybody was amazed at me. Less than fifteen minutes after he was in the house I sat down and wrote a letter to James. Alas, what must I do with my Father gone, you cannot comprehend. No one has lost so much as I. Oh how my heart bled, and so many tears as I shed in my loneliness, for I am an object of misery and cannot do without the help of others. But, at times I can surrender it all to the Lord and say, He who has provided for me so long will still provide for me. But for me it is nevertheless a hard matter and a time of testing, for it is by brothers and a sister that I have to support now. Sometimes I say if I had to crawl on my bare knees and so get my Father back I would gladly do it. But the Lord, who according to his decreeing will carries everything into effect renders no account of his deeds, but a great comfort and a pleasant recollection remains for us nevertheless. For to his God and the Lord Jesus rich in love who is the only way of salvation he always kept clinging, howbeit with frequent lamenting over his sins yet carrying on a continual struggle against sin and having as his sole desire to be the Lord's. Oh happy entrance into that land of Eternal rest where all trouble and pain ceases, and to have the privilege of meeting (as we may believe) those that precede him, as her whose womb bore him, and his eldest brother, and her who carried us, he has not been freed from all trouble and is now serving his God in perfect joy. For to him were confirmed the words we read in John 16, verse 33, last portion, which once came with marked force to his mind when we were still living in Kapelle. Yes, to the last of his life, even for in me he had to witness many troubles, but now it has ceased. Oh that you might continually betake yourselves into his presence, and that with a desire to arrive there too.

On his forehead, and his nose full of clotted blood, and his right arm out of joint, I certainly examined him 3 or 4 times for, it was you see, my dear Father. Father had been frightfully maimed; his skull behind his left ear was split open more than a finger's length, and fully so wide that one could lay a finger in it. His left ear cut through the middle; his nose between the eyes partly beaten in.

O what a privilege it would be for our dear Grandmother to be able to say, behold hear me and the children Thou has given me. Oh, do seek after it, one may have satisfaction here, of course, in the world, but when death comes we can take nothing with us and then as a naked soul to appear before the great judge can bring nothing but Eternal misery. Oh how Father too did long at times to hear this some time from you. Uncle Adriaan wrote in his letter that you no longer had a brother now to pray for you, but even though you were far away he made you, now and then, the object of his prayer at the throne of grace, feeling the burden of your souls. Oh, it is occasionally my prayer too that through God's grace you may be made seekers while there yet is to find. Oh, when once one may experience the sweetness, joy, and refreshing there is in the service of the Lord then one is constantly desirous of it. Oh, it is certainly a sweet service that gives afterwards an Eternal Peace, since the service of sin brings naught but Eternal sorrow. But, possibly some of you have learned to pray the prayer of the publican, O blessed and happy is he then who for Jesus' sake has found grace in God's sight. That this may not offend you is then my wish, for it is being done in love. What else now concerns our situation. I wrote you in my last that Father married again in 1857 with a widow who was living here, a native of Gelderland, seventeen years younger than he, with whom I am now still living. Until when I do not know, possibly until fall when I think I shall go live with Jannetje.

My condition is critical. As I told you before, I became ill in 1856, having nerve attacks and repeated distress. I spent more of the next two years in bed and had to be carried in and out. I had at least four doctors and spent a lot of money but made little progress. The first time I had an attack was when three persons died unexpectedly of cholera. Since that time is has become worse. But still I was always able to do my work until the time I told you of, even when I had taken bad colds. For the present I am using no medicines and am still very sickly, and did not mend after Father's death. There is not a day that I am free from nervous spasms and convulsions. Sometimes I am, of course, discouraged. All I can do is stay at home. When it is summer I can occasionally go to Jannetje's, but no farther. She doesn't live as far from us as we did from the little orchard at Kapelle. Also, I must spend a part of the day in bed. What is to become of me I have no idea. At times, however, I have a lively faith that the Lord will in his own time give deliverance. When I see what I am by nature and how many blessings I have the privilege of enjoying and what the Lord Jesus suffered, and that I have nothing to say, I have as yet lacked nothing and our allotted portion of bread has always been granted to us. Mother, too is very good to me. I enjoy much friendship from her and she has much patience with me. At times, too, my desire has been that I might be released sometimes, indeed to be quit of my troubles, but sometimes also from a desire to be with the Lord since I might take for granted that the Lord was charging me to his account. My guilt and sin were forgiven me, and since I had learned to know myself as a poor unworthy sinner, although it is accompanied with continual conflict and continual fear, that I

119

have not surrendered fully to the Lord, yet with a continual adherence and a continual desire to be the possession of the Lord.

In my former letter I told you that Jannetje and Isaac are both married. The former in May 1855 and Isaac in March 1859. Jannetje has had three children, the first died when seven months old. Now she still has two. One, Gerard, who will be three in September and one Susanna who will be a year in July. Both dear children. That little boy Father made a lot of and he of him. They have a fairly good living. They have two cows and a piece of land which they have bought from Father. Her husband's name is Jacob de Swarte, a native of Cadzand, 5 years older than she is. Jannetje too is weak but still she can mostly always do her work. Her husband and children are fairly well. Isaac lives in Michigan and works in a sawmill. He has already lived there four years. He has a wife from North Holland. Her name is Trijntje Wagenaar. They have one child Cornelia. He thinks, nevertheless, of becoming a farmer too later on. He and James had bought some forty acres of Fathers when we moved here, which is not their possession. They rented it when they were in Michigan and are doing that still, but this winter James sold his 20 to Isaac for 350 dollars. So it is then his (Isaac's) intention after he has earned more to settle there. It is good land; better than we have here. 27 acres of it is being cultivated and the rest is timber still. Isaac and his wife and child are also enjoying good health. His wife we have never seen. James too used to work in the sawmills until last fall in October. At that time he entered the high school (Academy) at which he still is. That is in the city of Holland, Michigan. He is there to be educated for the ministry, for which he has had a desire for a long time already, but frequently with the fear that he himself did not possess what he wished to present to others. He thought that if the Lord wished to use him in his service He himself would open the way. It is then his constant desire to be engaged in the Lord's service, yes, even should it be among the heathen. He has unusual gifts which we cannot help being jealous of, and the spirit that has been in him since he was still a child is not yet extinguished. If he pursues the entire course to learn English, Latin, Greek, Hebrew, and what more besides I don't know, then he must be there 5 years where he is now and 5 years at another high school (college) in New Jersey. Oh how happy Father was about this and desirous that he might yet be an eye and ear witness of this, but that has not pleased the Lord. But he was privileged to see offspring of his offspring. But what is more, that the prayers offered for us in secret and in pubic have been heard, for so far as I may believe we are all treading the way he has trodden. We do occasionally think over our lot here that we four who are still living should be enjoying this privilege of having been bought and freed with Jesus' blood, but with the Lord this is to be sure not wonderful, and he certainly wishes to reveal the glory of his free grace in redeeming sinners. The depraved heart does indeed at times well up, so that Amalek prevails, just as the Apostle Paul himself laments in Romans 7. But then there is sorrow and prayer from the heart for forgiveness. I have not written this to plume myself with it. I hope the Lord may guard us against this, that about what the Lord Jesus bought at such cost we would be proud. Oh may it serve to stir some of you to jealousy, and should we see each other no more this side of the grave, then may it be on the other side.

As for financial conditions here, in general, that is not so good as a few years ago. Wages are lower and trade as well in lands, as in products, is not so flourishing. Nor are provisions as cheap as when we came here. Crops this year, up to the present, are in general quite fine. It was unusually dry this spring so that people who had lived here thirty years had not known it so. In the beginning when we first came here Father bought a hundred acres of land, but has sold it all except 31 acres which are still partly encumbered. But next summer when James comes home we shall probably sell it. Land is priced higher here than in Town Holland (Sheboygan County) but we will nevertheless lose some on it at that, because it is less valuable than a few years ago. Mother also has twenty acres which she had when she married Father on which she thinks she will go to live. She has no children. She is a strong, healthy woman used to working in the field. Now we have a request to make of you, to make inquiry if it is possible about Mother's relatives, who of them is still alive, whether Uncle Jan of Dordrecht is still living. We have learned that Uncle William lives in the area of Hulst, and Aunt Mie's husband of Ellwoutsdijk has died. Inquire about it sometime if you can and write about it then. Now we hope that you will not allow this letter to go unanswered but will reply to it soon. Even though Father is no longer living, realize then that this blood flows in our veins. O, Aunt Martins, if you are still alive, you certainly have not forgotten us. I think it still comes vividly to my mind how you clung weeping to his neck that last day. Herewith I now close and hope also to receive one from you soon. Cordial greetings from us all. Mother also, though unknown to you, greets you. Jannetje and her husband, Isaac and James greet all nephews and nieces. We sign ourselves your loving blood relations and I your loved niece,

Catherine J. Brandt

[The next set of letters chronicles the interwoven story of the Bril, van Ouwerkerk and Risseeuw families as they settle in Milwaukee and Sheboygan County. Sara van Bortel was born 16 March 1796 in Cadzand, Zeeland. On 27 January 1819 she married Abraham Pieter Bril in Zuidzande, Zeeland. When he died at age 30 in April 1828, she was 5 months pregnant with twin girls and had 4 children under the age of 10: Pieter Johannes b. 1819, Abraham Pieter b. 1821, Johannes Izaak b. 1823, and Jacobus, b. 1826 who died in 1838. On 24 November 1830 Sara married Pieter van Ouwerkerk who was born 13 July 1803 in Zuidzande, Zeeland and died 27 March 1865 in Town of Holland, Sheboygan County. They had four children: Pieter b. 1831, Maria Pieternella b. 1833, Pieternella Sara b. 1836 and Jacobus Hendrik b. 1840. On 30 April 1851, on the ship Eensgezindheid, Sara van Bortel and Pieter van Ouwerkerk set sail for the United States with most of their combined families. The oldest son, Pieter Johannes (b. 1819), who had married Sara Baarendse, was the only member of the family who did not emigrate. Johannes Izaak Bril (b. 1823) was married in February 1848 to Esther B. de Meyer and in May 1848 they left for the U.S. Two other Bril children had married before emigration: Abraham Pieter (b. 1821) married Maria Meulendijk and Magdalena Pieternella (b.1828, one of the twins) married Daniel Tellier, and they and their families were on the same ship. Sara Willemina Bril (b. 1828) also accompanied her mother and step-father, along with her husband to be, Hubregt Risseeuw (b. 1821). Sara and Hubregt were married 26 July 1851 in Milwaukee.]

Letter from Abraham Pieter Bril, married to Maria Meulendijk, to Pieter Bril at Zuidzande, NL

Milwaukee   13 November 1851

Dear father and mother and brothers and sisters,

I have to say hello to you. We are still healthy. We are all right. On our trip we were well too. We had to go on to Milwaukee. When we arrived in New York they went to the office. No one told me and they paid for us till here. But at the moment we were at Rochester we had to catch something from our belongings. Otherwise we should have stayed there. Our belongings were packed up under other people belongings and that is the main reason that we are here in Milwaukee. And if it depends on others, they do what they like to do without asking. But therefore I am doing well here. First I worked with an American farmer, just a fortnight but I earned 4 sixpence there and had full board. We eat there pork and slices of bread. They were greased too. Afterwards I became a hodman in town and there I earned 6 sixpence. Now I am working for another boss and maybe I can work there for the whole winter. And I earn 6 sixpence a day too. I have to do nothing as plastering, it is different here from Holland. There you should have to work for 8 penny these days. Father think this over, if I should be better here than in Holland. We eat more pork and flesh here in America than as long as we are married. If all your pork or flesh is gone, we go to town and buy as much as we like. In Holland we could not do that. Pork cost 5 cents a pound, flesh cost 4 cents a pound, but these are American cents. An American cent is 2 ½ cents in Dutch money. I already bought a permit on which I can count that there are 12 decameter potatoes in it. I paid 8 dollar for it but it is only lent and not my own, but they told me it was in loan. And I asked some people how much a smithman can earn. The son of physician van Houte, who once lived in Sluis, you must have known him father, is just an apprentice and earns 6 sixpence a day and he told me there were people who earned 10 to 14 sixpence a day. Here they work from 7 in the morning till 6 in the evening. I already bought a stove for 5 dollar and a half, on which we can cook 4 pots at the same time and bake a bread. Anything else, we don't cook we can buy it easily.

For a barrel of flour, which is having a weight of 196 pounds, we paid 4 dollar. We couldn't do that in Holland because a cup of wheat was all we could afford, and those were sweepings. To shoemakers it is very good here. My brother-in-law Tellier has a lot more work than he can do. For a pair of shoes you pay a dollar here and sometimes 10 or 12 sixpence. And for a pair of boots you pay 20 to 22 sixpence. For maids it is good here too. My sister Maria earned a dollar a week. Pieternella earned 5 sixpence and if she could speak the language they could have earned more. But now my sister Maria married to Jacobus Verdouw and Sara married to Hubregt Risseeuw. Father went to Sheboygan and there he is living at the house of the widow Verdier. My brother Jan went to Sheboygan too. He bought 80 acres of land there and paid 230 dollars. Brother-in-law Tellier has 40 acres and he bought a cow. Father and mother I have to send many greetings from Uncle Henderik and his wife. They are healthy. And greet Mr. Moens from us and ask him how his grapes are doing. My wife was a fortnight with Uncle Henrik and during that time I worked in the city because they live 8 miles from the city. I wrote a letter to Uncle Engles and he wrote me back and told me he gave a letter to Izaak de Wilde. That letter Uncle Engels received on October 26 and I know from that letter that you all are well and they were too. They wrote me Elizabeth earned 5 sixpence and Maria is learning to make clothes. Father, I am curious how the potatoes are doing because here it is the same as last year with you. They cost 3 guilders a bag here, but I can better can pay 3 guilders here than in Holland. I am curious to know how the trips of brother Piet went. Tell him I am curious. I don't know what to write yet.

My address is:
Milwaukee State Wisconsin

Greetings from me, Abraham Pieter Bril, Maria Meulendijk. Our little boy is well too.

◆◆◆◆◆◆

Pieter van Ouwerkerk to his stepbrother Pieter Bril at Zuidzande

Town Holland   18 September 1851

Dear brothers and sisters,

We received your letter from July in good health and the whole family is healthy. We hope that you enjoy the same. We received just one letter from you. To our regret we heard that your wife was not well. Your question is if we paid more than we agreed. No, we did not pay more. The harvest is low. The rye and potatoes are very good. We sold 5 hectolitre potatoes for 50 sixpence a hectoliter. Calculated by 2 ½ bushel here. We like it very much to be here. We are alive. We have to work hard, especially father, but he still likes it. We already have two heifer calves and chickens too. Boelen and I will milk seven cows next summer, so the prospects – if the Lord blesses us – are very good. Jacobus is very content. He drives the oxen and he can shout the chants. We have a very dry summer and have had a lot of damage from it. We milk 5 cows now, almost six, so we are busy with milking and churning. Yet the milk is not a very big quantity because of the dryness. But it is raining at this moment so it'll soon be better. We live three hours from the nearest village which is Sheboygan Falls and four hours from Sheboygan. Jacob and Pieternella are walking to Sheboygan every fortnight with butter and eggs. But I think it'll be nearer soon. Three miles from us a pier was built. Ships arrive there and there'll be shops so it will be nearer soon. Jan, that place is called Amsterdam. So that place is going to be big. They count on three thousand Dutch people. There are two reverends here and there are still people arriving. These days we have Mr. van Altena, in earlier times physician in Biervliet and burgomaster. So we hope we don't need him but nevertheless we are happy he is here. Three miles is an hour. Piet, I have to tell you, this is the first letter I write to you to tell something. It was my intention to write you before, but one cannot write something before you are in America and still I don't know what to write. The people who are here don't want to go back to their fatherland, because they live here undisturbed. Who is so lucky that he can buy forty or eighty acres land. He can find a fair competence. But for the time being it is with big trouble, because this land is not like the land in the Netherlands. Here you have to see first that you have the trees pulled up. So you go there and there is a lot to saw, but it goes as it goes. I cannot say that the success can be as in Holland, you know, but not so soon. Because in the second or the third year you can get a reasonable harvest, but sometimes it is just low. If it was a tree here and a tree there it was easy to do, but they grow very close to each other, so before the land is available to crop it needs a lot of patience, work and money before you can earn a living on it. There are other parts in America without woods but they are more expensive than woodland. You can buy the woodland for 10 shilling, governmental price, and second hand it costs three dollars, sometimes six or seven dollars an acre. More I cannot tell you at the moment except we are by the Lord's kindness still fit and healthy and we hope you all are too. Greetings to all our relatives and people known to us and we hope soon to receive a letter from you and hear how you are doing. Your dear mother wishes to ask you if the old neighbors are doing well. I stop with my pen but not with my heart.

Your faithful father,
Pieter van Ouwerkerk and J.J. van Ouwerkerk

Piet, this is your dear mothers sign Sara van Bortel
Pieter L. van Ouwerkerk

Piet you are curious to know from us how the little Sara Bril is. She is very well and she should like to live with us. And Cor is talking English like a Jay. And Piet earns still his 6 sixpence a day.

◆◆◆◆◆◆

Pieter van Ouwerkerk the third to his stepbrother Pieter Johannes Bril at Zuidzande.

Town of Holland   12 April 1852

Dear Brother,

I have to tell you the state of our health. We hope to hear the same from you, because we are very desirous to get a letter from you. We didn't get a letter from you as long as we are in America so you can understand that mother is not satisfied. If you write, send your letter from Sluis. And if you sometimes will give a letter along with an emigrant you can do that too. They can take it freely. Just seal it because they don't ask for anything if you gave the letter along with emigrants. In that case you have to write the address like this: Aan Pieter van Ouwerkerk, Sheboygan County, Cae du Groive (Cedar Grove), State of Wisconsin. It will cost you nothing and if they post it they have to pay nothing either. So brother, write us how your business is going and if those girls of P. de Lijs are still baking. I asked it before in my first letter, but they didn't tell the answer. I can tell you that we all are still healthy and

124

we have a good life by the kindness of the Lord. See brother, we have had quite severe winter but the last 8 days we had nice weather and at night it is freezing a lot and by day it is nice weather. At the moment I am busy making syrup and sugar. The Saturday before Easter I made two buckets of syrup. O, what a free and fruitful land. Brother, we heard that the daughter of Verlare from Oostburg is coming too and write us once if it is true or not. Look, P. Soufrouw is her lover and his mother is against it but she didn't tell the reason. Everyone has to do what he wants to do in this case. So did I, which I'll fulfill as soon as I am able to do so. Brother, give her (his girlfriend Janneke) your brotherhand to the one who is mine and see her as your sister. I intended to go to the city of Milwaukee on the 15th or 16th to get a job. As soon as possible I'll send money to her. See brother, if you are writing about P. Soufrouw, write it in a little letter and don't tell anybody. See brother, I stop with my pen but not in my heart and be greeted by Father and Mother and Sisters and Brothers. By me too.

I am still your brother and yours faithfully, Pieter van Ouwerkerk the third is greeting you again and goodbye from all of us. Write me once when you receive this letter and if you send one how much you have to pay.

◆◆◆◆◆◆

Pieter van Ouwerkerk the third to Pieter Bril in Zuidzande

Milwaukee   15 June 1852
After rain comes sunshine

Dear brother,

I have to tell you the state of my health and the health of the brothers and sisters. They are all in a reasonable condition. Father and mother too. On May 25th I received a little letter from Father and at that time they were all well. They were very busy with planning and sawing. The harvest looks to be very well at the moment and the vegetable garden looks to come right. On June 5th it was freezing hard. A lot of plants in the gardens were damaged by the frost. But now it is pretty warm. The American sun is getting rid of the Dutch smell. We lost it already, but the new people haven't yet. Dear brother, there is not much to tell. At the moment it is difficult to get a job in town. The reason is that the water is very high in the river because of the long period of frost at night. They could not make bricks. They would lay bricks it there were bricks. But I am working with the gasworks for three weeks and I earn 6 sixpence a day. It is well paid but now we are closed for three days because of the water. Those pipes have to be dug 4 feet deep. Brother Abraham Bril is working with the brick layers for 6 sixpence a day. Well paid, but he is obliged to spend half of his wages in the shop.

Brother Hubregt is working with the same boss under the same conditions. Under these conditions it is easy to get a job, but it is more storestuff that shopware. For one who is married it is bad stuff. It is just good for the winter. Brother, this is not to the point. I have to tell you that I was able to send money to my dear Janneke Zwigtman. She and I, so I think, hope and believe, for I didn't know her so well and I loved her so and still love her, or I wouldn't send money. At the time I was with her I swore not once but a thousand times I should never let her down and I am still thinking the same by the Lord's kindness. I don't regret it but I have seen boys who had to leave one in such a way. See brother, I send 40 dollars via Jozias van der Plasse, notary at Milwaukee. He has sent it to New York to Mr. van Steenwijk. Mr. van Steenwijk will send it to Wambroezi and Crooswijk at Rotterdam. Mr. van Steenwijk shall write a letter to Wambroezi and Crooswijk that they have to send the money to J.H. van Ouwerkerk, my dear uncle. Brother Pieter, be so kind to let my uncle read this letter. I hope he will read it for my sake and most for that orphan (Janneke) and her delicate fruit (Janneke was pregnant). Dear uncle, I shall write more but I don't have enough time. Be so kind to ask the gentlemen Wambroezi and Crooswijk if the money has arrived because she will be anxious to know. I hope she comes as soon as possible. Brother and uncle work for my good, like I trust you to do. The money will leave Milwaukee on the 15th of this month to New York and it can arrive as soon as a letter. So write to Rotterdam soon dear uncle. Greetings to Izaak from A. Bril and his wife and children. Tell them they are still fit and healthy. Greetings to grandfather and mother from me. More I cannot tell you, we all are well by the Lord's kindness.

I still am your faithful brother and cousin,
Pieter van Ouwerkerk

Greetings to all relatives and people known to me,
P. van Ouwerkerk – and your wives too.

◆◆◆◆◆◆

Pieter van Ouwerkerk senior and Sara van Bortel to their son (and stepson) Pieter Bril at Zuidzande

Town of Holland   15 March 1853

Dear son, daughter and grandson,

I have to tell you the condition of our health, by the blessings of the Lord, we are all well. We received your letter on March 2 and it was a great pleasure that you and yours and all the neighbors and relatives are still prosperous. Now I like to tell you how we are. Pieter and neighbors, you are surprised why I am writing so little. The reason why is that if you come here you can write things you heard from other people, but not by experience. And by experience I can tell you now and write the truth like I'll do to you and all people I know. I can tell you that as long as I am in America I didn't have to pay charges. Jacobus goes to school every day. We have to pay rent. My first residence was in Milwaukee on the Dutch hill in the house of P. de Zwarte and there I paid 10 sixpence a month. Something else, as long as were on the ship everything went well. But from the moment we arrived you needed 10 eyes instead of 2, for the reason people would take all your stuff away as soon as it is unloaded if we were not attentive. You asked me about Uncle Izaak Lemoine (LeMahieu). He lives one hour from us and we stick together a lot of time. And Hendrik Orlebeke, Klaarbouw (Claerbout), Jan Kaljouw, de Bats, Antonie de Met (called Mette) live all at the same distance. Jacob de Raaf lives a quarter of an hour from us too. He is our physician. A lot of Dutch people live near us. I'll not name them because there are too many of them.

I like to tell you that I bought 40 acres of wooded land for the governmental price and that it is 10 sixpence an acre and to purchase the deed is 3 dollars, so it is together 53 dollars. But the wood is not land to cultivate yet. First you have to pull out the trees and burn them, but if everything goes well with the burning you can make from every 6 acres, 10 or 12 dollars for the ashes. After that you have to make a separation and then you can saw whatever you like. We have a lot of oak wood we can make a lot of money from. There are a lot of maple trees too, to make sugar and syrup. And a lot of other kinds of trees. I can assure you that it'll need a lot of work to get it ready. If there are people who were thinking that they could earn one's keep without working, they should be mistaken in America. A farmer here is a workman too. That is the reason why a lot of people's hope was deceived. They came with a lot of money but it is all gone now. A day's wage is so high in America that they lose their money soon. It is not like in Holland where you have to work for 50 cents a day. The difference is very big. I work in Holland to earn 50 cents most of the days. Here you can earn 6 to 8 sixpence a day during the harvest. But sometimes you cannot get people to work for you. So, a lot of people come to America who cannot or wouldn't work, but who had a lot of money. Other people bought a lot of land to speculate on. All their money is in it and they have to pay all charges (taxes) every year. However it is not so much, but that is the way they lose it. There are people who have 80 times 80 acres. Say that they pay two dollars of the 80 acres for taxes. That makes 60 dollars for the 8 times 80, and that every year. It is going to rise high. Now they pay interest with their own money. This is the way it goes for a lot of people. But, if you can work and like to work you are the boss, because the one who comes with money has to work and the one who comes without money has to work too. Something else now, tell Maarten Albregtsen a good millerhand earns 40 dollars a month. Someone here earns 40 dollars but he is a head hand. It is not a windmill. It goes with water and all is grinded at one time, grain and grit.

The bosses here are not permitted to pass criticism because the servants leave them saying America is so big! But with you it is very different. You have to keep your mouth shut and sometimes that is very difficult. So it is with a lot of workers. If they have a lot of trouble they have to go. It is very different here. The more children you have the better. They earn a lot of money. Of course, they have to speak English. If my children would like to serve, none of them would be home. The already speak English very well. Jacobus Hendrik most. He speaks, reads and spells very good. Pieternella could earn a dollar a week sometime ago. She is walking out with the son of the former burgomaster of Biervliet. Willem van Altena is his name. His son's name is Pieter. I have to tell you that the land we bought is next to the land of Jacob Verdouw and the land of Jannis Bril. First we thought it was all swamp, but we had it measured out and there are 25 acres we can saw on. The rest is more swamp, which is lowland, overgrown with spruce firs. It is a better quality wood than the spruce firs you have. That land is very wet and for that reason you cannot use it directly. But if we have 30 acres, we can live on it and then we have 10 acres for firewood too. That will be enough for the rest of our life or for 20 or 30 more years or as long as it pleases the Lord that we'll live. And we sincerely hope that the Lord will give us a number of years together. In that case we'll have, without accidents, a good life and a lot of joy when we are old, if the Lord pleases. We have to thank the Lord every day for the benefits he gave us our whole life. Now we started to fell trees and build a log house. It is a fashion here that if you build a house you ask your neighbors and then it'll happen that the walls are built in one day, without a roof and without windows. And not small houses! These log houses are not cold as you smear it well with clay or mortar.

I have to tell you we had a reasonable harvest. We have threshed 74 bushel rye and we had a lot of hay. We are threshing grass seed and we sell it for 14 sixpence a bushel. If we like to thresh it all, we can have 20 bushels. We can sell hay for 10 dollars per 2000 pound. 4 ½ of your ounces is an American pound. I would like to tell you the prices of the grain. Wheat is 70-75 cents a bushel. It was 90 cents too this year. Rye 40-45 cents, oats from 22 to 25 cents, the barley 30-35 cents, potatoes 31 cents, peas 75 cents. It is all a bushel and American cents. 2.66 bushel is a hectoliter. Butter is 14 cents a pound, eggs 10 cents a dozen, pork 6 cents a pound, flesh 5 cents a pound. And if we go to the mill our grain is ground and sifted, and after it is ground we have flour, grain and middlings. We just eat sifted bread. I am not writing this to boast about it. Oh no, but this is the way of the country and we eat very well. I have to tell you that horned cattle makes a good prize. A yoke of oxen, 5 or 6 years old, make 60, 70 and sometimes 80 dollars. A yoke is 2 oxen. The milk cows make 20 to 25 dollars and all proportionally. If someone has to sell something, he can make a profit. These days we can make a profit from wood. The reason is that they build a pier. A pier is a kind of a quay for ships and steamers. That pier is 800 feet long into the lake. It was built by Dutch and American people. We can get rid of our wood there. For a thousand staves we get 15 dollars. Those staves are 35 Dutch inches long, 10 wide and 1 thick. And we can sell firewood too for 1 dollar a cord. A cord is 8 feet long and 4 feet high and 4 feet wide. Who has 40 acres wood, a yoke oxen and cart, can earn a lot of money. But you cannot earn it without working. And if they come, they don't have to do it on my saying so. It is the truth which I write. Everyone has to do whatever he likes. So did I. I am not complaining, but I am sorry for the poor people who have to ask for their bread in Holland. If they were here they could earn it. There are poor people here too, but those are the people who are handicapped or who don't like to be good. There are not so many poor people here as with you. Sometimes it is bad if you come here. The first year you cannot understand anything and if you have just a little money it is very lean. But it gets better fast most of the time. However, it goes one bad and another good, just like with you. I have to tell you that sister Maria van Ouwerkerk had a son on January 14, 1853. His name is Pieter. More I cannot tell you. We like being in America and make a living. Greetings from all of us. Greetings to all our relatives and friends from us, and from me too, who is called your father and mother.

Pieter van Ouwerkerk, Sara van Bortel

♦♦♦♦♦♦

Pieter van Ouwerkerk Jr. and Janneke Zwigtman to Pieter Bril at Zuidzande.

Milwaukee   16 November 1853

Dear brothers and sisters,

I read in your letter that you all were in reasonable health which made us happy. We saw that you had another blessing of the Lord that you can see your wife recovered and that you can see your fruits (a baby, maybe a twin). I was not so lucky to see mine, but it is the Lord who did it and what the Lord does is well done. Now I have my beloved wife with me and I hope that we'll see again our fruit. Something else now, there are bees here too. They cost 5 dollars a hive. A lot of bees were in slices of trees and there are a lot of swarms in the woods. I paid 16 cents for a pound of honey. Nowadays Jacobus Hendrik van Ouwerkerk stays with us. He came walking. It is his plan to leave next week with the steamboat to go home. He grew a lot. He is 149 Dutch centimeters tall. He speaks English and German and spells and reads English too. Father and mother are reasonably well too. They have a passable way of living. No abundance, but a good life. It is my intention to go to the woods in December too. Father and I should learn together if we are healthy then. At the moment we are with Daniel Tellier, and Pieternella is here too as his wife. Abraham Bril, his wife and son are of a reasonable health too. He is working with the bricklayers and earns 7 sixpence a day. Hubregt and Sara Bril are well too. He works with the bricklayers too and Sara gathered flesh, but is not fat. Jannis Bril, his wife and children are in a reasonable health. Jacob Verdouw and Maria van Ouwerkerk and children are well. Daniel Tellier and son are in reasonable health. The little Jacob is growing. Magdalena gave birth to a young daughter, but the 7th day after it she declined. The physician said her milk was spread and there was a lot of blood in her milk. The baby died shortly after her mother. This is all I can tell you and we like it to be here. Brother, if you write, write us news. Also, I want to thank my brothers Abraham Zwigtman, Pieter Bril and Izaak Verhage for everything they did to help my wife, and if you are in trouble yourself I'll help you as much as I can. I hope you'll receive this letter in health. Don't forget to tell us where brother A. Zwigtman is living. Greetings from us who call themselves a brother and sister, niece and nephew. Greet all of your wives and people known to us, grandfather and grandmother and all the relatives.

Pieter van Ouwerkerk and Janneke Zwigtman

P.S. Dear friend Verhage write to me. If you can get used to sleeping with your wife, I can! Write to me if brother A. Zwigtman has a wife or a girlfriend yet. The dollar is a present for brother Abraham Zwigtman from his sister Janneke Zwigtman.

Pieter van Ouwerkerk and Janneke Zwigtman

♦♦♦♦♦♦

Pieter van Ouwerkerk to his stepson Pieter Bril at Zuidzande

Town of Holland   11 December 1853

Dear brother and sister,

I have to tell you that we are, thanks to the Lord's kindness, still fit and healthy. We received your letter of October 2 and we read in it that your wife gave birth to a daughter. I went to Milwaukee to visit all the brothers and sisters.   They all were well. Yesterday we shot a deer with 5 Americans. Aunt lives in Sheboygan. She bought a house there for five hundred dollars and here she has built a new one. We have two oxen and two heifers, two sheep, and 10 chickens. We farmed two years for the half of the harvest, but now we are farming for the second bushel of the three bushels. Two of them for us. From the cattle, we raise half of it because we cannot live on that half. If you start to farm you need a lot of things. A yoke oxen cost 70-80 dollars. A cart 50 dollars. A plough cost 4 to 10 dollars, and a windmill 15-20 dollars. A cow is 15-20 dollars to up to 30 dollars. A sheep is 2 ½ dollars. Now you can go farming, but not before you have all of this. You don't have to think lightly about it. If you don't have anything to start with then you have more to do than you like. Now we are still going. And if I am tired of working I can take a rest now. Here you can do what you want. The charges (taxes) are not as high as they are in Holland. For roads you have to work 4 days if you have 80 acres. These are all the charges we have, but in Holland you can work for the taxes. Now I have to tell you that Pieternella married your brother-in-law Daniel Tellier and his plan is to come to his land next spring. If the plan is not changed, then we are nearby to each other except Abraham. They are still in Milwaukee. If you cannot handle your business any longer or it goes downhill think this over. You can come to America. And if you and your wife are inclined for it, but as long as your business is going well you have to hang on because it is difficult here. Try it anyway if you like to come. We should like to see each other again. But I should not mislead you. It is to warn you before you lose everything, because then it is too late to come to America. You have to do what you like. I would regret it to mislead you, because that is not a small thing. Now I have to stop with my pen but not in my heart.

                                    I stay yours faithfully,
                                    Piet van Ouwerkerk and Sara van Bortel

Piet, greet Arij Masclee from us. He is the workman for Poessenier. We are doing well here. There is still a lot of land for sale if you like to come. My sister Pieternella married Daniel Tellier and I was a witness on November 23. J.H. van Ouwerkerk

◆◆◆◆◆◆

Family of Pieter van Ouwerkerk to Pieter Bril at Zuidzande

Town of Holland   16 May 1854

Pieter,

I read in your letter that you feel you would like to come to America and you ask me what we are thinking about it. We think first that you have to do what you like because we should regret it if you came here and you didn't like it. I have to tell you that we like it here. But at first everything looks strange, particularly to those who have no friends or girlfriend it could be difficult. However, we should like it when we can meet each other again in good health. There is still enough land to buy; woodland and clean land. You don't have to think that you don't have to work, just like in Holland, but the money we earn we can keep. Up to now I didn't have to pay charges (taxes) and if I am tired I rest. Piet, it is not to mislead you, oh no, but I write you the things I thought over. At first, if you see that your affairs are going down so you cannot make a living from it after some time, I should think that you have to come to America before it is too late. Because if your money is gone it won't come back. Not that I like to tell you to come or not, oh no; it is your own will. We can make a living here working. But if I could make a living in Holland and could keep it and had good prospects for my children, I should not leave my fatherland. Now people have to leave because of the poorness that prevails. In this country there is room enough for poor and rich. Pieter, if you come, bring your violin and your rifle too, because there are still wolves, bears and deer too. This is all I have to say. If you are willing to come over, write us soon. In that case we will write you another letter to tell you what you have to take with you. Greetings from us who call themselves your father, mother, sisters and brothers.

Pieter van Ouwerkerk, Janneke Zwigtman, Jacobus Hendrik van Ouwerkerk

On behalf of father I wrote this. Pieter van Ouwerkerk, Sara van Bortel. Greetings from all of us again.

◆◆◆◆◆◆

Pieter van Ouwerkerk Jr. (married to Janneke Zwigtman) to his half-brother Pieter Bril at Zuidzande

Town of Holland   13 November 1854

Dear brother and sister,

I cannot refrain to write you to let you know that we are in reasonable health at the moment. The whole family except Maria Verdouw. She is ill many times. She is tormented by worms. There is nothing in particular I can tell you except that we rent aunt's farm for 3 years for the sum of 40 dollars a year. But if she sells it we have to leave. In that case everything will be valued and then they have to take over. This summer she had a public sales day for her cattle and utensils. We have a milk cow and a two year old heifer who was with the bull and a yoke of two year old oxen. We also have two one year old heifers and two calves. We sowed 6 acres with winter wheat and 3 acres of rye. The rest of the land is in summer fruits. We have a yoke of work oxen together with Jan Bril. We have a cart, a plough, harrow and sled. But there is still a lot to pay for. Brother, be so kind to greet brother Abraham Zwigtman. Tell him we like to receive a letter from him and tell him we had a sweet little baby which was born too early. And that we are in reasonable health. Brother Pieter, we don't know what is wrong that you do not write a letter to us. We are waiting for a long time but it is in vain.

◆◆◆◆◆◆

Hubregt Risseeuw and his wife Sara Wilhelmina Bril to brothers and sisters

Milwaukee   25 January 1855

Dear brothers and sister.
I have to write you some words because we have been expecting a letter from you the whole summer. We counted on the fact that you could have given some letters for us to the emigrants for free. Now I let you know how we are. By the Lord's kindness we are fresh and healthy. Our little boy is by the Lord's kindness fresh and healthy till now. Last December 16, 1854 he was one year old. He can walk alone now. His name is Hubregt Pieter Risseeuw. Mother walked this winter to see all of us and stayed 5 weeks. She left on January 3rd, 1855. Brother-in-law Verdouw came with his cart to Milwaukee and mother went home with him. Mother told us that they all; father, mother, brothers and sisters, are well.

Front: Hubregt Risseeuw and Sara Willemina Bril
Back: Anna and Peter
Photo courtesy of Mary Risseeuw

Brother Pieter was ill last summer for 3 weeks, but now he is well again by the Lords kindness. Brother Tellier's wife gave birth to a son on October 16th 1854. The name of this child is Pieter Tellier. His wife's breast began to ulcerate and now it is 3 months later and not better yet. Brother-in-law Abraham Bril's wife gave birth to a son in the month of October 1854. The name of the child is Izak Bril. And young Abraham goes to school and is growing well. Little Jacob Tellier is growing well too. J. Verdouw has 2 children and J. Bril has 3 children. P. van Ouwerkerk has 1 child and D. Tellier has 2 children. A Bril has 2 children and now we have 1 child too. I have to greet you from mother and by the Lords kindness. We hope and wish the same to hear from you.

This winter it is two years ago that my wife and I walked to the woods and were there for four weeks. But now we are planning that, if the Lord may give us life and health, we go next summer to visit father, mother, brothers and sisters again. We won't walk. We'll hire a cart to go there. Now I let you know that Uncle Pieter Bril died on November 29, 1854. He was ill for only 6 days. Uncle Bril went to Jacob Bekkens to visit and there he became ill and died. Mother spoke to Uncle P. Bril before he died, but he already was too ill to speak with. And all the children of Uncle P. Bril are well by the Lord's kindness. Two children of J. Bril died on their trip at sea. Abraham van Peenen, who is married to Sara Willemina Bril, lost their child too on the sea trip. Pieter Bril's children are still alive; all four. Last summer a lot of Dutch people died. Most of them from cholera. Izak de Zwarte died from cholera, and Jannis Looisen, and Abraham Wijkman, and Jacob Maljie (LeMahieu?) died from consumption. And others which I cannot name at the moment, and several other Dutch people you don't know. Dear brother and sister, we heard that you have the intention to come to America, if the Lord'll save your life and give you the health to do, but we don't know if it is true. Because sometimes people are talking and you cannot trust it. You'll know it best yourself. It should not surprise us if we hear how many people have already left and how many would like to leave, if they could, for the United States. We can understand it, because since the time we left the poorness hasn't become better. It just became worse. Everything is so expensive for you and no income. But dear brother and sister, nevertheless I should not recommend it nor dissuade. I think that everyone who likes to come has to do his own will. And if he is not making it, he cannot reproach it with anyone. I would regret it if I would recommend it to someone and at the moment they are here and it is not going well, they maybe could say it is your fault I am here, you better had let me stay where I was. You have to make your own decisions. We are doing well. I can write that to you, but not for all people. The people who are too lazy to work will not do well here. The ones who like to work and can work will have a good life here and can buy his own piece of land and he cannot with you. And you almost cannot make a living there whether you like to work or not. Maybe you think I should like to dissuade you, oh no, not really. But in the beginning it is difficult, most in case of the language. Otherwise you can earn your money very simple here and it gets better all the time because there are a lot of Dutch people in America and one is helping another to get a job. Well brother and sister, if the Lord may save your life, and your wife's and children and may give you the health to come to America. And if you may come, I can recommend you to stay close to your belongings during the trip and don't leave without your belongings. This year a lot of emigrants were traveling as soon as they were in America and their belongings were to follow them. I cannot recommend that because if you at your place of destination, your belongings will come 5 or 6 weeks after you. So this is the best I can recommend to you. As soon as you are in America and start to travel, you have to take care of your goods and in that way it travels with you. That is the most easy. To all of you, brother, if you are coming during this year you only have to write when you leave from Holland as you come to us in Milwaukee. Write us as soon as you can because from the moment we know and can calculate when you will be here we can look for you every day. And write us the name of the captain and the name of the ship, because we read the newspaper, so we can see when you arrive in New York or in any other place. We can see it in the newspaper. Then we better can calculate whenever you will be in Milwaukee and where you will arrive. There is a Dutch inn and the innkeeper always takes a look if there are any emigrants and he will take you to your place. And if you come there as a Dutchman, if I am not there, ask where I live and you can stay here. By the Lords kindness we are able to wait for people. And now brother, I have another request for you. If you are coming, if you like or are able to, to bring 2 blankets of wool with you and a costume bodice for my wife. My wife says it is not important if it is not the best you can get, but your wife will know best what she needs. Here there are wool blankets too, but they are not as good as the Dutch. This question I ask is for if you are coming and if you are able to advance the money till you are here. Then you can get your money immediately. If you may decide to go to father, mother, and other brothers and sisters, that is all right with us too. Take it with you if you can, we will get it from there. Well brother, now I am going to write you something else. On March 9, 1855 it will be 2 years ago that I bought 2 acres of land for the sum of 300 dollars. It is good land. I sold one acre early. The reason why I sold that acre was it was too hard for me to work on it. I have to go to the city to work and I said to my wife we are better with one acre and to work in the city, than with two acres and stay at home a lot of time. Because it is not possible to do it all in the evening. I sold that acre for the sum of 156 dollars. I had that acre from March 9 till November 9, 1854 and I had six years time to pay it. I paid it off in one year and 8 months. This autumn I could have sold this acre for the sum of 300 dollars. The land, which is situated in the neighborhood of the city, is getting to be expensive. I think it has had a good profit in such a short time. But I did not have the mind to do it. It will be more expensive. We had, by the Lords kindness, a good year to work and earned a lot of money. And we had the luck, by the Lord kindness, to be in good health. Last winter I worked for 6 sixpences a day and after it for 1 dollar a day, and then for 9 sixpences a day. For the 9 sixpences a day I worked till November 28 and because the days became so short I worked for 1 dollar a day till December 14. Afterwards I worked for myself and now I chop wood for this winter for myself. We get this wood just for the work. Now I have 14 cartloads of wood at home and it is already dry wood. If you have to buy your wood, it is expensive. You pay 3 to 3 ½ dollar a cord nowadays. These are my wages of the year: in the month of January, 18 dollars and 25 cents; in the month of February, 14 dollars and 25 cents; in the month of March, 10 dollar and 12 cents; in the month of April, 1 dollar 89 cents; in the month of May, 14 dollar and 42 cents; in the month of June; 10 dollars and 34 cents. In that 4 months I worked a lot for myself. In the month of July, 22 dollars and 10 cents; in the month of August, 23 dollars and 29 cents; in the month of September, 24 dollars and 75 cents; in the month of October, 27 dollars; in the month of November, 25 dollars and 57 cents and in December, 11 dollars. In the whole year I earned about 205 dollars. In Dutch money I earned 512 guilders and a half. On March 28, 1854 I bought a cow for the sum of 27 dollars and a half including a churn. And the cow had a calf on May 12. After 7 months we got 32 dollars for it and we had free butter and milk all the time. The calf we sold for the sum of 3 dollars and 75 cents when it was 3 weeks old. The buttermilk we gave to our pigs and we made 2 nice pigs with it. I had a lot of Spanish wheat in my field to give to the pigs and chickens. We didn't have to buy that too because we have everything we need from the field and we can sell a lot too. The potatoes were not as good as last year but they are nice. I sold potatoes for 7 dollars. Now I go to work for the same boss in the beginning of March. He asked me to do that at the moment I stopped. We immediately calculated the work that was to be done and then he asked me if I would like to come back to work in the beginning of March or, if the weather would be nice, in February. And now it is the third year I will work for him. We worked a while last summer and my boss got his 5 dollars a day, but it was a hard job. The day's wages were pretty high in general this summer. The bricklayers' man got wages this summer of 14 sixpences to 2 dollars to 18 or 20 sixpences for a day's work. And the other workmen who were working in the city, their lowest day wage was one dollar a day and 9 sixpence. Now the price of the grains: wheat 1 dollar 30 cents to 1 dollar 40 cents to 1 dollar 50 cents; that is for a bushel. Well brother, I like to write you the price of the grains, but you can read it in the letter of my father. So brother I have a request to you, please give this letter to my father because I won't write an address on it and you can read it well. And the less they cost the better. However, those two letters won't cost a lot because they are written on light paper. I couldn't get lighter than this. Sometimes I think that if my father or my brothers could, they should pay their part. And brother, forgive me this bad handwriting, it is so difficult to write on this light paper. And please write as soon as possible. I stop writing because there is not much room left on this paper. Be greeted from us with regards from us, brother and sister, who call themselves Hubregt Risseeuw and Sara Wilhelmina Bril and Hubregt Pieter Risseeuw.

We hope and wish this letter will reach you in health.

◆◆◆◆◆◆

Jannis Izaak Bril and his wife Esther de Meijer to Pieter Johannis Bril at Zuidzande

Town of Holland Sheboygan County
31 September 1855

Esther B. de Meijer and
Johannes Izaak Bril
Photo courtesy of Mary Risseeuw

Today I like to write to you again some words about the time and the circumstances. Brother, I received that little letter from de Lijzer on August 20th. They came here fresh and healthy. I went out to get my book on September 9 and I did receive it. And I talked to that man too. Brother, I like to thank you so much for the book. Brother, a question from brother-in-law Hubregt Risseeuw. He asked if you didn't receive his letter from last winter. He wrote to you and his father. He didn't get an answer to it. I have to tell you that Hubregt Risseeuw Jr. died on April 4, just 17 months old. Hubregt was with us for a few days around

August 20 and he slept with us. Further, I have to tell you that our sister Pieternella passed away on April 20th and she was still in full possession of her facilities till the last gasp. And she said such a lot of things, people don't often hear that. Mother was with her all the time. Mother told me that she went so joyful to kingdom as if she went to the kermis and she shed no tears. She said she should like to stay here a little longer but her time had come so she had to go. She sent for all the brothers and sisters to say goodbye to them, and she said farewell to them in full possession of her facilities without one tear and passed away on the same moment. Daniel is keeping house with his youngest sister and he has such a lot of work that he don't know what to do first. We are, by the Lords kindness, fit and healthy. We had a good harvest and everything came in dry. Father, can make a profit to sell a load of wheat and he is leaving aunt's farm. He rented it for 3 years and now she withdraws her word. Now he is renting another farm for 60 dollars. 40 acres plough land for 3 years, or six if he gives satisfaction to their agreement. They are going to live an hour father from us now. The potatoes are very good. We had in 3 years no rotten potatoes. They taste good and cook totally into pieces. Brother, I am very lucky with my bees, from the 2 hives I had six swarms and together with the 2 old ones makes 8. Father had just one swarm and with the old one makes 2. My first swarm came on June 6, the last one on July 30. You can put them everywhere except one, the last one is to lean, but we have to feed them anyway. I am going to keep as many bees as I can so I have to do nothing else. My wife picked up two swarms this summer. I was not at home. Piet, I'll keep that pig till next year. It is just a nice one. I have another 3 to fatten. Something else Piet, mother was not pleased that you wrote so little and didn't sign the note. Piet, mother should like to see you so much

136

and your wife and children. Piet, my youngest son started to walk on his own. He is almost as tall as the eldest, and their hair is curling around their cap. We now stop having children. Something else Piet, Jan Orlebeke is here in our town and they are well. He has so much to do as he is able to do. Jan le Grand is in Milwaukee and he is doing well. Dina Tounaunis (Toussaint?) told Sara that as long as she is married she never derived so much pleasure from her husband as she had in the short time they were in America. Cousin Jan le Grand earns 10 sixpence a day. Cousins Jan and Pieter earn so much too. A. van Peenen works in a match factory. And brother A. Bril and Hubregt earn 9 sixpence a day with the bricklayers. But A. Bril always stays poor. He paid father 6 dollars now and Daniel two. Hubregt paid off his field already and he has a cow too and no debts. He could have sold his field for 500 dollar on credit, and if he can get the money he'll sell it. Then he'll buy a piece of land in the woods here and would like to be a farmer too. Piet, our so called Amsterdam is growing. There is a saw mill and now they build a corn mill. They are building a hotel too and there are already four stores and a school. It was a good place for van Ouwerkerk and for a tailor and barber, because they don't shave a person for less than 5 cents or 12 ½ cents of your money. Willem Tel (Tellier?) is still in Rochester. He drinks and stuffs himself, if they should believe him. His wife picked up the potato peelings from the street to eat last winter and he earned his dollar a day. Pieter Orlebeke was here and told me that he was in prison twice. He don't care. He is making good cheer and he is cheating whatever he can. Something else, I received a little letter from Jacob de Mejer on July 15th. It was posted at Rochester, but it was not written on who had taken it. It was written on June 1st and you wrote me that he had spoken with you about it and that you could not help him. And that he couldn't blame you that you didn't know him and that you have your own costs. I should like to help him but I don't have the money. I would have had the money, but Abraham Eernisse took the last 30 dollars; otherwise I would have sent it. And now I don't know where to get some. I hope father de Meijer'll keep his promise. I did what I could and it didn't help. Father de Meijer said when we left, if Ko would come he should take up the money to come to America. He has not to worry about his money. If you could come here healthy, you can send your money back in a year with the interest. Here you have to pay 12 per cent interest and I cannot get it otherwise. Now I like to see what you are doing father, you don't have to be embarrassed for your son and if you don't trust him what do I have to think of it, who has nothing to do with it. If I had it, I should have sent it a long time ago. My land and beasts are worth a thousand dollars now, but I should not like to sell it for that purpose. So father, if Ko was just healthy and could pay you soon, do what you like to do. I cannot help him. Next year I have to pay off my land and it is one hundred dollars. And that is all the debt I have. So father, help your son before he falls into poorness. You can earn enough money here. Father and mother, I have to tell you that the harvest is gathered again. The potatoes taste very good. We have just two rotten potatoes. As long as I am a farmer we haven't seen one rotten potato. Next year we'll have cows without accidents. We have 3 pigs to fatten again and again 3 for next year. I have 7 cows without the work oxen which I own together with father. Father lost 2 one year old heifers to an illness. This summer a lot of cattle died. The Americans call it "Bliekleek." Everything now has a good price: the barley is 7 ½ guilders, the oats 9 sixpence, the peas 7 ½ guilders, the white beans 7 ½ guilders, the potatoes 9 sixpence, the eggs 6 to 10 penny a dozen. Pork and flesh were sold last summer for a sixpence a pound, the butter 7 to 10 penny a pound. I have sold 4 young cocks for 9 penny a piece. Honey 6 to 8 penny a pound. Something else, while I was writing, a man came by and told me by about this opportunity for Ko de Meijer and he promised me that if father cannot or doesn't want to help, Ko has to write back soon.   Then he would give me the money to send it to him. So I expect an answer back soon. Write me how much he needs to come here. Pieter D. Tellier is going to live in the woods too. He sold everything he had in Milwaukee. He got 280 dollars for his land and 50 dollars for his little house. He sold his house to Frits Outkamp. I don't know to whom he sold his land. Now he is here and he came with a load of goods. I'll go with him to Milwaukee to get the rest. He has a cart now and oxen. He is going to farm now. He has not a wife. We advised against it, but he does what he likes. Piet, father threshed 130 bushel of wheat, 36 bushel of rye, and 50 of oats. 2 ½ bushel is a hectoliter. Verdouw has 113 bushel of wheat and 40 of oats. I have 45 bushel of wheat and 5 bushel of rye. I have a lot but I need everything for my own use. We threshed everything with a machine with 2 horses. It cost 5 dollars a day and they thresh to 150 bushel a day. And clean the corn and bring it to the garret, and put the straw on a lump with 6 men. Further we all are healthy here and in Milwaukee. We hope to hear from you the same and hope that you'll receive this letter in blessing and health. I stop with my pen but not with my heart, because there is no more place to write.

Be greeted, J.I. Bril, E. de Meijer, Jacobus Hendrik van Ouwerkerk, Sara van Bortel

Piet, this potato seed is of the blue "Pienoogen" or white potatoes with blue "eyes". Father has 300 bushels of it.

To Pieter Johannis Bril, Zuidzande
Kingdom of Holland, Province Zeeland

Cedargrove Wisconsin 1 November 1855

With the Cunard line via Liverpool
Paid 5 cents. Postmark EP November 19, 1855
Postmark New York November 6

◆◆◆◆◆◆

Sheboygan County

[Derk Jan Haartman (bap. 25 November 1787), his wife Hendrika te Bokkel (bap. 21 May 1791), and their 6 children left Aalten, Gelderland, Netherlands on 4 August 1846. After arriving in Milwaukee, Derk purchased 40 acres of land. While living there, Hendrika, three sons and a daughter died. Derk, and his sons Derk Jan and Evert became some of the earliest settlers of Sheboygan County and on 1 July 1848 purchased 640 acres of land. This letter is presumed to have been written about 1848.]

Marriage announcement in De Nieuwsbode
of Derk and Hendrika's son, Derk Jan

Gibbsville, Wisconsin to the
Netherlands
D.J. Haartman to relatives

We eat meat until we are satisfied, which you, on the whole, cannot do. Too much must be bought from all kinds of business which we do not have here, as we can also make more. In the short time we have been in America we have made more than in all of the time we were there. All the taxes levied there! We have to pay only once per year. It is collected at our home and I am asked to pay less on all of my land than on the small parcel of ground at Haartman (a farm), so you realize we save more money than where you are at Haartman.

By God's grace we have made such progress that we have 300 gulden outstanding in interest each year, which we can also loan out at interest, if the Lord spares us from disasters, to which we are exposed at all times. I have experienced the proof of this in '46 in the loss of my wife and four children, who were taken from me after long illness, from which we recovered and to which we might also have succumbed, but the Lord spared us. For which we cannot thank him enough with our stammering tongue.

You will probably say that because of loaning out money this must be a country in which to make progress, and that is true, but you must realize that there is much work to be done since there are plank roads, railroads are being built, canal ways, saw mills, and grain mills, which are very costly matters since daily wages are high here. Carpenters earn 10 to 12 shillings per day, masons also, but day laborers earn one dollar, hired help ten dollars a month, maids 10 to 12 shillings a week. And you may ask, the medical doctor or pharmacist, do you have them? Yes, but not very many come here, and mostly Germans, and not as many come as formerly, for according to reports, in the month of February 8,175 emigrants arrived in New York, among them 500 Netherlanders.

You will probably say, you write about everything, but what is the situation regarding religion. There is freedom here also, and in other areas. One is not forced here to believe what the church believes.

We will close here for this time although I could write about much more. If we could converse with one another, we could say much more. Now in anticipation of your answer, about circumstances, what is going on in the family circle, as well as other matters, with warm greetings we are your dear friends,

> Brother-in-law and cousin
> D.J. Haartman
> and sons, D. J. Haartman

My address is:
D.J. Haartman
State of Wisconsin
Sheboygan County PO
Gibbsville Town 14, sec. 32

◆◆◆◆◆◆

[Heine Jakobs Baar was born 12 August 1819 in Uithuizemeeden, Groningen to Jakob and Fenje (Kooi) Baar. On 17 October 1846 he married in Uithuizemeeden, Trijntje Alberts Scholtens, the daughter of Albert and Grietje (Rijpma) Scholtens. She was born in Uithuizemeeden on 18 January 1826. They emigrated from London on 24 September 1853. This letter is from the Dutch Immigrant Letters Collection, Archives, Calvin College, Grand Rapids, MI, Box 4, Folder 1.]

Gibbsville, Wisconsin   16 December 1853

O dear Parents, Brothers, Sisters, and family and other friends!

O dear parents, we had a very difficult trip for body and soul. We left London on Saturday the 24th of September and because of violent western winds we were 14 days in the Channel before we sailed south of England. After 15 days that we saw the last land and we sailed on the great sea with a good wind. But it was of short duration. After being on course for 2 days we had a violent wind from the west so that on the 15th or 16th day our dear girl became sick and the sickness increased violently. It was on Monday morning at 1 o'clock on

140

October 24 that the Lord took our dear one and she was buried at sea. Oh, parents and friends who have lost children know how heavy it can be for a person. Three days later both of our boys became ill. The doctor gave them medicine and by this means Albertje was feeling better in three days. He was otherwise more sick than Jacob. But Jacob then grew worse but that passed.

On Monday the 7th of November we received a pilot on board and on Tuesday November 8 in the morning we saw both light and land. And then the steamboat brought us inside so that we came before noon to Staten Island which is a good half hour from New York. Then we received the doctor on board to see if there were any sick people on board and there were four sick ones. We thought that Jacob was as well as before, but orders were given that the sick had to go to the hospital. And so my dear wife had to go to the hospital with Jacob. They had to leave us from the ship, parents and friends. As we remained on board to the next day and then we were all brought by steamboat to shore. The ladies and children together, but our Albert was always with me. It was Thursday when I with my son was by her. But then we still couldn't learn whether there was a turn for the better. I must let you know that when my dear wife was placed under such a situation she was very patient and good natured. I visited her again on Friday the 13th of November and then I journeyed to New York. But my wife and son had to remain in the hospital. The doctor said that he was much too weak to travel. Then we came to New York, all this was paid for by the Captain.

On Saturday the other Hollanders departed from New York. But the doctor said that we should remain because in his opinion Jacob was some better. The following Wednesday I went to get them but they refused it because he was so weak. The following Friday, I went back to her again and after many requests to the doctor we received permission to travel because Jacob was somewhat better but he was still very weak. His mother never left the side of his bed.

I took them out of the hospital. And on Monday the 14th our little son Albert became somewhat ill. Then on the 19th we left New York at three o'clock by steamboat to Albany and then by train we came to Dunkirk. We arrived on Monday around 5 or 6 o'clock and both of our children could not stand up. At 3 o'clock Monday afternoon we journeyed to Detroit. Wednesday at 10 o'clock we went by train to Chicago and arrived there Thursday evening. We stayed there and on Saturday at 8 o'clock in the morning we got some medicine again from the doctor for Albert. Jacob got much better but Albert did not improve. On Saturday evening we came to Siebajt (Sheboygan) at about 8 o'clock and there we stayed until Monday morning. And then we journeyed 10 miles or three hours and 20 minutes to L.T.B. and he received us as one of his best friends. And here was an opportunity to rent a house, and we rented one not very expensive but particularly because Albert's illness became worse. And we could not travel any further. And what's more, on Thursday the 8th of December my wife gave birth to a son. So we stayed close to R.T.B. for eleven days.

She had a very easy delivery and she finds herself in good health. The first blow on the water was very big, but the 2nd was not made better, that the God of heaven and earth on the 16th of December once again deprived us of some of our children that He snatched away our

141

son Albert through death. So that with great sorrow we saw him laid in the grave. Jacob is still weak but as far as we can see him getting better and stronger from day to day. He walks around the house and we took him outside. Oh parents and friends we have often said, we are experiencing that we were departing in the anger of the Lord, oh that the Lord gives, that out of the death of our children, our dear little sprouts, that a strong lesson might be learned. He gives, that we might in retrospect experience the testimony of David, before we were oppressed and we wandered away from God and we must remember God's commandments.

Parents and friends, we often think about the healthy days we had with our children in Holland. Oh may the Lord give that we as worms in the Earth might humble ourselves before Him. That we with Psalm 34 bear witness, God is close to the brokenhearted, and what more follows, and that the Lord gives that we may realize this and we may love Him.

We write to you of the death of our dear children and wish that our parents might mourn over them. We hope that the Lord may withdraw his rod. But we must be thankful that He has saved our own lives and so far we have not had one unhealthy hour. Oh that all of us may continually bend our knees before the High Holy God, and that He may guard our paths. My paper is too small to add more writing. America is not what people report in Europe. However, many things do look good to us. We sorrow because of the calamities which we experienced, but we do not regret that we came to America. We hope to buy wooded land since that is plentiful. ??? are too young to give us land. Now we are obligated to buy land. Others tell us that it is cheap. When it is the Lord's will and we are living, I will write about this matter again. We did not write sooner because of the difficult circumstances under which we lived and we did not dare either.

Oh parents, friends and acquaintances, greet P.J. Luidens. The letter to Hoepke I have delivered. It was close to us. P. Jonker's letter I could not deliver. Please pass greetings of J. Kruizenga to all his friends and acquaintances, they are all well. Reinje is here, our midwife. There are good friends here. We also had a doctor look after my wife. She had an easy delivery.

Every other Sunday the Reverend Zonne preaches for us. We do not live far away from Reverend van der Schuur. Our little son who was born recently I wish to name again Albert. Johannes Boelkins is still in Milwaukee. They lost their baggage. They rented horses and a wagon to bring the family, but their little one died and Hendriktje became ill and they were unable to come. So far they had been very healthy. The day before we arrived a ship came with a thousand souls. The cholera was on that ship. They came from Liverpool; and 170 people died. People report that it is better to travel from Holland. I will write more in 14 days.Please greet P.J. Hamming and his wife and R. Vos and J. Goedhuis. Please tell J. van Dam that I cannot go to Pieter Willems Diekema. Greet all the relatives and write to us if you can. Our address is: H.J. Baar Wisconsin Sheboygan County, Town Gibbsville

I sign,
Heine J. Baar

♦♦♦♦♦♦

Grades Heinen
Photo courtesy of the
Sheboygan County Historical
Research Center

[Grades Heinen was born 19 October 1827 in Aalten, Gelderland, the son of Jan and Harmina (te Brinke) Heinen. He died 24 October 1908 in Sheboygan County, WI. On July 21 1854 he married Willemina Wandrina Wisselink, the daughter of Garrit Jan and Johanna (Nyeboer) Wisselink. She was born 2 February 1826 in Aalten, Gelderland and died 12 March 1879 in Sheboygan County, WI. Shortly after their marriage, on 21 August 1854 they sailed from Rotterdam on the ship *Leila*. Grades' brother Abraham, his wife Johanna W. Scholten, and their three children accompanied them. Grades served his new country in the 27th Infantry during the Civil War.]

Sheboygan Falls, Wisconsin to Aalten, Gelderland   31 October 1854

Dear father and brothers and sisters,

I can let you know that we are fine thanks to the Lord and we hope you feel the same. If it were different, we would feel sorry. Now I will let you know about our trip. We sailed from Rotterdam on the 21st to Helfensluis (Hellevoetsluis), and on August 22 we sailed from Helfensluis, but the sea was a bit choppy so that soon we had all become seasick. The seasickness was not bad and after two days most of the people had recovered, and then we continued our trip. We were sailing against the wind but we found the ocean not bad at all. We were not in danger. We were with 224 passengers on board, but three died. The oldest daughter of Garsoord (Anna Geertruid Gantvoort) and two children. The ship was called *Leila*. It was a three-master. It went quite fast and since the weather was quite steady we had almost no storms, except for two or three hours, and that is all the storm we had.

On September 23 we could see land, and then we were happy and merry at 5 o'clock in the evening we arrived at New York. That is a big city where we stayed only one day, and then we were on a steamboat for two hours, and then in railroad coaches, and then to Dunkirk, and then by steamboat to Toledo, and by train to Sikago (Chicago), by steamboat to Milwakije (Milwaukee), by steamboat to Sigoigan (Sheboygan), and then we continued for two more hours. There we stayed in a place that we liked very much. There were three empty houses, so there was no shortage. We live close together.

Brother-in-law Berend Hendrik and I go to work together and then we work just as you do and I earn 25 nickels a day with board, and we do not have to work harder than you do. We can earn as much in one day as you do in a week, and the groceries here are cheaper. Your rye bread is not used here. People eat wheat bread, meat and bacon and it is cheap here. Everything else is equally the same. Potatoes are abundant here. I have not seen them like that in ten years.

We have experienced no hardship. We would not prefer to be back in Holland. We never had it better in Holland that we have been in North America. But if a person can speak the English language than it is even better, but there are not many Dutch people. Gerrit Houwers lives nearby and Gesink from Varsseveld. Brother Abraham is feeling very well. He lives four hours away from us. I visited him for a few days for the fun of it. He was at Hendrik Kolste's with his wife and children. He still had no home. You should write us a letter first and then he will write. He wanted to make wooden shoes. They are expensive over here; there are many Dutch people, but others don't use them. The big wooden ones cost eight nickels and the small ones six and wood does not cost anything. There is plenty in the woods. They cut it here three feet about the ground. They don't know another way over here.

Dear father, brothers and sisters, write to me and tell me how it went with the buckwheat and potatoes. Here everything is fully grown. Have this read by Bullens, father and mother and brothers and sisters, that we like it here and we still have not wished we were back in Holland. And compliments Gerdhinderik Fukking (Gerrit Hendrik Fukking). I have not yet given the letter to Harmejan (Harmen Jan). He is not in Milwaukee anymore but he is in cibargen kontrein (Sheboygan County), three hours away from us, but I will send it to him. I do not know what else to write. My regards to Mr. te Bokkel and to his wife and children if they are still healthy. Here I stop with my pen but not with my heart. My hearty greetings and those of my wife. My regards to D.W. Heinen and G. Kappers.

My address is:
Gradus Heinen, Sheboygan Falls, Wisconsin, North America. Write to me when you have received the letter and what it costs.

◆◆◆◆◆◆

To Holland   6 December 1856

Dear father, brothers and sisters,

I cannot stay away from writing you a few words to let you know that we still in good health and we hope the same for you. We received the letters which you sent on May 4 that told us you are feeling well and hoped we would receive the letter in good health. We received it on the 27th of November and we don't know why it took so long for the letter to arrive. The letters cost 9 stuivers. Send regards to B. Draaijers and tell him we handed his letters over. We are letting you know that the Lord blessed us with a daughter on September the 2nd. Her name is Johanna Hermina. Regards to Bullens, his father, mother, brothers and sisters. We received a letter from them in which they told us that father and Jan Henderik had been ill and that they recovered, thanks to the Lord. That was very nice for us to hear and we read that the family expanded. In the letter you wrote to us that the widow Gussinkloo died. Write to us where the children went. Regards from brother Abraham and wife and children. They are all well. You were curious to know about his youngest son. They call him Jan Hendrik. H.J. Scholten is also in this area and they are still in good health. He is doing fine here. The spring rain was normal and we had a very dry autumn. Not much rain has fallen to now and we have about one foot of snow and it is cold. The crops were quite good here. We have one hundred and fifty bushels of winter wheat. We did not thresh the buckwheat and oats. We let someone do it with a machine and two horses. That cost me seven dollars. For that price I cannot thresh it with a vlegel (a stick like a broomstick with a hole at the end with rope attached and a cudgel to swing by hand). The wheat is not as expensive as last year. It now costs one dollar a bushel, so that is still a good price. Bacon is three to four stuivers a pond (half a kilogram) and butter two shillings a pond, so everything is equal. We have six horned cattle. I have sold the oxen with the yoke for 110 dollars and I bought 4 year old oxen with a yoke for 90 dollars. We have four pigs. We have a good farm here. We leased it from a farmer. If we had not come we wouldn't have had this in Holland. I bought a three year old heifer from a neighbor. He wanted fifteen dollars, but I got it for working thirteen days. So I still earned nine shillings and board. The Americans are good people. We cannot stop thanking the Lord for sending us to North America because we have a good life here.

Write to me as soon as possible and give our regards to all friends and neighbors. Here I stop with my pen but not with my heart. Greetings to all of you from me and my wife, W.W. Wisselink, and regards to B.H. Wisselink and wife and children if they are in good health.

My address:
Mr. Grades Heinen Sheboijgen Countij Wiskonsen unitue states of Amerika Gibbcsville

◆◆◆◆◆◆

To Holland   27 January 1856

Dear father, brothers and sisters,

We cannot forget to let you know that we are still in good health, thanks to the Lord, and we
hope you are the same. We have the letter which you sent to brother Abram. We received it
in good health and it told that you were still in good health. Now I will let you know how we
are doing. We have leased 80 acres for seven years, including a house. We have cut the
trees on 20 acres. We moved there on April 22. It was heavy work, but we don't need much
money to pay for it. I have to pay a tax this year of five and a half dollars, plus working three
days on the road. This is about all we have to pay each year. One year it will be a little bit
more, another year a bit less. The crop was good. We have one acre with summer wheat, so
that was not much, but we got ten bushels out of it. From half an acre of buckwheat we got
twelve bushels and we have half an acre of potatoes. They were good, because we got 80
bushels out of it. From an acre of Turkish grain we got 40 bushels. You can use it for people
and for animals alike. We fed an old pig and a sow with that grain. In the spring we bought
a bag full of grain that was 10 years old and on Scintjapik (St. Jacob's Day, July 25) we
bought a cow and a calf. Because the calf was four days old we paid 30 dollars, so we have
almost enough. We also had an acre with grain which was also good, so we have enough
food for the year for us and the animals. In summertime there is plenty of food for the
animals in the bushes. In the summer, half of the time I can work with the oxen without
giving them food. In the beginning of September I seeded seven acres with winter wheat.
Here, this is the best time to seed wheat. We pray to God the Lord that He will bless it and
much might grow on it. I used land which was not ploughed. I just threw seed on it. It is
possible here to seed land twice without ploughing. You still get a good crop. I have a
harrow with ten iron picks and the wood is like you have. The plough is much bigger, and
with a good yoke of oxen it is possible to work an acre of land a day, so we get good, loose
topsoil. You won't believe how that works. We can harrow so the roots are at the top to
remove and a crop will grow as good as on already used land. After five years we will
remove the stumps, but not the big oak stumps. They stay longer. You must not think that
we have as much work on the farm as we had in Holland. We don't have to take care of the
manure or the furnace. Labor is expensive here. When the days are short I will still be able
to earn four shillings plus board, and in May, six shillings during the hay season. I have
hayed seven days at an American farm. I hayed and cut grass and he paid me one dollar per
day plus board. The food was as good as what the best citizens of Aalten would have. We
can speak the English language good already. We also understand it quite well. It is a
difficult language to learn, but it is not as difficult as people in Holland think. I live full time
among the American people and they are very good people. We live about half an hour from
brother Abram and that is still fifteen minutes from the church. That church has a
Hollandschen teacher. His name is van der Schuur and he preaches in Dutch. He is a real
worshipper of Christ and we like that very much.

And now, dear father, brothers and sisters, I read in your letter that the crops are as expensive
as here. The winter wheat costs twelve shillings per bushel, rye a daalder (one and half
Dutch guilder), a bushel of potatoes three and a half shillings, and butter ten to twelve stuiver

146

per pound. Everything is equal here. Everything is expensive, but the wages are high too, so it is much better here than in Holland. We had it good in Holland, but here it is much better. Maybe you think it is not good over there for a farmer because the wages are so high, but at the wheat farms here, there is not as much work because we have nothing to do with manure. The work does faster here than in Holland. A person who can plant real well can plant three acres in one day and over here they thresh with a machine pulled by two horses most of the time so they can thresh one hundred to two hundred bushel per day. So it goes with all the work over here. We like it but the winters over here are long and cold and last year we had so much snow. This year we don't have so much snow, but it is cold. 7th, 8th and 9th of January it was so cold here. It was never so cold in Holland. People here say in the last ten years it was never so cold. But, in summertime it is much warmer than by you. My regards to Bullens; to father and mother and brothers and sisters. We learned from the letter which Berend Hendrik received that father and Hendrik had been sick but that they have recovered thanks to the Lord's blessing. We are happy about that and that mother is still in good health. We heard that Derk Willem got married to Johanna Wamelink and we wish that you will have fun together and hope that God the Lord gives you his blessing. It gives us lots of pleasure when we heard that you all are still doing well. We have been in good health because of the Lord's blessing and we have not experienced sorrow in America. Berend Lubbers visited us one day with his horse and buggy. Regards to Nijenhuis, Bullens, Straks and Pakkebier from Berend Lubbers. He is still in good health and he looks very well. He is living in penselfenij (Pennsylvania) which is 60 hours away from us. Dear father, brothers and sisters, regards from brother Abram and his wife. They had a baby boy January 22 (Jan Hendrik). Thanks to the Lords blessing she recovered real well.

Now, father, brothers and sisters, I expect a letter real soon. Write to me how much this letter cost and how much Abraham's letter cost. I paid ten and a half nickels for this letter and Abraham's letter cost two and a half nickels. If the costs are the same for you we would like to receive a letter from Bullens because we would like to know how they are. Regards to all of you and to friends and neighbors and to ten Bokkel. I don't have any more news to write. Here I stop with my pen but not with my heart. Greetings from me and my wife, W.W. Wisselink. Goodbye to you all.

My address is:
Grades Heinen Shebouigen falls Weskonsen noord amerika postafen gipsville

♦♦♦♦♦♦

[Johanna Aleida Heinen was born 1 August 1842 in Aalten, Gelderland the daughter of Willem Heinen and Hendrika Heebink. Willem was a brother of Grades and Abraham Heinen.]

Aalten, Gelderland   2 May 1865
Johanna Aleida Heinen to H.J. Grotenhuis

Dear uncle and aunt

I have received with pleasure the compliments from you. With God's grace you are still healthy. I was very happy that I heard from you. I am still feeling fine and my father and mother and the other children are also. I live in Aalten at Adolf Freriks and my parents live close by us in the barn of the house of A. Freriks. Hendrika lives at Jannes Blekkink on the market and then there are still five children at home; three boys and two girls and the youngest is two years old, and then there is

Marktplein – Aalten.

The house at the rear of the photo is the house of Adolf Freriks where Johanna worked. It is now the Freriks House Museum. Photo courtesy of Evert Smilda

Hendrik. Father gets lots of help from him. He does tailor work with Father every day and he does it real well. My father also had no bad luck. The great God blessed him with good health and those whose trust is in God is not built on sand. Mother is even stronger than before.

Dear uncle and aunt, I still think of you all the time and I thought you were going to forget me because I am now all by myself here. But I have to console myself and have to think God is a father for orphans. He will take care of me. I did not have the privilege to know my own mother, but this mother is so good to us, just like our own mother. I now can look after myself. This year Hendrika and I were confirmed by the Reverend Pape. I cannot write more than that Uncle Christiaan Heebink passed away last year. Freriks' second wife is already gone for five years and Elizabeth takes care of the house, so the children of the last wife are well taken care of. So, I am from a real small household. I pass your house all the time and also Uncle Heebink's house and I look with special interest at it now. You must also send special compliments to Uncle and Aunt Heebink and his children. I would like to see all of you sometime, but we cannot think about. But, we hope to see each other in heaven. Now I must end with the pen but not with the heart. Write to me when you have a chance, or let the whole family write together. Further greetings from all of us.

Goodbye. Your niece,
Johanna Aleida Heinen

◆◆◆◆◆◆

Aalten, Netherlands   18 July 1868
Johanna Aleida Heinen to H.J. te Grotenhuis

Dear uncle and aunt,

We received your letter in good health from which we noticed that all of you are still in good health and I was glad to hear that. I was looking forward very much to hearing from you people, but it is a greater pleasure for me to come to you. When I hear how it is at your place then one cannot stay here because things have not improved after you left. When I look at what you wrote I think often I should be with you people because when I read how many acres of land you bought over there, and Uncle Abram Heinen and Uncle Grades Heinen, they would never have been here what became of you there. You can almost not get a room rented and land here is so expensive to lease. You can get 8-9 guilders a "schepelzaat" and then still you can almost not get it and the earnings are poor. Aunt, I am still living at Adolf Freriks' till May and then I plan to get married and then to come to you. I have a boyfriend who is a good man who conducts himself well. His name is Jan Willem Sonderlo. We don't see a way here to start and many tell us I would rather go to America to your aunt. I almost went with Lammers, but we could not get ready that fast. I am not looking forward to the trip because it costs so much, but we have to trust the Lord and because of God's mercy we shall come. We expect that you will help us to settle, but aunt write to me if I have to bring linen cloth or what you think we have to bring. My father and mother don't like it very much, but I cannot see that because they cannot help me because they still have bad luck. Much happened within two years because two of their children died. They were sick for a long time and Heintjen was 12 years old and Mientjen was 7 years when they died and Hendrik is blind in one eye, but he can still see very well. Hendrika lives at the Mayor's in Bredevoort and she is also doing well there. We still are with five children. Now, cousins, I wished I could see your likenesses, but I cannot remember them very well, only that I came to you on Sunday to play with Tonija. I can remember noting from that period on I have also worked, but now I am not in the mood anymore. How is Gerrit doing there? I read nothing in the letter how he is doing. I have given your regards which you gave me, and I tried hard to give your regards at Lochem. I am curious if you received her letter but you have thought that I waited long to write but we did not know what to do but now we have decided if the Lord keeps us healthy to start the trip in May. I read in your letter that Uncle and Aunt Heebink and children are still in good health and that Gerhart got married. I have asked Lammers once more and he said you are doing real well there and that Gerhart got himself a Dutch wife. I did not understand why she did not write a little letter to you. Why that is I don't know, but write me back real soon. I expect a letter from Uncle Heebink too. When I pass your place it looks so strange to me because when you were here I was still a child. I think often about all of you. Now I have to end this letter. Greetings from me to Uncle Abraham and Uncle Grades Heinen and to Uncle Heebink and aunt and children. Now Aunt, my father cannot tell you about me because he does not know what is the best for us, so we have to come to you. Greetings from father and mother and Hendrika. Now I have to finish. I stop with the pen but not with my heart. I call myself your loving niece,

                                                        Johanna Aleida Heinen

Don't look how I wrote this letter. I was afraid the letter would not arrive. I sent one to Uncle Abram to see what he thinks of it, but write to me what you think of it. I ask you kindly to write a letter back. Aunt, if the Lord agrees that I come to you I shall tell you much about Aalten. I finish now because I wrote everything that I was thinking.

◆◆◆◆◆◆

[Christiaan Jan Snoeyenbos was born 10 October 1828 Aalten, Gelderland and died 28 April 1911 in Baldwin, St. Croix Cty, WI. His first marriage in 1847 was to Janna Willemina Wiggers who was born 26 August 1830 in Winterswijk, Gelderland and died 5 December 1864 in Town of Holland, Sheboygan County. They had seven children. On 10 June 1865 he married Aleida Brethouwer who was born 8 September 1843 in Aalten, Gelderland and died 30 September 1914 in Baldwin, WI. They had 10 children. Christiaan, Aleida and some of their children followed the migration of the late 1870s to St. Croix County. These letters are from the Dutch Immigrant Letters Collection, Archives, Grand Rapids, MI, Box 63, Folder 15.]

Christian Snoeyenbos, Aleida Brethouwer and children
Photo courtesy of Mary Risseeuw

Holland, Wisconsin   24 June 1859
C. Snoeyenbosch to cousin

Dear Cousin,

I take up the pen to do what you requested. But first of all we inform you that we received your letter of May 10 on June 14 in good health, and learned from it that all of you were enjoying a reasonable state of health which pleased us and hope you may receive this letter in good health. That is our hearty wish.

Dear friends, you wrote in your letter that you understood our letter very well. We are happy about that, especially the writer. You asked how anyone can get started here. A person who does not bring money with him, dear friends, there is no possibility of acquiring one's own land. That which we bought 12 years ago for 3 gulden an acre now costs 57 gulden, and renting farmers here do not make a good profit. I would advise such people to go to a new settlement where land is available for four shilling per acre. Such places can be located in the state of Minnesota and in Iowa, I think, but that is not the place to make money because there it is a case of being money poor. There a person will learn things he had never dreamed possible, but if he works hard he will be an independent farmer in 2 or 3 years.

My friends, I do not think it is necessary to write more about how things are done here. You can get books aplenty which describe this is detail and accurately, so if there should be someone who wishes to have more information about this, let me know.

You asked in your letter about Esselinkpas. He is in Milwaukee, in the state of Wisconsin. His wife and son have died. His youngest daughter is married to C. Schreurs. His oldest daughter is still not married. He himself is still fond of a glass of gin.

Further, G. Wesselink and his family live about 2 hours from here. They are all well and also Miena Mentink, married to A. Greupink, G.J. Mentink and J. Mentink, the children of J.A. Mentink. They are all well. They live in our neighborhood, as well as many others from Winterswijk. There are no sick folk or ailing ones among all of those you know, as far as I know. There are very few sick people. This is a very healthful part of America. But it is a very lean year as I wrote in my former letter. We also had a dry spring. Everything except rye looked bad. On June 5 we had a heavy frost which did a great deal of damage throughout all of North America. It is very dry now and we have mostly north or west winds.

We will close for this time. We wish you the blessings of the God for your soul and body, for time and eternity. May he give you and us rest in Him. For, ah, his dealings are always majestic and glorious.

Receive greetings from all of us,

                                        C. Snoeyenbosch and wife and children
                                        G.H. Wiggers and wife

◆◆◆◆◆◆

C. Snoeyenbosch to cousin

Herewith, dear cousin, I direct my pen to you. You who wishes to make a trip soon. You asked what we think of that. We think it would not be a bad idea for you. When you have a healthy body you can soon earn enough to be able to buy a piece of land, because you can earn three times as much here as you can in your country. Wages are low at present, but, in comparison with yours, they are better. Our hired man earns a hundred fifteen gulden in six months. It is true you cannot earn that much during the first year because you are not acquainted with the work, but there are some who earn more. There is not much work in the winter. Workers are hired here for six months as a rule. But then you can make wooden shoes. They cost from 6 to 9 stuiver (five cent piece). They are made of linden wood which is easily worked and costs little if any money. It is true, if there were not so many wooden shoe makers it would be better, but we discussed it with our brother-in-law who has a store where he sells many wooden shoes and he would take yours if you make good ones. For board and a room to make wooden shoes you would pay about 4 gulden a week. But be sure you take wooden shoe tools with you because they cannot be purchased here.

We would like to have you bring us a piece for a woman's skirt of the best quality, and a small piece of goods for every day trousers which you consider to be strong and the best. The length makes no difference even if it is a complete piece, if you can, but do not go to any trouble. If you feel you need your money, do not bring any of all of this, except a half dozen pipes with a small mouthpiece with an eight sided copper tobacco container of the best copper which will last me for life. It must not be more than 2 and ½ inches wide and 4 inches long, and as deep as the cooper smith feels is proper.

Further, as you plan your trip you should know that the months of July, August and September are the best when the weather and wind are the steadiest. Then you must plan your trip as follows: from Rotterdam to New York, and when you arrive there the first person you meet will want to help you better than anyone else, but do not pay any attention because the best talker will be the one who will deceive you the most. Go to the immigration house and there make arrangements for the train to Chicago. From Chicago go to Sheboygan by steamer. When you arrive in Sheboygan ask directions to the Tis Wils boarding house. Ask that innkeeper to direct you to the merchant Sprangers. He is a Hollander and he will tell you what way to take in the city to find us.

I will close here. The Lord be with you and may He protect and take care of you wherever you may be. Receive hearty greetings from all of us.

C. Snoeyenbosch

◆◆◆◆◆◆

152

[Gerrit Jan Droppers was born 11 March 1829 in Winterswijk, Gelderland the son of Garrit and Janna Gertruide (Vardink) Droppers. He died 2 February 1892 in the Town of Holland, Sheboygan County, WI. On 24 July 1857 in Sheboygan County he married Wesselina Gezina Ramaker. She was born 21 March 1838 in Dinxperlo, Gelderland the daughter of Lambertus and Hermina (Klos) Ramaker. She died in the Town of Holland, Sheboygan County, WI on 18 December 1892. These letters are from the Dutch Immigrant Letters Collection, Archives, Calvin College, Grand Rapids, MI, Box 21, Folder 14.]

Town of Holland, Wisconsin to Kotten, Gelderland   5 March 1860
Gerrit Jan Droppers to Uncle and Aunt Vardink

Worthy Uncle, good nephews and nieces,

We inform you noble people that in the morning, between 2 and 3 o'clock on March 2, father passed away at the age of 68 years. Father had said, early in the winter, that he would not recover. He was suffering from a progressive disease. The doctor said that it was 'forestwater.' I don't know. Father did not suffer a great deal of pain or discomfort. Father also said that he had no desire to recover. He said, "The Lord's will be done." Father was always healthy and well while in America. He was active both in body and soul. He was always very well satisfied. He always had a friendly relationship with us, and conducted himself as a father ought to live in his own house. He gave a good example to his own family and to the larger circle of relatives. He nurtured his children in the truth and caused them to be instructed. He always, at every opportunity gave leadership, both by way of counsel and example. For this we have never been able to show the measure of respect which is due to him. Now a few more details about his dying. From the time that his strength began to decline, Mother always cared for him alone. The last night I assisted him twice in leaving his bed. Throughout he maintained his mental health. One hour before his departure from us he said that he was distressed and that he would not leave his bed again. Then he laid himself out straight and he never moved his hands or feet again. And he passed out so quietly, yes, as quietly as when a lamp goes out. In a sense this was a cause for happiness. Yes, this separation of our father is a warning for us: Prepare your house, for you shall die and here and now is the time for preparation. If our soul is hid in Christ, then death is the glad tidings to deliver us into the rest that remains for God's people. If we can say as the church, the bride, the one I love is mine and I am His, the lines have fallen unto me in pleasant places; yes a beautiful heritage is mine, already here in the land of the living. May it be so.

I suppose you would like to know where we live. We live in the woods, fifteen miles from Milwaukee. We moved to this area in the first part of April. We built a house here. Prior to this we lived with our neighbor for a time. This neighbor lives about five minutes from us. These are good neighbors who come from Zutphen. There are other Dutch people who live nearby where we live. There one comes from this area and another comes from a different area. There is also a Berenschot, who comes from Voors, still another Berenschot named

153

Melis, who traveled with us. Also, there are some here who came from Clymer (New York). There are also many Winterswijkers who live here. A church is being built here and Reverend de Zonne is also here. You asked about Hanna. One the whole she is well, but not better than in Holland. Geziena, Alijda and John Derk are living in Milwaukee. They earn good money. Geziena as much as in Holland. Alijda earns two and a half guilders a week and Derk lives with a confectioner and earns fifteen guilders per month. He has a good position. Money can be earned here if a person is able to understand English. He has always associated with the English.

We have heard that there is civil war by you. When we heard this we were very disturbed. When I heard that my brother had died I was deeply disturbed. However, beloved, human life is short and filled with unrest.

Something else – tobacco, coffee, tea are just as expensive here as by you. We delayed writing because we wanted to see how the crops would grow here. Everything grows well here. Potatoes, peas, beans and kale are in plentiful supply. And whatever else we have sowed and planted looks good. We didn't sow any wheat because it was too late and we couldn't clear the land in time. A few more matters. We bought a cow and a calf for 13 dollars. A dollar is 50 nickels. The letter you wrote to us we received on April 15. If and when you write again send it to G.J. Droppers in Milwaukee because the letter arrived promptly. In Rotterdam nothing befell us. The winters here are very long and the summers are short. The climate is very similar to yours. Give our greetings to G.W. Wulphof. Also to all our friends and acquaintances. With this I must close. Now may the Lord bless you for the sake of His Son. May it be so.

G.J. Droppers

[Although this letter was sent from Milwaukee, Gerrit Jan was residing in Sheboygan County. He may have been visiting his siblings when the letter was written.]

Milwaukee, Wisconsin to Kotten, Gelderland
16 January 1863
Gerrit Jan Droppers to family

We have received your letter and from it we noted that you are faring well. This made us very happy – the fact that, as you write, you live in a land where there is peace, is a great privilege. This is a gift from the Lord. Yes, Uncle and Aunt, nephews and nieces, you are doubtless eager to hear from us and inquisitive as to our circumstances and how matters are going with us. Yes, Mother is still well. She is still well at her advanced age. As for us, we are concerned we are reasonably well in the beginning of the year. At the present time we have three children. All are well and healthy and the other members of the family are reasonably well. Even so we are not all together, one is here and another there. My sister Janna's husband has gone into the service. My wife's brother has also gone into the service as a volunteer. They receive good remuneration; I believe it is twenty dollars a month. Janna's brother-in-law writes that he earns forty cents a day above his regular wage because he is a carpenter. The enemy had destroyed the bridges and they are rebuilding there. You undoubtedly know that the South and the North are at war against each other. Yes, there is a lot of violence. He writes about one battle when they were attacked by the enemy. The enemy had taken a position in a corn field of about ten acres. Corn usually grows to a height of five to eight feet. Yes, he writes that when the battle was over, he entered the corn field, but he writes that he could not endure what he saw. He could not endure the groaning, because the ground was wet with blood. Fifteen thousand of the rebels died and fifteen hundred of our men. And my brother-in-law has just recently entered the army. Yes, friends, you can well understand that the situation is very serious. It has lasted so long already and thousands of people have entered eternity.

Now, I'm sure you are eager to hear something about the condition of all of us. Mother is well and healthy. She is able to do the work in the home. Aleida and her husband are also reasonably well, and the same can be said about Janna and her husband. My brother Jan Derk and his wife and son and daughter are also well. His one son died the previous year, on November 26, 1859. He was about two years old. I and my wife and daughter are well. Our daughter reached the age of one and half years the previous month. My sister Diena will write you a letter herself. So be it.

Now, something about the activities of the church. Much is sacrificed for and much work is done among the heathens. Also, the work among the blind heathens continues to spread. If only we were more prayers and workers for God's kingdom here on earth. But what can I say about our church? I can't say much that is favorable. Why are God's children so colorless? How has the fine gold been tarnished? And if that were the only problem, even God's children rise up against each other. In our congregation conditions are still reasonably good. We don't have a minister at the present time. However, it is our prayer and desire to receive one from the Lord, if that is His will. It is my hope that the Lord will supply all our needs for body and soul. In nature all things are reasonably well. We may rejoice in the blessings of the Lord. Everything is reasonable as to cost. Last year we bought a horse with which to do our work. We paid about 20 dollars. We bought a yoke of oxen for 60 dollars and a very good cow for 18 dollars. Receive greetings from Mother and all of us. Please allow all the members of the family to read this letter. I hope that this letter may be received by all of you in good health.

G.J. Droppers

◆◆◆◆◆◆

[Abraham Heinen was born 30 November 1822 in Aalten, Gelderland and died 9 January 1892 in the Town of Lima, Sheboygan County, WI. On 20 April 1849 in Aalten, Gelderland he married Johanna Wilhelmina Scholten. She was born 12 August 1826 in Aalten, Gelderland the daughter of Hendrik Jan and Berenden (Houwers) Scholten. She died 15 June 1898 in Town of Lima, Sheboygan County, WI. Abraham, Johanna and their first three children sailed for the U.S. in 1854 with Abraham's brother Grades.]

Children of Abraham Heinen and Janna Scholten in 1909
Back: Hendrik Jan, Arend Jan, Jan Hendrik
Front: Hermina Berendina, Aleida, Berendina Hendrika, Johanna, Janna Gesina
Deceased: Hendrika, Berentje and two infant sons named Abrahm
Photo courtesy of the Sheboygan County Historical Research Center

Gibbsville, Wisconsin to Aalten, Gelderland   20 May 1872
Abram B. Heinen to relatives

Very loving brothers and sisters,

We could not forget to write you a few words and let you know that because of the Lord's blessings we are in good health and hope and wish to hear the same of you. We have received a letter from you on March 10, 1871. I just had a letter that I sent to brother Berend. And now we have not received a letter again and then I read in your letter that brother Willem does not feel well and now I have heard it said that he is dead. I wonder if that is why we did not get any news. And now I will let you know about the weather. We have had a long winter and with it sometimes cold days. We were late with our sowing. On April 20 I sowed barley and on the 23rd we began with wheat sowing and now we are finished. If we can, we still have to sow the buckwheat, but that is still a month too early. And now I let you know that Miena (Hermina Berendina) was married on the 1st of March to Hendrik Willem ter Beest. And Hendrik Jan was hired for 5 months by an Englishman and he earns 90 dollars there. On the first of April he went there and on the first of September he will come home again and then he goes threshing. And I will let you know that last fall two railroads were built. The one is 3 miles west and the other 3 miles east of here and that one comes through the place where we first lived. It is now a good time here. Everything is quite expensive again. The wheat costs 12 shilling a bushel and so is everything is like that. Brother Jan I have heard that last year your place was sold and that you now are a farmer yourself. Let us know once whether you have bought the place and how much it cost you. And write us once if G. Assink still lives at Wesselink (a farm) and it goes with him. And write us once if it goes well with the wife and children of brother Willem. How many children are still at home? I have also heard that both the older boys are tailors at Wenters (Winterswijk) and I do not have more news. Write me once if you are yet thinking of going to America because I know of three who went to get people from Holland. The first one is Roelof Laarman. He lives near us and his family lives by Gour in Overijssel. And the second is one with the name of Wondergem. He also lived nearby us for a short time. W. Winkelhorst bought his farm. But Wondergem is not thought of much around here because he likes to drink gin and then there comes Chris Gijsbers of Bredevoort. He is from Nebraska. There is a man here who sold his place and all that he had and has gone to Nebraska because his children were there. And he has gone only three or four weeks, then he was back again and he said that it had cost him a lot but he was glad that he was here again because it did not suit him there. There was always so much wind. Every time someone leaves here we hear that it doesn't go well. Now I must end with the pen but not my heart. Receive the blessing of the Lord for soul and body. Hearty greetings to all of you and also from Grades and his wife and children. H.J. Heinen, I have heard that your wife gave birth to a young son. I wish you much happiness and blessings. And now I ask you that you write us a letter once so quickly as you can.

My address is Mee A. Heinen, Noort Amerika, Schoigen faals Post Offer, Gipsville.

                                                   A. B. Heinen

◆◆◆◆◆◆

[Jan Willem Korschot was born 3 March 1807 in Winterswijk, Gelderland the son of Derk Jan and Hinders (Lammers) te Korschot. He died 1 June 1882 in Sheboygan County, WI. On 10 May 1837 in Winterswijk, Gelderland he married Berendina ten Damme, the daughter of Aelbert and Aleida (Loytink) ten Damme. She was born 1 May 1814 in Winterswijk, Gelderland and died 2 December 1895 in Sheboygan County, WI. They immigrated around 1855. Delia (ten Damme) te Selle was a half-sister of Berendina. This letter is from the Dutch Immigrant Letters Collection, Archives, Calvin College, Grand Rapids, MI, Box 38, Folder 13.]

Oostburg, Wisconsin to Winterswijk, Netherlands   10 June 1874
Jan Willem Korschot to Mrs. Delia te Selle

Highly regarded brother and sister,

Just now I take up the pen to write you a few letters and to let you know that we, by the Lord's blessing, are still quite well and the same we wish for you. Now we wish to hear once again, since it is such a long time that we have seen each other, and also a long time that we have heard anything from each other, so that it seems that we are no longer brothers and sisters.

But yes, brother, as long as we are on this side of the grave, shall I think how it goes with my brother, if you are still alive or dead. But may you still have the privilege of being alive, then let us know with a bit of paper and ink, because how soon we can come to the end and then it is closer, say, when we travel through the valley of the shadow of death we leave our earthly friends.

But our best friend will never leave us even through the grave and death. Yes, brother, may we learn to know that friend. What a great privilege for every person, but it happens so often as the writer says, our hearts are as hard as rock. Even in view of our sin, it does not enter, no it is bound by the stuff of the flesh, and concerns our flesh and blood. We can hardly persuade the narrow flesh and blood.

Now, brother, I cannot write you much that is special. We and our children have food enough. We still have our youngest daughter with us. She is not married. We have 50 acres of land; then we rented out 20 acres to the daughter of her housemaid and her husband. And we have 3 cows and 2 calves and 2 pigs and one horse.

Now I let you know that the people tell us that your youngest son was called into eternity. Let us know once about it and write us a big letter about the circumstances in Holland – about the brothers and sisters and children. So we will expect a letter soon, and herewith I close with pen, but not with the heart, and wish you the blessing of the Lord, soul and body, and name you my brother and sister.

J.W. Korschot
B.D. ten Damme

◆◆◆◆◆◆

[Gerrit Willem Bloemers was baptized 14 April 1794 in Winterwijk, Gelderland, the son of Harmon Jan Dijkbosch and Christina Nijhof. He died 12 July 1889 in Gibbsville, WI. On 6 June 1819 in Winterswijk he married Janna te Selle. She was baptized 18 September 1796 in Winterswijk, the daughter of Teunis te Selle and Willemina Wilterdink. She died 14 August 1870 in Gibbsville, WI. In 1865, Janna's nephews, Jan Hendrik and Harmen Jan te Selle also emigrated.]

Gerrit Willem Bloemers and Janna te Selle
Photo courtesy of the Sheboygan County Historical Research Center

Wisconsin to Winterswijk, Gelderland
Gerrit Willem Bloemers to Derk Willem te Selle,   January 1865

Dear friends and other relations,

We let you know that we are still in good health and we hope you are likewise. We want you to know that we have received Jan Willem Korscot's letter in which we read about your good health and for this we are glad. We have also read that many of our friends and acquaintances have been called to an irrevocable eternity. They are, so to speak, only a little head of us, but let us hold on to our calling in the Lord so that through Christ's justice we may enter into his kingdom that he already prepared before the start of the world. But, enough of this. Each of us should find out for himself whether we are entitled to a share of that kingdom.

We will inform you of our current circumstances. The yield was rather good, except for the summer wheat and the hay which suffered a lot due to the persistent drought. All the food for cattle and people are expensive. Bacon is 14 cents a pound, beef is 10 to 12 cents, butter 32 to 34 cents. This makes good cattle quite expensive. We sold a yoke of oxen for 133 dollars and a young horse that is going to 3 years old this coming May for 125 dollars together with the gear. Clothes and cotton fabric are as much as three times as expensive as in former years, including tools that contain iron.

The day's wages are also much higher than before because in March the war will have been going on for 4 years and this involves a lot of expenses and brings poverty to many. Surely you must have heard that they must draw lots here and the last time they drew lots for conscription, Tobias drew a bad number. With a lot of pain, and after being away from us for 23 days, he got out of it because he occasionally spits blood. Otherwise it is to no avail; they don't care whether they have many children or are old people. In the latest conscription, five times a hundred thousand were selected and now they need three times a hundred thousand more. Still, we enjoy many privileges here. Everything in the South is being destroyed and burnt.

There they have to draw lots from the age of 45 down to the age of 20 and then they can also buy below and over those ages and then they will cost from 1 to 8 hundred dollars. This is for a year. Dear ones, what more shall I write of this. You know what the Lord says about it in his Word. A house or country that is divided against itself will be destroyed and it is the same over here. What more shall I write to you about the war. Where should I begin and where should I end.

Now I let you know that I intend to send you a book through a man born in Noord Brabant who is going to visit his parents. He lives close to us. But from where he will forward it, Arnhem or Rotterdam, I don't know. My wish is that you may receive it in good health and that you may draw blessed fruits from it for yourself and for yours. Perhaps you will occasionally encounter strange things in it, but in that case examine what the Word says about it. Should it come into your hands, read and read it again, and write me some day what you think of it.

Will you please inquire whether my three sisters are still alive because I have received no news from them at all. Write me whether there are some in the family in whom the Lord has worked and whether the Lord has added any newcomers to his kingdom, and how you, your wife and your mother have been. You must not think that I am tough. No, I just wish to admonish you like a brother. The Word teaches us that if we were not born again he shall not inherit the kingdom of God. So we may admonish one another as long as we may be in mercy today, and even though we have merely received one talent, we should make use of it and not bury it in the soil like a useless servant.

Furthermore, we let you know that we enjoy rather good health, except for Mother who has so much gout in her one leg that she has to walk with crutches. But her heart is still very healthy. As for me, my deafness is increasing and the strength of the body is declining for I shall be 71 years old on 14th of April. But I cannot thank the Lord enough for the favors given to me, a poor sinner. J.W. Korschot and his wife are also well, as are Dulmes and his wife and children. We also let you know that we have a family of 6 children: 2 boys and 4 girls (one little boy died) and they all are fresh and healthy. Please be patient with my poor writing and do write back soon. Do not give this letter to anyone else. Convey it orally, as I do not want them to know about the book.

There is something else I should report to you. This summer I went to see my brother in Michigan since we had not see one another in 18 years. There I saw many acquaintances from Holland and most of them are going fine. I really enjoyed being there. I have to stop because writing is becoming rather hard for me. It is probably the last letter I will write to you. Not to put an end to our friendship, no, far from that. Please remember me to all of my family and friends and acquaintances. Please write back soon.

G.W. Bloemers

◆◆◆◆◆◆

Wisconsin to Winterswijk, Gelderland
Gerrit Willem Bloemers to Derk Willem te Selle   6 June 1865

I let you know that my first attempt to send the book did not work. That man got as far as New York and there he was robbed of his money and had to come back home. I received the book and the letter back. I think I have another opportunity to send it. We have received the two letters: the one to our job and the other to our grief about the things she wrote. We cannot agree to that request for the time being, because due to the war we have to pay a lot here as well.

The materials for clothes and all other things are equally expensive. Gold and silver is not to be seen anymore. All we have is paper money and it would be no use to you, even if she was here. She could be helped with food though. Just tell this to Dela ten Dollen and give her our regards. I also let you know that Gerrit Jan ten Dollen has also been drawn for military service, but he has bought himself out for seven hundred and ten dollars and that for just one year. Aleida's brother is also in military service, but those drawn for the army will soon be back home, because the South has surrendered and they have captured the Southern president and they have also got the assassins of the Northern president. Now it seems that there will be peace. That war has taken an awful lot of human lives because the bitterness was great. Thousands and thousands who were in captivity in the South have perished due to starvation. You cannot imagine just how much that war has cost and this setback will not be overcome in the next few years because the South had prepared itself, whereas the North had yet to collect and gather everything first. Besides, the Northern president had a kind nature so that at first he wanted to spare a lot of things and the rage got fiercer and they started setting fire to and destroying things. It has pleased the Lord to put an end to all that. Now I should remind you that 4 months have gone by between the first and the last letter, because the first letter and your book came back and since writing is so difficult for me, I decided to send it anyways.

So, should the book come into your hands, please let me know how you liked it. After you have read it closely and looked over the bible texts. I also let you know that it was extremely hot here for fourteen days and we had a persistent drought, but now while I am writing this, it is raining a little and the fruit has some promise. Please remember us to old brother Konings and give our regards to all friends and acquaintances.

G.W. Bloemers

◆◆◆◆◆◆

Holland, Sheboygan County, Wisconsin to Winterswijk, Gelderland
Gerrit Willem Bloemers to Derk Willem te Selle   8 February 1873
(written by A. Stokdijk)

Worthy nephew, D.W. te Selle,

Upon invitation of your uncle G.W. Bloemers, I am taking up the pen to write you some lines in his name and in his presence hoping that these lines will find you and your family and two sisters in good health.

As far as your uncle is concerned, well, taking his years into account (since he is almost 79 years old), he still is very well, however, the old man is very deaf, and has much dizziness in his head. Also, it goes without saying, he is becoming weaker and less able to walk, and also must pay attention to many different weather conditions. The desire of your uncle is that he would like to know that all is well with you and with the entire family, not just from his side of the family, but also from the side of his departed wife. You must know that your uncle, however old he may be, would very much like to know how each member of the family is in the temporal. But also, and above all, I know that – however pleasing and refreshing it might be for him to know that you are all doing fine in the temporal – he would be delighted in particular to hear from you and the family that you all are doing so well that you can write: "Dear Uncle, we know that when our earthly home, this tabernacle is broken up, we have a building close to God,. A house not made with hands…but Eternal in the Heavens." That

162

your uncle for himself may believe this, I have no doubt. And that you and the entire family also might share in this hope is his sincere desire, and his highest longing. Not only here, but also his prayer to our God and Father. That the old man has written you about this before is quite sure. And that you are convinced of the fact that he means well by you, you would dare not deny.

It has befallen the old man well upon that way, and when we ask the older folks (in heaven) how did you come out with Jesus whom you have chosen as your deliverer, and your Leader, for your eternal hope, then they would all say, "All of us has befallen it well, yes as good as it was and is for them to be near the Lord, that they consider others as Strangers here below." They all would say to us that with Jesus they were never cheated or disappointed and possess a hope they do not want to exchange for the entire world.

And O, how wonderful it would be for him in his old age, that there are souls who have obtained a love for Jesus, and that is also why your uncle, once more wants to invite you to give heed to that great salvation. Considering his high age, it could be the last time that he is able to say this to you. So take heed to your days. I know that your uncle is sincere, and yes I know that he also likes to see and to hear very much that all of you are getting along quite well as far as the temporal is concerned. For that he is not reckless at all. He is with his family where he has it very good. And now after the passing away of his wife, he will also feel stronger than ever before how well the Lord still cares so much for him. So well cared for that he is unhindered and free from all necessity beyond the temporal. But above all his soul would fare well when his children and grandchildren, yes the entire family, might walk in the truth. The grace is not denied, no, no, a Christian would, if possible, bring all people to Jesus. A Christian prays and pleads many times, hidden from view. Many times sheds tears of sight, and in the inner chamber, in the night when most of the people are asleep. From this we see a great love, a great interest. Even as Jesus stood over Jerusalem and said while he wept, "Oh if only on this day you might know the things which bring you peace."

I want to invite you to write your uncle, especially how every member of the family is doing, and also how his two sisters are doing, if they are still living. Also if they are doing well, will you be so good to make them acquainted with this. And bring hearty greetings from him to them and the entire family. From your two brothers who went to America he has not received a letter for a long time. This spring it will be two years that Harmen Jan has written them. They live in the state of Nebraska. Nevertheless, he has heard from others that they are doing well after the temporal.

You will understand that your uncle still lives with his son Tobias and wife, and that he, in his old age, enjoys the privilege of being together in all freedom and comfort with his children, and not only that, but also with his grandchildren. Of who, Solomon says, that they 'are a jewel for the elderly." His children possess a total of nine of these jewels called grandchildren, of whom the oldest Janna is 20 years old; Anna, 18 years old; Hendrik Jan is 15 years; Gerrit Willem, 13 years; Dina, 11 years; Gezina, 9 years; Mina, 7 years old; Jan, 4 years old; Albert, 1 year. Thus 9 jewels crown the head of a man of 79 years old and living in a household.

Now, what else your uncle would also like to know is, how is the churchly situation with you in the Netherlands? He feels that if it did not take a turn for the better from when he left the Netherlands, then the situation of the church is not the best. Not that there are still some true Christlike congregations with upright ministers, or that there were no pious Christians anymore, but how things are in general. Isn't there a great falling away and departure from the true Christian teaching? If you still hear about conversions, or being born again to a living hope though faith in Jesus Christ and the Word. When you see churches and enter therein and hear and see what goes on there, and sit by yourself at home and read the Bible, and see what the despised man of Nazareth, Jesus Christ, teaches us about the way of salvation, and his disciples, those despised fisherman, what they learned, and not only what they learned, but how they lived; what would then be your answer? Is in your place the congregation of Christ visible to the world, or is the world with you in the church, or has the so-called church taken on the garments of the world? Your uncle longs for your answer. Tell him once your thoughts, because wc all know very well, or should know, that we are approaching the end of his time. We must remember that the day of the Lord is drawing near, and that that day will come, after all, when people expect it the least.

And it is quite plain that, in general, very little thought is given to this. It is evident that there are many who say, "Oh it is and will stay as it always was in the world. Where is the promise of His coming?" But when we see what the Bible says about that, then it is the language of mockery. Mockers and those who bear the name of Christians, we must not give need to hear them. O troubled Christendom, we might well say, "Did you learn Christ that way?" No, mockers are not Christians and it makes no difference who or what he is. Even the most fluent or talented preacher: when he mocks the return of Christ, he is not a called minister of Christ, and he himself is not a Christian. Surely we are in dangerous times, there is so much agitation to move and to go ahead, but where is the movement ahead in Christendom? Nevertheless, it is also true that there are crying voices from all directions: East, West, South and North. "See the Bridegroom is coming." Faithful watchers who God still gives, also in our days, and those calling voices, increase from day to day until the day is there. Fortunately there are still many who are awake here. And how is it with you, or don't you hear anything about this? We know that there are in the Netherlands, but if there are some with you, or is still everything still asleep?

O, may the Lord cause all to understand, not only to help us to recall that the day of Jesus is near, but also that we impart the Mercy of God in Jesus Christ through conversion so that Jesus Christ may live in our hearts by faith so that we with joy may long for that day. Because, otherwise, all our knowing will not help us. If we long for Jesus' return, then that Jesus must be our daily life. If we pray for His return then we must first pray that He may live in our hearts. If we long for the New Jerusalem, then we must first have our new birth from that Jerusalem, for when we understand that, my friend, then we can call ourselves fortunate people. And then we know for sure that our Lord Jesus Christ shall come when He has prepared a house for us in the house of our Father, the New Jerusalem. And worthy friend, may my wish and prayer be fulfilled. Then you uncle, I myself, will all our friends and acquaintances may receive that grace to know Jesus here and to long for his return, and to meet you and yours there, to be with the Lord forever. Amen, so be it.

And now, my friend, upon the invitation of your uncle, I have written you a little. I may have added a little of my own, but this I know, that whatever I have written, it will have the approval of your uncle. And with this I commend you with yours to God and the words of his Grace.

Your uncle's friend, brother and servant,
A. Stokdijk

We have had an early hard winter here. On November 12, 1872 the winter started. There is enough food and fodder here for people and cattle. The coldest it has been here is 22 degrees below zero. In other places as cold as 40 degrees. The photo of your uncle is enclosed and you and your family and all other friends hereby receive the hearty greetings from old man Bloemers, his son and daughter, as well as their children. Hoping that you will write back soon.

Address: G.W. Bloemers
            Gibbsville, Post Office
            Sheboygan County Wisconsin
            North America

◆◆◆◆◆◆

Written on the backside of this letter was the following:

Derk Willem te Selle to C. Grutters   28 February 1873

Highly esteemed friends,
C. Grutters and wife and children

I received this week from my uncle, your brother-in-law and brother G.W. Bloemers from North America, this letter. As he asked me to let you know the content of this letter, I send it to you, and also the portrait so you can see him on it, and also read from his letter how he is doing. So you can also send it to your other sister. They would like to have it and see it very much. But Grutters, will you be so good as to send me back this letter soon? The old man is longing for a letter in return from us, so I can give an answer to a few questions he posed. We have for many years not received a letter from him. It is true that he provided us, by way of one of my brothers who was also with him, a few letters. I would also gladly have brought this letter, but I am not able to face walking all the way to your home. Furthermore, I let you know that I myself, my wife and children, and also my mother, we are still in good health. We hope and wish this also for all of you. Greetings from all of us.

Derk Willem te Selle

Esteemed nephews and nieces. We thank you sincerely because you have sent us these tidings and noted from it that you are still healthy by God's blessing. That delights us greatly

165

that you are still alive about which we are happy, and as far as we are concerned, we cannot do much more. We are both old and if you need money for this, then be so good as to send a foreman. The writing is very difficult for me.

G.Z. Bloemers C.A. Gruter

◆◆◆◆◆◆

Gibbsville, Wisconsin to Winterswijk, Gelderland
Gerrit Willem Bloemers to brother Gerrit   19 May 1883

Dear brother,

We have received your letter in good health and saw that you also were still well. We are glad that we can send one another a few words again with the pen. We are not privileged at this time to do so orally. We do not know whether we will be able to do so again. We will leave that to Him who directs all things. Brother, we see that you would like to come over to us. That would please us. But I cannot see that you would like it here. We are in a village here and for that reason I think you would not feel at home with us. But it would be better for you in the city of Milwaukee. That is about thirty miles away. We are about 12 miles from Sheboygan. There is plenty of work there and an opportunity to earn some money. But it is not possible to make much at shoe making by hand because in America it is done by machine. You cannot understand that because here they have molded boots. They are called rubbers. They cost three dollars. They are good in water and snow. This winter I bought a pair of rubbers at the market in Cedar Grove for six gulden. They have a market day there every month. If you order a pair of boots at the shoemaker's you pay eight dollars, and the leather is not as expensive as it is where you are. So the labor is well paid. Anyone who wishes to and can work can earn more in America than where you are in Germany. However, last year some young people have returned to Germany. But I think they were the slaves of strong drink and not as much is consumed here as where you are. And it is expensive here but that does not bother us. People eat and drink very well here. Black bread is not eaten here. Hogs eat rye.

We have two hogs and three cows and 15 chickens and a cat. That is all of our stock. We have purchased a small place of 32 schepel. Large enough. It cost us $650. Uncle loaned us the money, and there was no house or barn on it. Now I bought a house and we moved that on it. We are busy building a barn. We make our money on the milk. Cheese is made from it. We had saved quite a sum of money. But it disappeared when we built the barn and moved the house, but that is not too bad if we remain well. Then we will have some more. We do not need much money because we have raised more food than we need. I am better off here than I was in Bredevoort. There I needed a great deal of money for a few living supplies. If you come here we can furnish you with board for a half year for less than it would be in Bredevoort in a week. A person has to work hard here in the summer but not much has to be done in the winter. We have had a long winter with a great deal of snow and cold, but now the weather is fine.

Brother, now as to travel expenses. They amount to at least 100 gulden, so 120 or 125 gulden, because the trip by land is more than by sea. We traveled 500 hours from New York. If you come you must get off in Milwaukee. That is the best city for you. There you can work in a shoe factory and make some money. There you can also get leather at the factory, and work by the pair if you wish. And then you go on to Oostburg. That is a small station and then you are less than an hour from our house. Then you can see if you like farm work. There is plenty of work here, otherwise you can go back to Milwaukee. There you will find many Germans and Hollanders.

So, Gerrit, do as the Lord leads you. With this I will close. Hearty greetings from me and my wife and from our Jan who is doing well.

W. Bloemers

◆◆◆◆◆

[Harmen Jan te Selle was born 4 December 1844 in Winterswijk, Gelderland to Jan Albert and Dela (ten Damme) te Selle. He died 22 June 1919 in Firth, NE. On 27 April 1866 he married Berendina Aleida Ruesink in Town of Holland, Sheboygan County, WI. His brother, Jan Hendrik, was born 22 Jan 1838 in Winterswijk, Gelderland and died 13 March 1921 in Firth, NE. On 28 September he married Hanna Berendina Onnink in Winterswijk. She was born 2 December 1841 in Winterswijk and died 17 March 1929 in Firth, NE. Their brother, Derk Willem, was born 26 July 1877 in Winterswijk and died there on 12 February 1904. These letters are from the Dutch Immigrant Letters Collection, Archives, Calvin College, Grand Rapids, MI, Box 73, Folders 3-5.]

Gibbsville, Wisconsin to Winterswijk, Gelderland   26 November 1865

Harmen Jan te Selle, Jan Hendrik te Selle and Hanna Berendina (Onnink) te Selle
to Dela (te Selle) ten Damme and Derk Willem te Selle

Dearly beloved parents, brothers and sisters and other friends and acquaintances,

We are letting you know that we are still in good health and we hope to hear the same from you. If it were otherwise, we would be very sorry to hear it. As you know, we left you on October 6 and we arrived at the Bloemers house on the 6th of this month. They were happy to see us arrive in good health. Yes, friends, come quickly to see us to hear out of our mouths some news of Holland.

We were asked if there were more people thinking of coming to America. We told them that there were indeed a few who would like to do so, but who sometimes lacked the money. Others who could afford it do not want to because they are worried about the trip, and

167

consequently, there were not many who came. They told us here that those people would be crazy to bring the land owners so much yield and to toil from dawn to dusk and yet not have enough bread to eat. I will not write anything further about this, for we really cannot say much about America as yet.

First of all I will give you a brief account of our trip, of which I have already given you some details, I think, as far as Rotterdam. So I will start from that point onwards. On Saturday the 7th of October at 2 in the afternoon we left from there for Hull where we arrived Sunday night. But before I proceed I should let you know that we were in the company of 2 Americans. One by the name of J. Vogel, who had fetched his family from Holland. The other had been to Holland just for fun. Those two were of great use to us, for they had a good command of English and could speak to the people and then they told us what we should do. We arrived at Hull when it was getting dark, but they told us just to follow them. There were 33 Dutchman with us and we proceeded until we came to an inn. But that group was too big for one inn. We split into two parties, but we stayed in one house with two dwellings in it. There we had to pay 12 nickels each for two coffees and a night's lodging. Monday morning at eight we left Hull for Liverpool by train, which was quite a pleasant trip, although we encountered such amazingly high mountains and rock cliffs that the train had to go through over and over and over again. One could wonder how it would be possible to pass underneath, sometimes for long stretches, and it was so dark in the coach that we could not see each other. But there were also some lovely acres of farmland and meadows with cattle grazing. We also saw camels or beasts of burden. There were many factories that belched so much smoke that they sky was dark from it and not as clear as it is by you. One could also see the state of the houses and they were black.

Monday night we arrived at Liverpool and we had to stay there till Thursday morning. Otherwise the departure could have been on Wednesday the 11th, but when you are told to wait another day you cannot do much about it. There we spent 5 guilders and 14 nickels, which was not much for such a long time for the three of us. On Thursdays at 2 in the afternoon we embarked with a group of a thousand men. The wind was quite in our favor. It was slightly to the north. After two days we came to the coast of Ireland. There another two hundred men joined us in a small boat. Subsequently there were 1200 altogether on the ship. You will say that was quite a lot and it would be full. Indeed it was, but that ship was pretty big, measuring 460 feet long and 40 wide. I do not know how deep, for she lay quite high on the water.

There were all sorts of people; French, English, Irish, German, Italians and only 23 of us Dutch. There were also three blacks, but those are mainly to be found in New York. Thus, we sailed on, but the wind started to turn against us and on the 15th it started blowing fiercely and straight in front of us. The ship rocked slightly so that many had to throw up, but it only lasted 24 hours, although the wind kept blowing against us. We sailed on slowly. On Thursday the 19th the sea started to get a bit more turbulent so that the water washed over the deck several times and many of us got wet and we were laughed at by the others. I, as well as Jan Hendrik, found out for ourselves: we got soaking wet. I lay down in bed fully dressed and I soon dried up. This went on for 2 nights and a day, but everyone stayed below since no

168

one felt like getting soaked again. It wasn't too bad for seasickness. Most had to throw up and so did I and Jan Hendrik, but just once and I was only bedridden for one day. There were women who suffered longer, but only one 6 month old child died.

I shall also tell you about our food. Many did not like it, but we cannot say we didn't. In the morning we had fresh bread with ample butter on it and coffee with sugar. In the afternoon we began with soup and then potatoes with meat. So much meat one could hardly eat it all. In the evening, tea with sugar and sea biscuits, as many as we liked, and again with butter. Saturday we had rice instead of potatoes with either molasses or sugar on it. Sunday we had pudding, and so we cannot say we had it that bad.

We sailed slowly on and after traveling for 17 days we arrived at New York on Sunday afternoon the 29th. The wind had been against us all the time, otherwise it could have been done in 12 or 13 days. We had to stay offshore from Sunday afternoon until Monday afternoon when we were taken to Castle Garden and there we had to pay for the remaining trip to Milwaukee: 46 and a half dollars as well as 6 dollars for the excess weight of the luggage. We were taken from Castle Garden to an inn. There that man Vogel made an agreement for a dollar a day for each of us, but when we came to pay we were charged two dollars. We did not like that too much: six dollars for the three of us. I'll tell you a little about the city. It was the prettiest that we have seen on our journey. The houses were so high, sometimes 5 or 6 floors. It was a very big city and we were told there were around 2 million inhabitants. This city was divided into three parts with two rivers separating them.

Tuesday the 31st at 7 in the evening we left New York for Buffalo by train, where we arrived on Thursday at 6 in the morning. We could not leave any earlier than at 2 in the afternoon, but at that time some of our goods had not yet arrived. So some had to stay behind to see when the goods would come, particularly the bedding, since the chests had indeed arrived. I and another Dutchman stayed behind and the others went on to Detroit. Many wagons arrived, but our goods were still not there when the fifth wagon rolled in, At 10 in the evening one chest of ours arrived, but the bedding did not arrive until 12. At that time we could not leave any earlier than at 2 the next afternoon. We arrived in Detroit between 1 and 1:30, where Jan Hendrik and Hanna and that man Vogel had waited. The others had moved on to Grand Rapids where they were going to settle.

◆◆◆◆◆◆

Town Holland Wisconsin to Winterswijk, Gelderland
Harmen Jan te Selle to Dela (ten Damme) te Selle   21 October 1867

Very beloved Mother and brothers and your wives and children,

We write to tell you that we are still well and in good health. We have learned from your last letter that you are also well, for which we are very happy. We have also heard Jan A. Sikkink tell quite a bit about what has happened in Holland since we left. Thank you, mother and brothers, for the trouble you took to send us what we asked you for. It is very fine material and we certainly do like it.

It will soon be New Years' and Christmas. Why don't you come and visit us and we shall have a cup of hot chocolate again. J.A. Sikkink and Dulmes have also arrived safe and sound at J. Sikkink's place. He lives two miles from here. When I heard that they were there I went to see how they were. "Well," said J.S. Sikkink, "I'm eager to talk to J.H. te Selle some time, but it is so far from here I've been told, and I don't know the way, and it is such a busy time that I can't even borrow a horse to get there." I said, "Well, it's indeed a busy time, but I can't work anyway. I will hitch the horses to the wagon and take you there." "Well," he said, "that would please me very much." So, the next morning I hitched the horses to the wagon and took them to Jan Hendrik, because he lives 9 miles from our place, which is a 3 hour distance. But it has not been so good here for the newcomers because land is getting more expensive. The prices range from 40 to 50 dollars per acre and I think it is bound to get far more expensive still, because it is amazing how many people keep arriving.

I will tell you a little about the work we have done during the year. In the beginning of the year, in the month of March, we began to build a barn. During the previous year we had already had boards sawed for it and had cut wood during the winter so we could start working on it right away and could finish it soon. We had 2 carpenters, and often even 3, but that cost a great deal of money. Just the carpenters cost us $72 plus board, and they slept here during the night. We had German carpenters who were too far from home to go back once in a while. We don't have the tiles for the roof that you have, but what are called shingles here, which are sawed from cedar or pine, about 6 inches wide and 17 inches long. The roofs here are much like those of your windmills. But they are very expensive and we had to get them from a place 24 miles from here. We needed 17, 000 of those for our barn. We had most of our own boards and wood, and the work we did ourselves was not even counted as part of the cost. Still it cost us about $400. But, then again, it is quite large; 45 feet long, 35 feet wide and 17 feet high – that is, up to the roof.

In the beginning of this letter I wrote that I had told Sikkink I could not work. You will probably wonder why I could not work. I will explain briefly. Our farm hand and I were mowing the grass. You will probably say, "Do you mow the grass yourself?" Don't you take care of yourself? But is an easy job here. Even boys aged 14 and 15 can do it here. But as I was saying, we were working together and here one doesn't strickle with a strickle as you do, but with a whetstone almost one foot long. However, I had broken one stone and only had one left at the time. I first wetted my scythe. With my left hand I held the scythe upright in order to wet its lower part and our man was standing a few steps from me. I wanted to throw this whetstone to him and in doing so, I hit the point of the scythe with my arm right in the wrist so that the blood squirted all over my arm. The farm hand tied his handkerchief around my arm so tightly that the bleeding stopped. The doctor was sent for immediately to bandage me and it healed very well. At first I feared that my hand or fingers would stay stiff, but they are alright again. But the thumb and forefinger are so numb that I can hardly hold a pen to write. Do not blame me for the poor writing. So four weeks went by while I could not do anything. I could hardly even dress or undress myself. That was really a nuisance and unprofitable in the middle of a season of haying and threshing, and me being unable to do anything.

Now I will write a few words about how the crops were this year. First of all, the hay yield was quite good. We brought in 22 loads of hay for the horses, and because I could not help, we had to have a few acres moved for half of it and for that the people had to do the haying with us and bring the hay into the barn. The wheat has also been pretty good. We have had most of it mown by machine. Then about 6 acres can be taken care of in a day; the work being done with two horses and two men. We have had it threshed already. That is done here by machine too. It took a day and a half with 12 men and 4 horses. Now we have 270 bushels of wheat and 43 bushels of buckwheat. I do not know about the oats because I am going to cut it for the horses. We had 3 acres of oats and 3 of peas. We have not yet dug up all the potatoes. So far we have already dug up 60 bushels. The corn is very poor. I am not sure if you know what corn is, but you call it Turkish white wheat. The wheat is very high priced. It costs 41.80 or 41.90 per bushel. So we have already sold 100 bushels and delivered it to the city. I think we will make 350 dollars on the wheat.

I could write much more, but the paper turns out to be too small. As far as I know, Jan Hendrik and his wife are still in good health. Greet all of our friends and acquaintances. Greetings to you too from me and my wife.

Harmen Jan te Selle

P.S. Tell Mrs. Toebes that Janna te Brummes sends her her regards and wishes her good health. Derk Willem, when you write let me know if your leg has healed well.

◆◆◆◆◆◆

Harmen Jan te Selle to Derk Willem te Selle   21 October 1867

When you write us again, please let us know whether brother Gerrit Jan has already got married or not. When we left Holland he was to get married in May. I have not heard anything about it. Please write where he is and what he does.

Some time ago we sold 30 acres of land. Most of it was forest land because forest land does not fetch a great deal of money. Besides, we have enough land to farm and lumber is not worth much here. It would cost too much money to cut it and turn it into arable land because day wages are too high here. Leaving it fallow does not bring in much and the earnest money is very high here. We got 750 dollars for it and we have the money put out at 8 percent, which comes to an interest of 60 dollars. That is more than lumber would bring in. Because the wood is just used for firewood. We have 15 more acres of that and before we have burned all that wood I think several years will have passed.

We still have quite a large farm: 40 acres of arable land, 10 acres of hay land and 10 acres of pastures for the cattle. We have 2 horses, 2 big heavy oxen and 2 young oxen over two years old and two year old oxen as well as 2 young calves and 2 colts and 2 cows. We sold 4 sheep in May of this year, so we only have 2 cows left at the moment because we cannot get any money for the butter here. Only shop goods. This means that one cannot keep so many cows and there is no need to keep any cattle for the manure. Just having yokes is the most important thing here. Altogether we have 18 head of cattle.

When you write me please let me know whether some of the young folk, like my friends there, have already gotten married. And whether the boys down at Harmshuis are still at home. I have to end here, but I should like to make a request, brother. Should there be an opportunity, I should like to have such a large size Bible like the one you have. For as often as I read and do not understand, I always think, "I wish I had that big Bible." I have to end here. Greetings from me and my wife.

Harmen Jan te Selle

If you send me a bible, I shall give them the money back here.

◆◆◆◆◆◆

Jan Hendrik te Selle and Hanna Berendina Onnink
to Derk Willem te Selle   22 January 1868

Very dear friends, parents, brothers and sisters and your wives and children,

I take up the pen to write a few letters to you. It has been a long time since we have written. Up to now we are all in good health; our household and all the relatives. Drikka has been with us for half the time up to now. A week ago she left and went to the daughter of Heurneman's at the Wooldsche School who wanted her real bad.

We have less land than we once had. We had rented at extra 15 'schepelzaad.' But that land was sold and its owner went to a new region where the land was better and cheaper. But in those areas are still savages, otherwise we would also like to go there and sell our land here. We can get three hundred dollars more than when we bought it. The land is now twice as expensive as when we first came here. It now costs 50 dollars an acre, whereas in those days it was 25 to 30 dollars. At that time the wheat cost two dollars and today it is only one. Buying is getting more difficult, otherwise we would like you to get here as well, but at this time you would be ill advised to do so. But I think that in due time we will also go to a new region if only brother Harmen Jan would sell his land. He has already sold 30 acres and has got 70 left. We will first investigate the land there.

The land out there is still to be had for free, but people have to stay on it for 5 years before they are allowed to sell. The reason for that is to attract people to the area so that the entire country can be populated. The land that is populated there costs 5 dollars per acre. It is prairie land which can be plowed right away. That ground must first be broken up with 4 horses or 4 oxen. The soil is said to be like your peat: black, tough soil way down below where the lumps are turfed out. Once it has been broken it is much less compact than the clay here, which is so dry and hard this year that many people here do their farming with 3 horses.

There has been very little rain this year. It is dry all the time. At times the sky looked like it was going to rain, but it was driven away in no time. The water is low, but the crops are reasonably good. We have a hundred and twenty eight bushels of wheat, 90 bushels of peas, 15 bushels of oats. We have not yet harvested the buckwheat. However, we do have no less than a hundred bushel of Turkish wheat (people here say corn) which is fed to the pigs and the cattle. The white climbing beans are expensive. They cost 5 dollars. The peas are 2 dollars per bushel. The rye is also more expensive than the wheat and cattle are also cheaper than last year. It is a difference of one fourth. W. Wassink is working Korschot's land which we have rented for him. I was at Korschot's place when we received the letter. From it I gathered that Willem wanted to come, on what he had written to Oonk.

Then I said to him, "You can now reserve it for him, he refers to it, because you have written so." "Yes," said mother Berendina, "He will have, otherwise he would not have written that." Afterwards there were more people that wanted to have it. In spring we thought we had also got a big farm. It was a 200 acre plot and we wanted to rent it. The man who lived there had also rented it. He was a Zeelander who wanted to buy some land in Michigan near his relatives. The Bloemers heard this and Uncle came to tell us about it and he advised us to make inquiries. It belongs to an Englishman and he is a nice person to have for a landlord.

So we went there and he promised that if the man left, the place would be ours for a third of everything and I had to bring him this. But he wanted to pay for bringing it to him and he also paid for everything I improved. I was very pleased with this. And the man went on a trip to Michigan, but found the land too expensive there, so he stayed on the farm. So we could not get it and we stayed where we were. I would rather have something bigger and sell ours or rent it out.

I have another request of you, Derk Willem, from the widow Roerdink of the Veenderhuisken who lives quite close to us. She would like to have a spinning wheel from Holland. Would you be so kind as to send her one through some person. This person can get the money for the wheel and the freight from me or from her, and for all your trouble, have those who bring it here pay you. It should be a single wheel, without this arm, but with two manuals and four spools. Nothing but wool is spun here in this country.

We have 4 sheep, one Maycalf and a 2 yearling calf, two cows, two 4 ½ year old oxen, one horse and two hogs. We butchered three hogs, two old ones and a piglet and also one sheep. We kept it all for ourselves so we and the children have a joint each. So you can imagine that we do not lack for food. However, we have had hard luck with the cattle. During the haying time our horse died, or rather was trampled by cattle. The horse turned one at Easter. I had the horse in Sikkink's pasture since he had more pasture than I. And I rented him the horse to pasture. The horse was with the cattle all the time, but the cattle got annoyed with him. But it had a meek nature and yet it was swift to run and I thought it would look after itself. Here the animals are outside day and night. Eventually he had not been seen for two days. Sikkink then went to look for the horse and found him dead. His neighbors came to tell me that my horse was dead and I felt very sad about it because it was such a beautiful horse. Everyone who saw him and did not know would say to Sikkink, "What a beautiful horse you have got there." And now in the fall our best cow died. So we suffered a hundred dollar loss. The cow had bloated so much that its tongue hung from its mouth as she fell and died. Our neighbor came to tell me about it. The cow was on the road behind his barn where she had been taken to pasture. Only half an hour before Drikke had milked her and had not noticed anything wrong. But we must eat anyway. It will just take one more year to get out of debt and to get the land free and all paid for. This fall I earned 35 dollars in two days with my oxen (in a period of 10 ½ days).

The eight of us had taken a job of filling a hole in the road for 280 dollars. We read in the paper here that in Kotten, south of Winterswijk, an epileptic five year old child had fallen into the fire because of which the entire house burnt down. Whether it is true or not, it is your own fault you will say, but I wish we could get together for a chat twice, 3 or 4 times a year. I would prefer that to writing.

This winter the weather is mild. There has been no keen frost and there is very little snow, so that we often have to use the wagons. Otherwise we would ride in the sleigh, which is much pleasanter and much easier as well, as the sleigh can slide with a heavier load. Butter is now 25 cents. Three weeks ago it was 35 cents. A dozen eggs costs 20 cents, bacon is 11 cents, ham is 18 cents a pound. Two thousand pounds (called a ton here) of hay are 14 dollars, potatoes 75 cents a bushel, rye 90 cents a bushel, buckwheat 1 dollar twenty cents a bushel. But buckwheat is the worst here. If it is good it is a boom, otherwise it is not worth anything. We have some buckwheat that is good and we had two acres of it worth nothing. It was not even worth the labor. We had 8 bushels of seed. Had it turned out right, we would have had buckwheat.

We have to come up with 60 dollars for taxes. Four dollars and 91 cents land tax and 45 cents for cattle and agricultural implements. That money is used for schoolmasters, bridges, etc. around here. We live close to the school and three quarters of an hour away from the church, where we have a good preacher. We also have church on Tuesday and Thursday and once a week catechism for the young ones. Four times a week this preacher makes house calls home by home for the celebration of the Lord's Supper.

Our congregation consists of 46 households. We must support the preacher ourselves as he is under contract for $600. For this we pay 4 dollars. I do not know what to write any further, but I do hope you will not do as I did and wait so long to write back. The more letters the better. I would rather receive a letter than write one. I send our hearty greetings to one and all of you and please give my regards to Jonker and Einink.

                                                                J.H. te Selle   H.B. Onnink

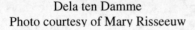

Dela ten Damme
Photo courtesy of Mary Risseeuw

◆◆◆◆◆◆

Town Holland Wisconsin   8 June 1868

Harmen Jan te Selle to Dela (ten Damme) te Selle and Derk Willem te Selle

Highly regarded Mother and Brother and your wife and children,

We let you know that we are all well and healthy and hope to hear the same about you. If it were otherwise it would make us heavy hearted. But brother, what is the reason why you have not written us a letter? I wrote you last October and have not yet received an answer. I don't think that you have forgotten us altogether, or are you afraid that it might bring too much expense? No, brother, do not be afraid of that because I would rather have you write three or four times a year than

only once, because if we have to pay a few cents for it, it doesn't make us any poorer. Therefore, write as soon as possible. Then I will know that you have received it. I will no longer let this delay me, but will inform you about this and that.

As to the circumstances here, I will first tell you that we have a new daughter on April 21. Wife and child are well and healthy. Her name is Dela, named after Mother. That name, here in America, is Dillije. So I invite you to come on August 1st to the children's meal. Now I will also write you a few lines about the weather. From the first of May it was very dry and cold here, so the grain, now up, has not made much progress. The grain stands well on the ground, even though it is not growing. So I believe that if we get warm weather and rain there will be some growth. I think we will get a nice little pile of seed because we have sowed 5 acres of wheat and 2 acres of rye more than we did last year. We have also sowed 23 acres of wheat. By your standards that means 57 schepelzaad. Beyond that we have 4 acres of oats, 2 acres of peas, also rye corn and buckwheat. We have had 40 acres under cultivation. You will say that is 100 schepelzaad. How can your work all that? For that, you would need four or five hired men here, but that goes better here than by you. Here you don't have to mow sods like you have to do. As soon as the crop is off the land, then the work is mostly done in the winter, because in the summer the animals do not come in the barn. Then the manure is brought on the land, and the plowing begins immediately until it begins to freeze. While there is work, the land stays lying until spring when the time comes to sow. Then one goes over it with a cultivator. There are nine or eleven blades which are five and five quarters to an inch and a half – four sided.

One hitches either two horses or two oxen to it, according to what one has. With that, the land is made loose, then sowed, and afterwards dragged. So you can easily realize that we don't need as many people here as over there. But, during the harvest it is busy here. If we needed as much help here as over there, there would be no profit since one has to pay a hired man from 100 to 140 dollars, and the day workers a dollar to a dollar and a half. We have made very little money yet this year. We sold wheat and hay for about $100. But that is not all profit because the $80 daily wages and $100 for the hired man is subtracted. That's a lot. Wheat is rather expensive here and costs $2 a bushel and sometimes more than $2 a bushel. Rye is about $1 a bushel here, oats 75 cents, buckwheat $1, potatoes 50 cents a bushel, butter 25 cents a pound, eggs 1 cent each.

Cattle are still quite high. Cows 30 to 40 dollars and good, heavy work oxen are $130 to $140 a pair. Here they go 2 and 2 in a yoke. So one cannot buy them here except in a pair. We bought a yoke of oxen yet this spring for $130. This year we worked with 2 teams of oxen and broke up some new land. One cannot do that with horses. I gave you the price of cattle but I didn't write about horses. You may think that they are worth no money here, but definitely they are presently worth money! They cost from $150 to $200 and a young filly of three months old brings 440 to 450. We bought a young filly for 440 and some days ago we had ourselves a colt from a horse. I believe if they stay well they will become a good team.

Yes, beloved, what more shall I write. I could write you a little about the climate. It is very healthy here, even as healthy as over there, but there are times when it is not so healthy. Sometimes the winter can be very cold, and the west wind can be very strong. No person can then stay outside. In the summer it can be burning hot. Much hotter than over there. It's because at midday the sun is much more directly overhead. Also, we are at a much higher altitude, so the sun can become much stronger, but the summer is not as long here as it is there. Also the crops can ripen more quickly, so one hardly knows where it will go. In the summer the days are much shorter and in the winter much longer than by you. I don't understand how everything works. Also in the summer we have heavy thunderstorms. Here I must end with the pen but not with the heart.

Greetings from all of us, also J.H. and his wife.

H.J. te Selle

◆◆◆◆◆◆

Town Holland Wisconsin
Harmen Jan te Selle to Dela (ten Damme) te Selle   5 April 1869

Worthy and highly respected Mother and brothers and your wives and children,

We are writing to let you know that we are all still in good health and we hope to hear the same from you. If this is not so we would deeply regret it. I will take up my pen to inform you about all kinds of things. But I almost forgot to tell you that we received your letter of January 10 and learned that you are all well. But that letter was not agreeable. One can say that it is pathetic to hear such a thing about one of our brothers. It seems as if the devil holds complete power over him. Mother and Brothers, now that we hear those things about him, I'll also write you something about him. Almost a year ago he wrote us a letter, but also forbade us to write to D.W. te Selle that he wrote us that letter. And we wouldn't have done so if we hadn't heard anything from him anymore. He then wrote us that he was still in good health, and also his children, but he didn't write anything about his wife. At first we didn't know that he had gotten married. But finally it came out. Brothers, I got married again, but I cannot agree with that for she is a bad lot and she can talk about this and that so nicely when she is with someone else and then she pretends to be very pious. She is always the best. Have you ever heard me complain about Grada, that she was no good. Perhaps he wanted to tell me it isn't my fault. But how would it be at your place, would it be good for me over there. I could be a clog maker or a farmhand. Please write me how much farmhands earn over there. For it is my intention to come to you. And also write me if it is good for Janna, for that girl I love very much and I would wish her to have a good life as well. She now works at the sexton's and earns 40 guilders and they love her very much. And there were many more details that we could gather so that we knew he intended to run away just like that and leave his wife behind. We were taken back of such a letter. Well, says Jan Henderik, what must we do about it. I say, well if you don't know, I do. We'll write a letter from which we'll be clear what we think of him. Yes, but not too harsh. I say, yes, but he must not get much consolation from it. Well, says Jan Henderik, write one then.

I wrote Brother, to our regret, we received a letter from you. From that we learned that you got married again but with whom you don't write us whether it is an old woman of 40 or a young girl of 18. We don't know anything about that. But you write that you don't agree with her. What about religious matters? You shouldn't argue with her too much, or is about household matters. You shouldn't give her too many orders. If she is in her right mind she will know what she has to do or if she is really a bit strange, then seek to improve her. And remember the words of the Apostle, the wife's flaw will be sanctified by the husband and the husband's flaw will be sanctified by the wife. Oh Brother, do not admit such thoughts that you want to divorce her and then go to America. You will think they don't know anything about that. There I will be a free man. There I can still be an honest man. Brother you are mistaken. There are so many Dutch people here and we know more than you would think. And if you did a thing like this you would disgrace us very much and they would avoid you and say that man is from Holland and he left his wife and children behind. That is a profligate. There is not much to him. And if you do a thing like this you ought not to come to us. But if you come together with your wife and children and behave up to our standards then we'll receive you with pleasure. And I wrote more things like this, but it would be too much to write it all. Thus, I went to J.H. and he added some more words, but with some more consolation. For he considered the letter too harsh. If you write you must let us know from what family that woman came. We have asked W. Wassink who didn't know either. Brother D.W., you wrote in the letter that you wrote to me that you had enclosed another letter in a letter from ten Hennepe who is married to the daughter of the Sijbleskamp, but so far I haven't seen that letter.

Respected Mother, while I have a good opportunity, for G. Lammers returns back to Holland in a fortnight and I know him very well. I'll send you, Mother, a present, not because I think that you need it to alleviate your poverty, but for remembrance sake. Brother D. Willem, thus I will give 2 guilders to your children as a remembrance for her, you can buy whatever you like. I send you 7 dollars, but how many guilders that will yield, I don't know, for here one loses much if one wants to exchange banknotes for gold. I will give it to G. Lammers who can exchange it in New York and then he can deliver it to you in money, gold or silver or whatever. But, if you have received it, you must write me soon how much you received. For then I would like to know how much the difference was.

The winter has been very mild here and we didn't have bitterly cold weather. On 1 April we had some heavy snowfall, that it could be called a good December day. The ground is still covered with ice and snow, in some places still two feet, but still spring is not as early as in your country. It lasts until mid May before the cattle are fully fed with grass. This year's wheat costs half the price of last years. It now costs 95 cents to 1 dollar. Last year's price was over 2 dollars. The plants didn't grow as well as last year for it was very dry. The hay wasn't half as much as last year. Where low lands were concerned, it was extremely good but the high lands were bad. The hay costs between 8 and 9 dollars per thousand pounds. It hasn't been that expensive for a long time. Butter costs 30 cents a pound. Eggs are 8 cents per half a dozen. The horses are very cheap. The oxen are between 100 and 140. The two good dairy cows are between 40 and 45 dollars. The lean pigs are also well priced.

Still another word and that will be the most important one. Janna Ongna became our neighbor eight days ago. She married a man with three children. She is suddenly blessed with three children. She is our next door neighbor. You do know her, don't you? Janna Ongna from the Loderhuisjen. If there are still young girls to be found who would like to find husbands, send them all to us for there is a great lack of single girls.

Here I must end. As far as I know Brother J.H. and his wife enjoy good health. He is going to have a young son or daughter very soon, so you can easily see that America is a fertile country. Now kind regards from us all,

H.J. te Selle

Here is a portrait of our little Dela. She is 11 months now. She is sitting on a chair on her own, but it was difficult to keep her still for such a long time. I went to the post with that letter and then it was too heavy. I'll send that portrait with G. Lammers.

Yet another small note. Mother and brothers, about something my heart could not hold back any longer. I often think of Holland, that old native country, when I reflect how many people there fare and some of my own brothers, as well how they have to work from the early morning until the late evening and then have to be content with a sober meal. I often think, I wish they were here, and I think of myself how three times a day we are capable of filling our tables with as much bacon and meat as we can eat. Oh, how privileged I am compared to many of my brothers. Thank the Lord that he has given me so many possessions on earth, but before I decided to get married I often prayed to the Lord and asked just like David, shall I advance. When I left Holland, brother Jan Hendrik had trice as much as I had but now I have thirty times more than he has, so times can change. On Sunday mornings I can tell the farmhand to harness the horses to the carriage and thus I and my wife sit in the carriage and drive to church. Thus my eyes are often filled with tears when I think how the Lord has blessed me so much.

Town of Holland 12 April

Another small letter and I inform you we are still in good health. Brother Jan Henderik and his wife are still in good health too. He also had a young daughter on 4 April and wife and child are very well and healthy. The little one's name is Dela. Come and visit her soon and receive her regards, and from all of us as well.

H.J. te Selle

When G. Lammers comes to see you he can tell you more than I can write to you.

◆◆◆◆◆◆

Wisconsin to Winterswijk, Netherlands
Harmen Jan te Selle to Derk Willem te Selle   June 1870

Yet it was with spring, very, very nice weather. The land was very dry so that the planting and sowing had a good outlook, also the stand of wheat is pretty good. But the grass is short because it suffered much from the frost and in addition, there was a long time of drought. Then the clay becomes very hard, that it does not have a very good outlook.

As far as the potatoes are concerned, what they will produce I do not know. The year before we were very much plagued by the worms. They ate up everything that was green. And now it is much worse. It seems that they grow up out of the ground and as soon as the potatoes are seen, the worms sit on them in piles, and the worms cannot be compared with anything better than bugs. So we name them after 'plat Gelders' (dialect of Winterswijk), but they are four times as big and have wings. Where the potatoes are, there they go, and do not go away until they have taken everything. Where the price of grain is concerned, that is cheap. Wheat 80 cents to 90 cents a bushel; oats 40/50; rye 70 cents. Potatoes cost almost as much as the wheat, butter 18 cents, eggs 1 cent each.

179

The horses are also cheap, because this winter one could buy a good horse for $100. I bought a three year old for $82, a very beautiful horse. This fall one broke its leg and I had to kill it. Cows are quite costly. For them we have to pay from $40 to $60. Pigs are also cheap, for small ones 36 to 40 cents. We have 7, and when winter comes I will take them to market, then they are much, much higher in price.

Brother Jan Hendrik is no longer here. He went at least 500 miles farther west to the state of Nebraska. There the land is cheap. There they can buy 80 acres for $100, but there there is almost no timber. When they first arrive, they must build a house with sod, or as they say with you, pieces of turf. Wallboards are very costly there, and they have to drive 13 hours to get them. It is an entire wilderness, so they say. But how it goes with Jan Hendrik, I do not know. He sold his land and everything. On March 28 he left. But he has not yet written us a letter. He wrote a letter to his wife's father that he arrived healthy and well, and that the trip cost him $100. Also that the land was wild and hilly and that in places water was hard to get. There was a man who dug a well 100 feet deep and still had no water. Stone coal they could get from four hours away and cost 25 cents a bushel. They use this for fire because there is not enough wood. More have gone there, but I know of two who have returned who did not find things so well there. What it is further, I do not know. They write that there are many rattlesnakes, prairie wolves, etc. More I do not know much about it to write. I expect a letter from them every day, but I don't see one yet. Whether he has written you yet I do not know but he will most likely write you. I do not know how he has it there. Herewith, I must end.

Greetings from Bloemers uncle and aunt. Both are well. Also greetings from the family. Give our greetings to the brothers and all those who ask about us. Greetings from all of us as wife and children.

Yours, Hendrik Jan te Selle

◆◆◆◆◆◆

Town Holland Wisconsin
Harmen Jan te Selle to Dela (ten Damme) te Selle   22 August 1870

Worthy Mother and brothers and wives and children,

Because of the goodness of the Lord I am allowed to write you a letter and to let you know that presently we are all well and healthy. We hope the same for you. The letter that you wrote July 3 we received in good health. From it we noted that all of you are still well, which makes us very happy.

I sent the letter as quickly as possible to brother Jan Hendrik, so he could read the same and note how it is in Holland. But I have not yet received an answer back. I also wrote that in case he had not yet written, that he would not wait so long, but write quickly to you. I have 14 days ago received a letter from him, when he wrote that he was well and healthy which gladdened us very much. He bought land and a yoke of oxen and other items. But I hope that he will write you soon. Then you can note about his welfare from his own pen. But he

180

wrote that it was very dry there so that the grass stood dry and withered on the ground. But with us this is not the case. We have a blessed year, there is almost nothing we can say which is bad. So long as I have been in America I have not seen such a nice stand of crop as this year. Since it has been dry for a time, so the buckwheat and corn need a little rain. One could not wish for a better harvest, no heat to hinder us, no rain to prevent us from working, so that all was dry and quickly gathered in. Those who have threshed say that much, and good seed is produced.

But the wheat is presently cheap. It is hardly a dollar a bushel and that is not very high. If one has a day laborer to work, especially in the harvest, one must pay them a dollar and half day wages. That is 1 ½ bushels of wheat a day. So one can think that for a day laborer in America it is better than in Holland to obtain his daily bread. And for a day laborer, it is better to come here than for a farmer, because there is not much land to rent here and to buy. Land is expensive. So many came here the past year who had expected something else. They thought to get land to own here as they had rented in Holland. And that was disappointing, even though they observe the way of life that there is plenty and enough here. They cannot decide to say America is good, but a day laborer is better at home. He sees there is no difference between the day laborer's bread and the rich farmer, and this is surely true that even a day worker can even so have his bread as well as by working two days a week rather than in Holland 6 days.

Yes, loved ones, what I shall write I have written in the previous letter. I have written much about the price of cattle and grain, and more generally, therefore, I shall not write more. I had on the letter that I wanted to write to Janamoeje Bloemers. His brothers and sisters could have written but I thought I would write to you especially.

I must close with the pen but not with my heart. I, Harmen Jan te Selle and his wife and children, wish you all the Lord's blessing. Give our greetings to all the brothers and all the friends and to those who ask about us. Greetings from us all.

Harmen Jan te Selle
Write us soon again.

◆◆◆◆◆◆

Harmen Jan te Selle to Derk Willem te Selle   22 August 1870

Brother Derk Willem, you have written a letter which I have given a lot of consideration, and yet I have not come to a conclusion to advise you one way or the other. Therefore, I'll leave it to you. Yet I should say that it will not be as worthwhile for you as for your children. But I will put a few things in writing for you. First of all you should realize that the guilders become dollars here and things are no longer as they were when we got here. At that time a lot of gold was mined which is no longer of much value now. One dollar is calculated at 2 guilders fifty cents. Today I think you could get a dollar for two guilders and five or six stivers. Gold is of greater value than the banknotes. Today there is plenty for sale here, but very little for hire. If you can manage to buy forty acres, which would be sufficient for a yoke of oxen or two small horses, you can make a good living. And you can easily work that with one of your little boys and then you won't have to cut so many sods. In this way you could have your other children take on a job, because hired hands earn a lot of money here. There are hands here who earn as much as 120 to 150 dollars a year. Now you may think that they have to work extremely hard, but it is nothing worse than at your place in Holland. Therefore I say that for your children it would be better here. They could become good farmers here in the course of time.

But I should get back to you again Derk Willem. It wouldn't matter very much whether or not you would be able to pay for it all or whether you had a debt of a few hundred dollars. Though I must say that the interest rates are tremendously high: 8 or 9 percent at the lowest, but most of the time as much as 10 percent. So he who has a lot of debt cannot easily get out of it. To have much less than 40 acres here, would make things very difficult. In that case you cannot keep a team of oxen or horses, and with one ox or one horse you cannot work the land here properly.

I suppose you would like to know what such a piece of land would cost here. It varies a lot. At the moment the land is not so expensive as it used to be because the grain was cheap for a couple of years. Today you can buy 40 acres of land for 1400…1600 as much as 2000 dollars. Depending on the wooden buildings that are on it. Nor do I know how it would suit you in those new areas where Jan Hendrik lives. The land over there is quite cheap. Some say the land is very good there whereas others say it would not suit us there. I don't know what it is like there; up to now I have had only one letter from Jan Hendrik and he has not written much about it. I have been expecting a letter for quite some time now but so far I have not received a single one. I myself have written as many as two letters to him, but I haven't had a reply to either of them. He is in good health for sure because that is what someone has written who went there last fall. But he is not much of a writer and that's that.

Yes loved ones, what more shall I write you. I have written you earlier what it would cost to settle here, so I don't think it necessary to repeat this once again. Dear brother, I don't know what more I should write you about this. I have written as much about it as I could. Therefore, brother judge for yourself what you should do about it. You won't have to eat black bread. I haven't seen that again. Well, this should do. Have the kindest regards from us all.

Harmen Jan te Selle

◆◆◆◆◆◆

[Johanna Scholten was the wife of Abraham Heinen.]

Gibbsville, Wisconsin to Aalten, Gelderland   22 January 1892
Johanna Heinen to relatives

Dear friends, brothers, sisters and children,

I take up the pen in order to write you a letter. I must make know to you of our regret and deep sorrow that your brother, my husband Abram Heinen, passed away January 9, 1892. I cannot describe to you how heavy this loss is, but what shall we say or what shall we speak. The Lord reigns and He does not explain what he is doing. He was not feeling well for about a year. But he always went to church and everywhere else. He stayed home only 4 weeks. He was not in bed for a long time and was not in pain and did not suffer much but he had to vomit a great deal. He had a stomach disorder and how hard this loss struck me and the children. But we don't have to mourn as if we have no hope because he could himself testify that he was going to Jesus where it is better than here. And he persevered to the end and so the minister chose the text, "Be faithful unto death and I will give you the crown of life." And so I hope that the Lord will give all of us strength so that we can carry the cross that he has laid upon us with patience and that we may follow in his footsteps. In order that when our time is here that we also may be found ready. Then shall the dead have no King to make arrangements but just a messenger of peace." How true that we are parted for a moment then we shall be united again where there will be no sickness, no pain or no more sorrow. But all tears will be wiped away from our eyes. That is my wish and prayer. The funeral service was held in the church which was very full. I ask you to announce this news to all the friends and relatives we know. More I do not know what to write. Write soon and write if you did not receive the other letters that we sent to Hendrik Jan Rensink. In it we put 2 daalders (1.50 Dutch guilders) for a little suit for the little boy. Here I stop with the pen but not with the heart.

Greetings from all of us and those whom I have mentioned.

Johanna (Scholten) Heinen

◆◆◆◆◆

[Jan Cevaal was born 18 October 1886 in Middelburg, Zeeland to Jan and Cornelia (Vos) Cevaal. He died 18 October 1951 in Oostburg, WI. On 3 March 1921 in Sheboygan, WI he married Mary Vander Puy. On 27 April 1909, Jan arrived alone in New York with $15 in his pocket. A year later he had saved enough money for his sister Pieternella to emigrate. On 10 April 1911, Jan's father Jan (b. 28 March 1862 in Ritthem, Zeeland) and his stepmother, Johanna Bosselaar and their five children arrived in New York. Their voyage was also paid for by Jan. These letters chronicle many trials and triumphs by this family. These letters are from the Dutch Immigrant Letters Collection, Archives, Calvin College, Grand Rapids, MI, Box 12, Folders 18-20.]

Middelburg, Zeeland to Sheboygan, Wisconsin   9 July 1909
Abraham Cevaal to Jan Cevaal

Dear brother,

Your letter we have received in good circumstances and notes that you were still in good
health. I can inform you that we are also in good health. Since in your letter you had asked
how I was doing with my work at the factory lately, I will tell you. I was dismissed the 28th
of June with another man. All those men you don't know anyway because they came while
you were gone. One of them, Lindenberg, has also been dismissed, but all the others
remained; those old fellows. But Lindenberg was angry that he was fired since he had not
figured on that. Otherwise, it has been busy, with night work and even on Sundays, which I
have never done. On June 25 he left with the Frisna from Amsterdam, but he was not at all
ready. The painters all went along to Amsterdam and the porters, also Bosselaar, also Piet
Moes and Daane. All had to go along. Therefore Lindenberg was so angry. There were
some 40 painters from Amsterdam also to help, and so you can understand what a mess it
was. If you had been here you could perhaps have gone along also, for you were in good
standing with boss den Houdt. Greetings to you from everyone especially from Boeresie and
from Peene. He, Boeresie, did not go along to Amsterdam for he is not yet entirely well.
Therefore he desired rather to remain here, and the boss had told him that he anyhow still has
rations. It's still the same here in regard to work – slack, as always. Last week yet I helped
unload a lumber barge. Koo Coslijn was also with that. But that is hard work, and my
shoulders were opened because of it. Now this week I am working at de Pauw in his hay
barn at the Loskade, but that is also just a couple days. So it is again simply a struggle, and it
is in the middle of the summer at that.

It was really strange at first when you left. We questioned occasionally how you were
making out. But God made everything work out for good before we could give him thanks
for it. It was actually much better than you expected – you are getting so quickly
accustomed. I too am pleased that things are so much to your liking. With the election it has
been a busy time. You could not have heard the result, but it went well with the right side
getting the majority. Bechts 60, Lucks 40. Here in Middelburg, Blum was chosen.

Johannes has not yet said anything to father about having to get married. He comes home
evenings, sits down, and says almost nothing. Father has already asked what the trouble is
that he says nothing, but he just will not say it. Now, the 24th of July he will be discharged
from the service and then he will have to speak up, for Kuurt would like for him to get
another woman the following week. For Mina is already home two weeks and she will not
be in a good attitude because she has to eat and doesn't earn anything for that.

Rev. Letthuis died last week. I haven't yet seen A. van Slings for he has often been sick, but
is now improving. C. de Boer lately is keeping company with Wilhelmina of Uncle Piet.
The house of Zevenhuis must also be sold. Just so we can now remain in it. Did you get my
picture card? Father is also on it, but you perhaps couldn't recognize him. Now I must bring

this to an end, because it is full. I hope you may receive this in good health and that the Lord will continue to be with you. Further, greetings from us all and from your brother,

A. Cevaal

Give my greetings also to the family Kaat. Father would like to know whether you read De Zeewe?

◆◆◆◆◆◆

Jan Cevaal to Jan Cevaal
Middelburg, Zeeland to Wisconsin   8 September 1909

Dear Son and brother,

We were very pleased to receive a letter from you again, and to gather from it that you are still well and healthy. When people are so far apart so much can happen before anything is know about it. For, as you also wrote, there is just one step between us and death. May our constant prayer be, Lord teach us to number our days that we may get a heart of wisdom.

Now I shall write you some things about the family circle. Abraham is not home. Since September 7 and for 25 days he is with the armed services. Recently he worked on the city septic tank and Johannes also. That was hard work, that pushing a wheel barrow from 5 o'clock in the morning, but now that is finished for a new river well is being constructed at Vlissingen, and now the water is so low that a loaded ship can't come into the area. They earn good money. At present Johannes is working for Cornelisse at Heersche Way for 7 gulden a week.

Now I must write you something about Pietje (Pieternella) that will also give you pain. Shortly after you left for America, when I came out of church on a Sunday evening, Jan Volmers spoke to me and said that Pietje always had us believe that she walked with Pietje Volmers, but, he said, that was not true for she walked with a Corporal, a Bimmel from Domburg. It so happened that the Thursday evening before Pietje had asked whether she could go to Volmers because her girlfriend had a birthday. But there was nothing to that – she always walked with Bimmel. Then a little later, one evening after 10 o'clock while we were lying in bed, she went away leaving the doors standing open. During the night Coor woke and when your mother went to look, Pietje was not in bed. You can imagine how frightened we were, not knowing what to think. Then Abram and I went out hunting for her and came to the market. There stood two policemen of whom I asked whether they had seen them, and they had. In the meanwhile Abram had gone into the market and saw Bimmel run into the Noordstraat. He called to him, but he ran on saying that he had to be inside at 12 o'clock. When we came home Pietje was also home. They had come through Herspel. I spoke to her about how wrong her behavior was, but it didn't help one bit. Abram also talked to her a number of times, but she told him, "What have you to do with this? I have to know this for myself." When on Sundays we would go to church we would leave Cornelis with her, otherwise that Corporal would go to her. But then she left Cornelis and Maartje alone and she went walking. Two weeks ago we went to the beach at Vlissingen while Pietje and Cornelis were to wait at home. But when Cornelis came from school, everything was locked up and she had spent the entire afternoon walking the streets of the town in costume clothing that she had borrowed from M. Klap. It has happened that we thought she had gone to church, but she went walking. She wouldn't work anymore. She only wanted to be a maid servant.

I have struggled with this so long, that finally I gave in, because that wasn't any life anymore. Had not the Lord protested, accident would have happened, for often it was too much to bear. Saturday, the 4th of September she left and now lives at Cohen on Segeerstraat. You can well understand how hard it is to see her go against all warnings and choose to go the wrong way. Continually there ascends a prayer from my heart: "O Lord! Keep her upright on her way."

There, dear son you have the problem with your very beloved sister. O, if the Lord has heard your prayers, then don't give up praying for her. Who knows but that the Lord may be gracious to her. I could write much more about this but I must leave it at this. We have an unsettled and wet summer. There still is much in the fields.

◆◆◆◆◆◆

Jan Cevaal to Jan Cevaal
Middelburg, Zeeland to Wisconsin   November 1909

Dear son,

Your letter we have received in good health and from it have noted that you also are well. We're always curious as it becomes time for another letter. You wrote that Pietje had better wait until spring. I had also told her that, but she thought that she could come right away. We'll just wait until spring, if the Lord spares our lives. You mentioned that this summer you would be going to work in the city, but I thought that the factory where you now work is in the city. You must write about that because I had wondered whether there would be a street car to use, or whether you would go with your bicycle. We thought you were an hour from your work.

You wrote about getting married and starting a business, so we wondered – has Jan been keeping company with someone that he speaks of getting married soon? We have often talked about going to America, but that isn't so easy with such a family, very much is needed. Then when we read your letters we say not and then – I wish that we also were there because with us it remains nothing but struggle. You asked whether we had given Grandfather anything for his birthday. We did not because one doesn't know what to give him. That advertisement that your Uncle Arie placed in the Zeeuwse (newspaper) I found to be ridiculous. It's just as though he is his father alone and that he doesn't have any other family. You asked if he is quite satisfied at Arie's. That's going very well. Everyone is good to him. Your Uncle now prays and gives thanks with the meals and Willem also. Grandfather can do as he wills. Arie has restored the Bible in which he always reads. As to his service to God, then I am somewhat concerned that he finds peace too much within himself. It is not easy to be saved by grace. We always want to be saved by works. We always want to try to make ourselves better. And so I fear that he has not learned to see himself as a poor sinner. And to that we must come. As long as we still think that we can do a little from or of ourselves, then we place ourselves as obstacles in the way.

Today I spoke with Breel, but nothing will come of their going to American for he hasn't any money for the trip and his son is in the service for 6 years, at school at Schoonhoven. The house and barn has not been disappointing, but I had not estimated as high as you had. I still have some good news to share with you. Saturday, October 30, I received notice that I could receive 19.60 gulden at the post office from the Rijks-Insurance Bank. I don't understand this at all because I had had a letter from Utrecht that your health and surgical treatment had been certified and that for the rest nothing was receivable. So you must write what I should do with that money. If it's all right with you I'd like to keep it a while. Today I needed 3.75 gulden for the Zeeuwse. Pietje will now be a house servant at Meeuw on the wharf. Greetings from C. Vermeulen and Mideavine who work for Albers. Willem Goverse received a postcard from you, but he doesn't know your address, and expects a letter from you.

Now I'll close. We hope that you may receive this in good health, and that the Lord may spare you on all your ways. We are all well, and the family also. Abraham of your Uncle Willem is already back from America. He was a fireman on a petroleum boat. Now he wants a trip to W. India. Further, from all of us, hearty greetings.

Your parents, brothers, sisters,
J. Cevaal

Middelburg, Zeeland to Sheboygan, Wisconsin   30 May 1910

Dear Son and daughter,

We have received your letter and have noted that you both are still in good health. We also are all in good health and to our great joy we can announce that Saturday evening the Lord delighted us with the birth of a well developed daughter whom we've named Catrina. So far the Lord has made all things well, and again testified that he has no desire for our death and destruction but that we should be converted and might live and have a heart that gives thanks to his name. It's been a very strenuous time – we had to recover a daughter, but it's going very well now considering the circumstances, and with the child also.

We noticed that you have a new position. We congratulate you with it and hope it will go well for you. A letter came from Pietje; we had waited a long time for one. The money also came. Thank you and to Pietje also. It has come at a good time. The negotiations are going some better. Cornelis delivers radishes and black radishes every day and this earns a little, and every little bit helps.

Rev. Wagenaar spoke to Cornelis at catechism and said that he had received a beautiful letter from you, that he didn't know whether he could write as well as you. He really was pleased with it. He said that Schout had also received a letter from you. You asked about Putte; what he was going to do. He will work in the garden where he has farmed. It has been sold, for he had a debt of 3000 gulden. Abram lives on Spanjaard Street. He now works for Snoep, earning at least 8 gulden a week and if he satisfies he'll get 9 gulden, and he still has deterioration. Willem Polderman lost his life in a fatal accident. He was working with a disc harrow and had the horse of Nypjes nearest and in turning, the horse came out of the traces. Then as he tried to loosen the trace he got a kick in the head which almost instantly killed him. Uncle Arnout was also taken suddenly. Thursday he had been in town and Tuesday he died.

With our vegetables we are much ahead of America. The 29th of May, van Soelen had new potatoes at the auction. We've had beautiful weather the last half of May. The son of Lange has also gone to America. He was in the butcher business for himself at the Bree. He had loaned 300 gulden from Mr. de Heer for starting the business, 100 gulden from Marin Sanderse, and 100 gulden from a notary for which his father is guarantor, and also 30 gulden from his sister. He sold his home furniture for 50 gulden. He went through that all and with his wife from Sjsseren, she is a Smit, went to America – otherwise he would have gone bankrupt.

With Schout also we had a sad experience of "Patrimonium." Two delegates had to be chosen to attend the society gathering at Utrecht. There were 22 members. With the first voting M. Sanderse had 12 votes, so he was elected, but of the others no one had a majority. So another vote between Schout and Wondergem. Then Schout read 12 names for himself and 10 for Wondergem. After the election Schout had to leave, so Vander Kuip functioned as chairman. We had a few matters to deal with in regard to the Society gathering, and then as our meeting was ending, it appeared that Schout had taken all the ballots with him, something that never happens. This aroused our suspicion, and by investigation it was revealed that Wondergem had received 14 votes. At first he (Schout) would not make an admission, but when he saw that he couldn't get out of it, he acknowledged that he had bungled. Hence he would have to resign as chairman.

Abram sent 4 cards at the same time to you; one for you, one for your girlfriend, one for Pietje, and one for Kat. We can't imagine why you didn't get them. Be so kind and let Pietje also read this letter, or share it with her, and ask her also to write. Johannes doesn't yet have steady work, but he does have some work. Now I end this in the hope that you may receive this in good health and that the Lord may bless you on all your ways. Greetings from us all.

Jan Cevaal

Is Pietje still a house maid or is she in a factory?

◆◆◆◆◆◆

Middelburg, Zeeland to Sheboygan, Wisconsin   13 September 1910

Dear Son and brother,

We received your letter with picture and card in good health and from it realize that you both are also well. You look good on the picture. It seems as though you have still grown for you look so tall. We had to laugh about your plowing. I thought – wouldn't there be someone to teach him? For if in a four sided field one gets a difference of two rods, there is really something wrong, which surely could have been seen earlier. Tying the reins around your body is dangerous and I would not do it. We thought it strange that you are no longer courting. We had not expected that.

You asked if we are still thinking of going to America. We think of that all right, but it is not likely we can do that from Uncle's inheritance. For there are so many things that must be done, as the notary and estate duties. We don't know yet how much we have. Such things always take so long. Your Uncle Piet also won't be able to pay some on his new home from it. There won't be that much. He couldn't do much good with his house because it was too low. So he can't improve it by sections and therefore must do it all at once.

I'll ask your Grandfather whether he has a sermon book for you otherwise I can try the market. Jan van Wallenberg has died in an ill fated manner. In connection with the Queen's Festival he was on his way home in the evening, along with two other men and their girlfriends. They had a bottle of drink with them from which they were all to drink. Then three soldiers approached them and asked to join in the drinking. When this was denied there followed a sharp exchange of words, resulting in one of the soldiers drawing his bayonet and plunging it into van Wallenberg so that he immediately died. Abram says that you know him. His mother is a widow. It is frightening so suddenly to be in eternity. Well, may it be our daily prayer that we always are ready, for we are in danger every moment. David said there is but one step between us and death, and so it is with each of us.

Rev. Wagenaar is declining more and more, decreasing in body and spirit. He can't think clearly. Humanly speaking, he can't improve anymore, but the Lord has power for all things. How is with your potatoes? Do they come out with a machine or by hand? Potatoes are getting expensive here. For good ones you pay 3 gulden. I fear we'll have a bad winter, for if potatoes are so expensive then more bread is eaten and vegetable not needed. How is it by you with the growing of vegetables, such as carrots and red cabbage and beans, etc.?

When you go to church do you go to Sheboygan or is there also a church where you are? And is that a town or a village? How often is the land plowed for winter, and don't they grow wheat? Pouf Wattle is crippled. He has been in the hospital a long time. He had injured his hip and now walks with two crutches. Kop Lange works on a ship in Rotterdam. He had an accident and has not worked for some six weeks.

You wrote that Pietje would be so glad to be able to look around in Middelburg, but it is still the same and has not changed. She would not have it as good in Middelburg as in Sheboygan. Nothing more that is special to write about. We are all in good health and we hope that you may receive this in good health and that the Lord may protect you from all evil. Greetings to Pietje. Now then, greetings from your loving parents, brothers and sisters,

Jan Cevaal

◆◆◆◆◆◆

Middelburg, Zeeland   6 October 1910

Dear brother,

With this I would inform you that we are in good health and we hope this is so with you also. I've taken the pen to jot down some words. I received your letter and picture. It's a good portrait of you. In your letter you asked how much Father inherited from Uncle Arnout. But I don't know that, for that is not told to me, and I don't ask about it.

We also had some pictures made of Keetje and have put two of them into the letter, one for you and one also for Pietje. If you would give it to Pietje then I'll add a small letter otherwise it costs so much. You wrote about getting news, but I don't know much news having already written everything. You already know that Willem Barentsen is married, and that Cris de Boks is going to marry Wilhelmina of Uncle Piet Cevaal. Also a necessity. Keetje is also doing well. Ariel we had photographed when she had her birthday. So you had better think it over, for you only have one. From Uncle Arie she got nice shoes, and from us beads with a little container. Further, you can see for yourself when you come to Holland.

In regard to working conditions, I think I'll have work all winter in the gasworks where I also worked last winter. There one earns about 10 gulden a week with free fuel. When you receive my letter let me know that right away. More news I don't have and I hope you may receive this in good health and that God may spare you from calamities and misfortunes. Greet Pietje for I don't have any more time to send along a little letter to her. Also, greetings from you brother, J. Cevaal and wife and child. Congratulations on your birthday. We hope you may have many more such days and that we for a long time may be witnesses of that.

Johannes Cevaal

◆◆◆◆◆◆

Middelburg, Zeeland   31 October 1910

Dear friend,

Friday, October 21, we received your letter and picture. For that I first want to thank you, for that pleased us very much. I would have answered you earlier, but early last week I had some trouble in my right hand making it impossible to use. Now it goes quite well, but likely it will cause some strange twist in my writing. However, just so you can read it. It is really much better. The doctor said it was rheumatism. I had planned to write you for we must bring the sad news that on Saturday, the afternoon of October 15, about 3 o'clock Mother suddenly died of heart failure or spasm. We did not see her alive again. She died in her chair. Fortunately, her brother had just come in and Neal had not yet gone away, for as you know Gerrit's wife always worked there. She was also shocked. Cornelis had not seen Mother since Sunday, and I not since the week before when she seemed very healthy, but was always short of breath, showing some trouble with her heart – but who knew that? About 11 o'clock she acquired some pain in her head, neck and chest. But she walked yet until after midday dragging many things around. However, she didn't want anything to eat, although she did drink three cups of tea after midday along with two rusks. When Uncle Jan came about three o'clock she told him that there was something spasmodic in her head. She was sitting in Father's old captain's chair and all at once she threw her head back, made a throat sound, and was gone. What a plight, Jan, of which we knew nothing, and Mother dead. They came for us but didn't tell us that she had died. Just think that through because I can't describe it. I was deeply shocked and in those first days extremely nervous. I knew that all that does somehow draw together in my hand, but one must again go through it. There in that sound "go forward, everything must have its place again." And thus we came on top again during those difficult days, or better said, we were gently led through them.

Rev. Wagenaar died the morning of Mother's funeral day. He lay for two weeks, I believe, and was in much distress and was mostly unconscious due to the brain disease from which he suffered, along with other sicknesses. His wife will greatly miss him too for she is now all alone. Yes, it is as Job says, man born of a woman, is of few days and tired of unrest. Jan, you wrote about Jans. I expect her one of these days, for she wrote in a letter about the death of Mother, that she would come, for she was deeply touched. She has a one year old girl who is very delicate. I seldom see her.

It gives us much pleasure that you have it so good in a strange land; that compensates somewhat. And if you may remain healthy then you can bring something here, but you know what I wrote in a former letter. I am after all a weakling who weeps at all the flesh pots. Far in the south, lies my Spain; I do try to understand that. I believe that if I got my down hearted moments, I would try to get to the highest peak of a tower, that in the swaying of earth and heaven to seek the direction of my country, to send be blindly to my acquaintance, to everything I leave behind. But fortunately not everyone is as I, an emotional person, for then everyone would die of homesickness. But you surely will come here some time again. I hope that you may come again to talk, and that we may once again meet in good health.

What a beautiful summer we've had here. It's been nothing but dry, yet nice weather. It is a bit unnatural – sometimes it's warm and the fruit is disappointing, due likely to the previous wet year. As yet I have not received anything from my brother. I don't like that at all of him. You can understand that I don't write him again, since I definitely notice that he doesn't care at all for us. He will have to give account for that. He has a different character trait than I. My lord is again already some four weeks on a journey. We hear nothing from him. He doesn't even know about Mother's death. I'll give him your greeting and thanks when he comes home.

I don't have much news at present; at least nothing exceptional. You ask about a soldier who committed a murder. He is a Dieleman from Zaamslag, a first class fighter. Today I heard that the club to which he belongs has gone to Den Haag and he is in prison in Den Haag for the court martial. Now, has he confessed? Everything is so secret, one hears so little. So Jan, if all is well – until the next writing. My hand is getting tired. If I come across a nice card I'll send it. Best wishes from us all and hearty greetings.

Your courtship is over, in the American way.

J. Cevaal

◆◆◆◆◆◆

Middelburg, Zeeland   10 November 1910

Dear Son,

We've received your letter in good circumstances and not that you are well also. That Rev. Wagenaar has died, you doubtless have learned. I wanted to write you, but thought that you would know of it just as quickly through "De Zeeuw." Widow Blok has also died suddenly on October 15. At the grave side of Rev. Wagenaar there were many speeches. You perhaps read about that in the church paper that Abram sent you. Almost every Sunday we have a minister, but I don't think that will stay that way. We'll likely have to do without some time,

In your letter you did some figuring, but I don't believe we'll make that much from our household goods if we take our bed and other things with us, for that way the best is removed. And my business, I don't expect that many will run to it. It is easy to make an estimate but I have fears about making it. Are the living quarters by themselves, or are there neighbors?

Did you get the picture of Cornelis? You didn't say. Your Grandfather Cevaal is getting some weaker. He has to cough a lot. That is getting better, but he hardly makes any improvement. I have not asked him for any book. They are not so expensive. This cost 60 cents, if you consider the commission, the cost is 1.50 gulden. We've had a nice fall, but in the last days we've had much wind and storms. How does it go with your plowing? Have you learned quite a bit, or not?

With this I will end and hope that you may receive this in well being and that the Lord may lead you in all your ways. As far as I know all the family members are well. Now, greetings from your loving parents, brothers and sisters.

Jan Cevaal

◆◆◆◆◆◆

Middelburg, Zeeland   23 February 1911

Dear Son and brother,

We have received your letter in well being, and have noted that you're both in good health. I have delayed writing for I was waiting for a letter from Bakker. He's been here twice asking about it, but each time I have to tell him there is no letter for him. We were disappointed after reading your letter. We thought we would learn something about our trip but that was disappointing. Lately so many people are going to America that it is hard to get a reservation on a ship. All reservations are filled until mid April. So I think that it will be well into June before we can come, for we can't request a place before we have a ticket, and by that time Cornelis will be 12 years old and Kaatje one year; which means one person more and will cost 150 guilden more, I think. Therefore we would like it if you could send us a ticket as soon as possible. As long as we don't have that we can't make a firm commitment. It would be a shame if we had to pay so much more. I don't really know how that would go if the ticket were purchased and we had to wait so long due to lack of space. You've written about buying reed baskets but I think they would cost quite a bit. I have placed my vegetable business in "De Zeeuw," but there is no desire for it. They at Dhui have asked once or three times, how things are going with "De Zeeuw" and I've asked you already, but as yet I have not received an answer. So I've had to reply each time that I didn't know.

W. Huibregtse from Kort Noord Street is also going to America and the son of Alewijn Pramse and Jan de Jong and Wattze and another of Louwerse of Vlissingse way, and Jan Sturn in also in Sheboygan. So there is currently quite a bit of desire for America. We'll be happy when we're once on the way. Here there is nothing to earn. Last year I could do some spade work in the afternoons, but this winter we have not had any frost and after New Year very little rain, so they do that all themselves.

We have not called a minister yet. They are not in a hurry, for they want good knowledge first; for as they say, we can better be embarrassed for lack of a minister than embarrassed with a minister. Jan Sturn has written his brother asking him to buy two silver watches so that I could take them with me. But wouldn't there be some import duty to pay? Jan Sturn is now a farmhand, according to his sister, and earns 30 dollars a month. Thank you for your newspapers. Those people really had to endure a lot. If it were still that way I'd rather stay in the Netherlands, even if conditions were bad. With Abram and Johannes all is well. Abram and Sien are living in happy expectation. He has much regret that we go away. But that can't be changed. We can't stay here if we like to improve ourselves. Don't write anything about this to him. Maybe he will write about that himself. I don't know of anything more to write. We hope you are well when you receive this, that the Lord may spare you from all evil, and that it may please him to bring us to you in good circumstances. Greetings from your loving parents, brothers and sisters. Also greetings from Pietje.

                                                                    Jan Cevaal

Middelburg, Zeeland   August 1912

Dear Brother,

With this we would let you know that we are well, and we hope that is so with you also. I've taken my pen in hand in order to write you a few things. From your letter we note that all is well with you. You said that I should also write, but I don't always know what I should write, for if there is news, you can read that in "De Zeeuw." Working conditions are quite good for once. Up to the present I'm still working at the gas works, and with the approach of winter it gets even busier. Otherwise, it's quite slack with work in Middelburg, and not earning anything is for the birds. There should be some work not since the electric power is coming and that means there must be some digging done.

Some 3 months ago I moved and do not live in that house next to us. In that, I have more in the rear, a room and a kitchen, making for pleasant living. Behind the house is a pear tree, and then in my days off I have built a chicken coop. At the gas works one gets a leave every 6 days with the retention of salary. Then I bought two brooding hens, one from Uncle Piet and one from Kees Sturn, but I didn't work that out very well, because I have so many roosters too. I think if I once have 3 chickens that will be enough. Then I also have 2 rabbits, but recently one of them died. It weighed some 4 kilo. So that didn't work out either. Oh well, things can't always go favorably for always prosperity is not good.

You asked whether we were not yet thinking about going to you. However right now I have no desire, for whether sometime in my life I shall do that I don't know as yet, but not now. I know of nothing more to write than that Keetje is growing well and is a big girl and a lovely child. Everyone remarks about that. When you get this letter, then write back whether it came over all right, and write how it went with the death of Grandfather, whether it went better than expected. I hope this finds you well, and that the Lord may spare you from calamities and misfortunes. From us all, hearty greetings.

He who is named, Johannes Cevaal and wife and child

◆◆◆◆◆◆

Middelburg, Zeeland   19 July 1914

Dear Brother,

With this we let you know we are all well and that we hope the same may apply to you. I've received your letter in good circumstances and have noted that all is well with you. Last week the minister of War sent me a request for compensation. Whether I'll get anything I don't know, but we'll hope for the best. Next month, I must again be in the service, if I may live. You asked about working conditions. Well, that is only so so, for at present it is not busy. I've been in Vlissingen some 7 days working in the cabbages. But we shall hope that it will become busier. It's a difficult time for me to be in the service, that is just when it became busier with the cabbages and elsewhere. You wrote that I should give you much news, but I don't know any news except that Areel is married again, and that a girl of Uncle Willem married a widower who is 37 years old. Katje was only 18 years old, but not much was said about that. She worked there and had to get married, but we know of this only from an outsider.

Our Keetje hasn't been well either. Her face was full of pimples, something glandular, but now she is much better. Also she had pain in her ear. We had the doctor for her, and he gave us something to use as drops for the ear.

Last week we had a nice rain which was needed. Still the produce in general looks good. You wrote about the independence festival of May 5. That really must have been worthwhile to see. That was just like something which we had once with those suppressors, and yet much more. This summer we have even a world's fair, so if you have money you could very well benefit from it.

In May Keetje started school. She must be 5 years old in September, if she lives, and then she can just get used to it when the coming year she goes to the large school. This past week Grandfather Vos was hit again when on the way with a wagon load of baskets for the auction place. But he didn't hurt himself very much, nothing but his hand. He is always so pleased if one of us goes to him, for when you then go away he pinches your hand in a firm grip. He also likes Keetje very much. When it is New Year we always go to him, then Aunt Mietje tries to place a dime in his hand, but he says, "No, for Keetje, a quarter." Then she (Mietje) looks so stern. When it's Keetje's birthday, he always comes, for that he clearly remembers. He would surely be happy if he could still see you, but that will likely not be here.

With that I will end this, for I have written quite a bit – this paper is quite wide – in the hope that you may receive these writings in good health, and that the Lord may protect you from illnesses and all calamities. Further, hearty greetings from him who calls himself,

Johannes Cevaal, wife and child

Give greetings at home too and tell them that all is well with us.

◆◆◆◆◆◆

Abraham Cevaal to Jan Cevaal   17 October 1909
Middelburg, Zeeland to Sheboygan, Wisconsin

With this I would let you know that I have received both of your postcards. Therefore I have also taken up the pen in my hand to write you, and to inform you that I still am active and healthy. And I wish the same for you, that the Lord may spare you for a long time; also the people with whom you associate, for it's a great joy for us that they are so good for you.

You have been gone quite a while. The time does go by so quickly. And now you have written that you wonder when we will come this year yet. However, I am committed until May of next year, and hence I just can't walk away from that. Besides, my father and mother are so opposed, as well as my entire family, so it is not an easy thing for me, Jan, and then there's the need of money to travel as a family. It was different with you, for you were entirely alone. For us it is required immediately to have a house, and for it so very many things, along with my own responsibilities. I just see so many difficulties. However, it's still a long time and much can happen. Perhaps changing the situation, indicating that it would be to our advantage.

What do you think of it, Jan? You'd better write us exactly how things are. For you it really would be pleasant if we would come. Here it really remains poor – when one becomes old it's the same. But there is some hope that if one may stay healthy, he will have saved up something. That is appealing. So, Jan, think about it, and tell us just as it is. For myself, I'd be ready if father and mother were not so opposed to it. Are family expenses high, or are they reasonable. This is what bothers me the most. If we go to you would we be satisfied? Is life quite pleasant by you? How much do you earn per week? You, doubtless, can save some because you always were thrifty. Yes, Jan, I've always been sorry that I didn't' give you something, for Pietje had once said that you would gladly have had a gold ring. But I didn't know that before you left. Then they said that I could send it to you. But Abram said, "Don't do that." However I promise you Jan that if we may remain healthy and I have permission from Father and Mother to come, then we'll take one along for you. For I do get a bit of a desire to go. No one says that one must always remain. I can still go home and also write to my family. Jan, you should write a little somewhat like that. Then they at home could read it, Jan, and perhaps believe it.

My congratulations to you on becoming an uncle. They did not celebrate long. I was there recently and they are all well. They have really just a very small house, but they are well married. In reality, it was not a pleasant day when they were married, Jan. You mentioned that yourself, for there was so much lacking. I didn't feel at all good about it. Now a bit of time has gone by and maybe they can learn a little, for as to that girl, it is really sin. Now she goes to you full of pleasantness, but Jan, you can give them some money and that may not be such a large amount, but be careful, hear Jan. Now I'd better quit.

You better not look at the photos, if you have received our postcards. And now I again congratulate you on your birthday. May the Lord grant you many returns of the day, and I hope, with all health and love, so that again the following year if you have another birthday, I may express myself with the mouth rather than with a piece of paper. Further I wish for you, Jan, the best of health. Greetings to the family. Goodbye Jan, 'til we see each other.

Greetings from Abram

◆◆◆◆◆◆

Abraham Cevaal to Jan Cevaal
Middelburg, Zeeland to Sheboygan, Wisconsin   18 January 1913

Dear brother,

You will be glad to hear something from us. It's again been a long time since I have written you, but you likely have sometimes read a letter from us. We are, fortunately, all in good health, and hope that the same applies to you. I have received your letter and also the one of October. I had sent you a card for your birthday, but I got it back. We also received a card from Pietje, but still nothing from Father.

At present we have winter here. Last week it snowed a lot. For us that is very difficult if you must push a cart. You know about that somewhat from the last winter you were here in Holland. Father did write once that you don't see handcarts in America, so it's quite different from here.

It's almost four years that you are away. How quickly the time flies by. Don't you sometimes think about coming again to Holland? I have talked about that with Johannes, but he doesn't have any desire to come. Most people here cast it aside if you talk to them about it (going to America) by saying, "One has his bread here also." However, I don't desire to go to America in order to get rich, but it would be so pleasant if we could all be together, especially not that everything is going well for Father, for here there was much adversity for him. How I'd like to see him yet on his small farm.

With Grandfather, it's getting to the end, I feel. He isn't so sick that he is bed, but it's something from which he can no longer experience improvement, I think. The trouble is with his feet, which have open sores. It can, perhaps, last quite a while.

In regard to work here, it is not busy. In De Schelde at present there is much work. There you would see quite a change were you to come. It has grown considerably. They are going to build a 600 foot ship – so much has the hold been enlarged. Have you ever had a letter from Brois den Hondt? I must give you the greeting of Willem Holdemine. We have also received your card. You're becoming a first class horse keeper. Looking at the card I can see that they're good runners. You must surely ride with them. Received a letter also from Father. It came after I began writing this. Nothing special to share. I hope that you may receive this in good circumstances. Also, greetings from Father at home. Greetings from all of us,

                                                                                A. Cevaal

♦♦♦♦♦♦

Middelburg, Zeeland to U.S.A.   10 August 1909
Pieternella Cevaal to brother

Dear brother,

Through this letter I am letting you know that all of us are in good health and I hope for you the same. And also through this letter my hearty thanks for the gift that I have received from you. I have chosen a pretty watch with a chain with it, and I am very happy with it. My Maljers came with three and I picked out the cheapest because the other kinds were not much better.

John was married July 30, but the weather was not nice because it rained the whole afternoon. March was just two years then. If you ask, "Where is John?" then she says, "in America." She says everything and has changed, but is still the same lovely curly head. John has a house in Smoorsgang where the Mr. Putte has lived, who is dead and now he is moving in today. He worked by Cornelius after coming out of the army and working on the city hall and he is finished there now.

Abraham has lately written a letter to you and now I must ask you if you have received that already. Now I have to inquire once concerning the maid who served at Dr. Verheiden. She has gone to Yerseke and in mid-August she is going to be married. You must not think about this. You better see that you get an American lady. If you per chance write, then you must write whether you received "Trouw" regularly and whether you read the *Spiegel* completely. If you perchance want the *Spiegel* then you must write. I have saved all of them. I do not know of much news out of Middelburg except that Rev. Littoor and van Driest of Lanervel have died. But you perhaps know this already.

When John is married there will be a celebration by us as Knuyt has such a small house and we have a lot of room. We shall not celebrate in it much more as it has been sold and we will have to move this year. Mr. Hoorkamp is coming to live in it and a bakery is started in the garden. I have received your letter and we wish that your hope may be fulfilled that we may congratulate each other personally. If we cannot get a house we shall come to you.

Grandfather John Vos is not very good. He has a very heavy cold. And if you should write a letter than you must first let it dry as we have not had a letter without a blot. Now you have asked concerning a postcard and I have not written many letters. And what I have written first I should written last. But you must not look at it so narrow as then you cannot hold it any more. As I have written I must give you the greeting of Johanna France. At present she does not have it according to her desire as she so much wishes to be a housekeeper, but she cannot get anything like that. Pietje Volmer greets you also and many more acquaintances also and also others of whom I cannot write.

Now I shall end the writing because I have no more news. Again hearty greetings from everyone and greet also the family Kaat for us.

Your loving sister,
Pieternella Cevaal

♦♦♦♦♦♦

Middelburg, Zeeland to U.S.A.   24 October 1909
Pieternella Cevaal to brother

Dear brother,

I received your letter and Jan, I regret it deeply that I did it. But if I stay here I cannot avoid doing it. I read that I cannot come sooner than 2 years from now. This is a very big disappointment. I went to serve at Broekert's and I am employed there for a half year.   But I would there…….that is 14 days. So by November I am without employment. Now you wrote that I should go home but mother does not earn much with hawking in the streets during the winter and mother does not like me to come home. Now you said that I could come this winter and now you write that I cannot come sooner than over 2 years. I counted on it with everything. I needed a cape, however I did not purchase it because I thought that I would go to Jan soon. Now you wrote me that I should submit myself to that. But you know that I cannot get along with mother and that is easier said than done. To home, that is not what they want because to serve in the summer and to come home in winter that is not what they do. Now I do not know what I should do, I cannot go home because in the winter I do not earn my food and clothes and if I go to work in Middelburg then I am off almost every evening. And if I see him then I will go with him again. So now the only thing that I can do is to come to you. But now you wrote a letter like that. I hope to hear from you something different soon because I will leave the Broekert's because I could be with you before the winter. Father likes me to go because then I would behave myself better. I will not write any more now. But I do hope the best. Father prefers for me to go this year because if I stay in Middelburg I will not behave properly even if I badly want to. Father says that if Jan wants, he can get money in America because he knows many people and there are people over there who have a lack of workers. I received a while ago a postcard from you with printed on it "If you like to, you can do it!" I would like to hear from you soon and if you would write (send) the money over too. Because at home they count on me going this year and as soon as possible. You must send no letter anymore without money because otherwise it will be new year (before I will receive it). Now I will stop writing.

Be heartily greeted by your sister,
Pieternella Cevaal

Because otherwise I am desperate if I cannot come to you. Because I counted on it. And I told it already at Broekert's and they will not keep it quiet. So it looks strange if I do not leave now and go to America.

It is not written neatly, but it has been written during the morning and my ink was all used.

◆◆◆◆◆◆

Indianapolis, Indiana   31 July 1914
Pieternella Cevaal to brother

Beloved brother,

I will write you a letter to let you know that I am sick. I do not have anyone here that I know and I do not know what to do. Will you be so good and send me some money that I have money to buy food and also to pay for medicine. I still have 20 cents and that is all. So John, if you please, send me that money. If you can miss it, send me about $15.00 but do not tell the family of father as they will be worried. So, as you receive this letter, send it so that I get it by Saturday evening else I do not know what to do. Maybe you have to send it special delivery. So John, I hope you will receive this in good health. The best greeting from your sister.

◆◆◆◆◆◆

Grand Rapids, Michigan – Plymouth, Wisconsin   29 January 1915
Pieternella Cevaal to John Cevaal

Now I have here a letter especially for you because the other letter each one in the house could read and I could not write anything special. You indeed expected an earlier letter from me but from Pentecost on I have trouble with my eyes and so I could not write.

I went to Dr Scheps but he could do nothing for me. But as of last week they are far better. I have a remedy to wash them with rain water morning and evening and that has helped very much. It is at present very quiet by us now that you have gone away. John is gone now also and Abraham always goes to bed early so I am always alone. I think so often that I would like to come to America if father would let me and that would go yet this year. You said once that if I could come than it should be this year. When you write again then you must ask once if one of us will come. If you write to Abraham, ask if this year he does not wish to come. Because there is good work then I think he will do it and then I shall come along. The

200

worst is that there is so much money necessary but maybe that will come also.

At present I am not very busy with mother but if none of us is home here then it does not go at all. I have thought often of you John because you were always good to me. I hope that you will remember what you did to me. We shall never forget each other even though we are far from one another. When we are with each other we do not realize it but when we are separated then we are aware of it. We are glad that you have such a good boarding house as they are good people.

Now I shall finish with writing and I do not know anymore except that I have the hope that soon I shall come to you. And now I wish you God's choicest blessing. Be further greeted by your loving sister.

Pieternella Cevaal

♦♦♦♦♦♦

Indianapolis, Indiana   25 May 1915
Pieternella Cevaal to brother

Dear brother,

I have received your letter in health and hope that you may also receive this in health. Well, Jan, you are now studying. Well, I hope that you may be successful. You wrote that it is hard, well that I believe and it cost also a lot of money. Jan, I will try very hard to pay you off something. Jan, I waited long, but I did not know your address, so don't hold that against me. I don't really know what to write. There is a lot I know, but my head is so full I don't know where to start. Jan, the letter I received from you made me realize how deep a person can fall. Sometimes I got to sit down and think, well is that me. My heart aches thinking how my childhood was wasted and how I spoiled my youth.

The world is full of temptation but it holds no promise. What is it leading to with this great war. The world will not continue so long anymore. Well Jan, I have to close and I will write more often after this. Greetings from me your loving,

Pieternella

♦♦♦♦♦♦

[Jan Hendrik Wiggers was born 26 October 1834 in Winterwijk, Gelderland to Jan and Christina (Wiggers) Wiggers. He died in Oostburg, WI on 11 August 1919. On 1 May 1867 in Winterswijk he married Janna Aleida Esselink, the daughter of Hendrik Jan and Johanna (Mentink) Esselink. She was born 3 April 1827 in Winterswijk and died 26 September 1919 in the Town of Holland, Sheboygan County, WI. Jan's sister Berendina was married to Jan Slotboom. This letter also included a partial list of the people on board the *Phoenix*, which sank in Lake Michigan in November 1847. These letters are from the Dutch Immigrant Letters Collection, Archives, Calvin College, Grand Rapids, MI, Box 89, Folder 10.]

J.H. Wiggers to J.W. Slotboom.   February 15th 1909
Oostburg, Sheboygan, Wisconsin.

Dear relatives G.J. te Kulve, wife and children.
And also J.W. Slotboom, wife and children.
Also Johanna Slotboom widow of H.J. Berenschot and her many children.

The dearest wish of our hearts is that you all are healthy of body and soul. By this we like to send you this letter as our beloved ones and relatives. As you all can see above, all of your names are mentioned as our relatives. We trust that you will read together the letters we send you because our message is meant for all of you. We like to tell you that the last letter from het Holder, from G.J. ten Kulve and wife, reached us in a good prosperity. Maybe it was written by one of your children. We were very pleased to hear from you, our relatives. Although we should like to get a more comprehensive message from our old fatherland.

And now dear relatives we may tell you that we by the Lord's kindness are in a good health. So we can be each other's help and support, a dear privilege which we have to old age. If the Lord may save us till October 26 next I'll be in the 84th year of my life without any illness which hinders me in my work. Now we have half an acre and an acre is 2½ hectare by you and I can work on it all by myself with a spade. It is new here to build a house and barn apart. Most of the houses here are built of wood or planks, as they call it here. Almost every house has a carpet on the floor. And so, beloved, you can see how life is going here.

Dear relatives it is the dearest wish of our heart that the Lord will take you all in His love and save your body and soul and gives you His blessings for all your needs. But above all, dear relatives, we hope to hear the Lord's voice who tells us in His Word: come to me, all the people of the earth while we are still alive. I have a request to you, please visit den Plantkamp where my sister lives and ask if they have the letter about the death of Wilhelmina Esseling, wife of J.A. Rijmes. And by that opportunity ask her if Jan Esslink from het Dankershusjen is still alive.

◆◆◆◆◆◆

J.H. Wiggers to J.W. Slotboom, Ezinkbrink, Kotten, Gelderland, Netherlands
Oostburg, Sheboygan 60, Wisconsin   23 January 1914

With the hope that we soon will hear from our relatives.

Dear, dear relatives, J. Willem Slotboom and children and also Jan Slotboom, wife and children, G.J. te Kulve and children and Johanna Slotboom and children,

Your health of body and soul is the dearest wish of our hearts to all of you in the old fatherland. From the last letter of widow Berenschot we learned to our joy that you are all well and healthy. We thank the Lord, and only Him, for that, dear relatives. Now we can tell you again that we are healthy too. The good Lord saved us in our old age that we can help and support each other on our trip through life. There are so many people who have to go their way on their own. We think you also know them. We would like to tell you that we think about you in our daily prayers for the throne of mercy. Yes, dear relatives, it is our daily need to pray for you to support and strengthen you on the way of life through the desert of life, but also to be reformed as far as you need this.

Because without the Lord's Word there will be no entry into the Lord's Kingdom without a true rebirth. O beloved one's, it is our daily need, like the old poet in the 129th Psalm on Sunday: See through and know my heart, O Lord, that what I think is in your honor. Try and see if my heart is nourishing something evil and let me go on the way to salvation with firm steps. O beloved, where the urgent prayer of our hearts for each other will be by the Lord's mercy. There the Lord will fulfill His promise. Who's praying will be heard. Who's searching he'll find and who knocks the door will be opened. What a rich promise of the Lord to us poor sinners and we, who are unworthy, will forfeit everything.

And now, dear relatives, we can tell you that the other relatives are still living in prosperity. Janna Kobus, husband and children are all very well. Also the widow of Jan Kobus and her offspring share in prosperity and health. All of them are sharing, just like us, in a lot of blessings from the Lord. This year we had a wealth of blessings; so abundantly that there are not enough barns to put it in. If you could have seen it you would have been surprised: corn, still in sheaf's, standing outside. Now we have a winter like we have never had as long as we have been here. Next May 2nd it is 47 years ago that we left our old fatherland behind. At the moment there is no snow, just a little dusting of snow, but it is gone quickly. Until the new year began, livestock could graze in the meadows and the farmers were plowing all the time. Even now, livestock can be outside. There is a little frost which makes paths and roads like a concrete floor. It is like this in almost every state in America, also in South Dakota were cousin G.J. Krony is living. He visited you two years ago. Last summer he visited us in June. O, dear relatives, he had so much to tell about the old fatherland. And also about the many pleasures he enjoyed with you. At last, dear relatives, something about the state as follows: pork is 10 cents a pound at the market for a complete swine, but at the butcher you have to pay 12 cents a pound and meat is 11 cents a pound, etc. Eggs are 30 cents a dozen, which means 12 eggs. And now beloved ones, we hope that this letter may find you in good health, which is our heart's desire for all of you. Many greetings from us as your relatives.

Again, may the Lord bless you all. And also dear relatives we wish you a happy new year. To all of you that the Lord may bless your body and soul with the words time and eternity. So let it be. From all of us, your relatives.

◆◆◆◆◆

[The next letter was written less than a month before Jan Wiggers died at age 86.]

J. H. Wiggers to J.W. Slotboom
Oostburg, Sheboygan 60, Wisconsin

25 July 1919

Dear and beloved relatives J.W. Slotboom, wife and children, and all the other relatives,

The wellness of soul and body for all of you is our heart's desire. It was on July 25 that we received your letter that you were in an excellent state of health. We were very pleased to hear from our relatives there in our old place of birth, Winterswijk. And now it is June 3rd 1867, just 50 years ago that we left the old fatherland. We married on May 1st and left on the next day, the 2nd. If we look back on our life path and the guidance of the Lord on his path with us, O beloved, we have to tell you that the Lord, beyond prayers and thinking, made everything well on all our paths. And the Lord made everything well by saving our love for each other until we were in old age to support and help each other on the path of life. On June 3rd my wife began her 92nd year of life and is still able to run the household on her own. She bakes her own bread like every housewife does. She is baking it of wheat flour, what you call white flour, and also of rye flour..... (here ends this letter)

◆◆◆◆◆◆

[Hendrik Jan Haverkamp was born 20 June 1858 in Winterswijk, Gelderland the son of Gerrit Willem Haverkamp and Janna Geziena Damkot. He emigrated from the Netherlands on 5 August 1876 and married Hendricka Willemina te Stroete on 25 March 1884 in Town of Holland, Sheboygan County. She was the daughter of Antonie te Stroete and Gezina Doornink. This letter is from the Dutch Immigrant Letters Collection, Archives, Calvin College, Grand Rapids, MI, Box 27, Folder 36.]

Cedar Grove, Wisconsin – Winterswijk, Netherlands
H.J. Haverkamp to H.W. Korschot

9 October 1911

Dearly beloved friends,

W. Korschot and wife and children, I thought I should write you a few lines to let you know that we are all in good health and we hope to hear the same from you. I feel quite a bit better than at first when I was still with you but everything turned out for the better, for which I am very grateful. I had a very good trip home. It took 12 days and it was beautiful on the ocean. Everything was calm and quiet, a big difference from the first trip. When I got home it was just as dry as at your place, but that changed in the beginning of August and from then on we have had a lot of rain and at present it is so wet that we cannot do a thing in the fields. It is raining every other day.

From a letter written by Albert on September 17 I saw that the weather over there was still just as dry as it was during the past summer which is very bad for the cattle. We have had fairly good crops, the grain was heavy, better than expected. Corn or maize and potatoes also fairly good, actually better than expected considering the drought in the early part of the summer, but after the rain we had late in the season we still had plenty.

Well, Willem and Fie, why don't you two come and see us sometime like I did all unexpected? I guess I would recognize you seeing it is such a short time ago! If you yourselves cannot come, why don't you send both of your boys and the girl. They would come in really handy here. We have been asked why we did not take anybody back with us. There is a lot of work here and they can earn good wages. The best thing would be to come and look around once. Just come to my place and I will look after them. But I guess I had better let you decide. Father and mother might say, "Don't even talk about it. That is out of the question." But those strong boys would never be sorry, I can tell you that much.

Enough of this. Anyway, I hope you will take time to write back soon and let us know this and that. It is always a pleasure to hear from each other even after having met each other such a short time ago. Give our regards to your nearest neighbors and to sister Janna and family. Tell Albert that I got his letter the 28th of September, 11 days after he wrote it and tell him I will write him one of these days. With best regards,

H.J. Haverkamp
Cedar Grove, Wisconsin U.S.A.

◆◆◆◆◆◆

[The next two letters were written to the Edward Bruggink family. Edward was born in the Town of Holland, Sheboygan County on 19 September 1875. He was married to Pieternella Verhulst, the daughter of Willem Verhulst and Jacoba Joosse. Pieternella was born 28 November 1872 in Westkapelle, Zeeland. Jacoba Joosse's oldest brother Pieter was the father of the writer, Jacob Joosse.]

Middelburg, Zeeland   22 January 1925

Dear Bruggink family,

We received your letter of January 8th in a good health and we also got one from your sister Martina and her son Robert Wildgrube Jr. We were very happy to hear from you. Your daughter Elvira wrote that you still are able to do your housekeeping all by yourself and I thought: well, well, that old grandma Pieternel! In the photos everything looks nice and

205

cousin Bruggink with rifle and dog beside him to go hunting. That must be a favorite sport during the winter. There is also a car on it. Now I think that driving is attractive when one is living in America on a farm far away from everything. We have a lot of cars here these days. But there are still bicycles. In the Netherlands they introduced a cycle tax of 3 guilders each and it brought in 5,300,000 guilders and more. So you can say that there are 2 million bicycles. That means every 3½ men has a bicycle. My husband cannot walk any more these days but I still can walk a whole day.

I read in the newspaper that it is very cold where you are and there are a lot of snowstorms. Here it is the opposite; very mild till now. The livestock were outside in the meadows till Christmas but the last two months we have fog and sometimes a storm. Recently an English cutter stranded near the top of the dike in Westkapelle. Your wife will know how high that is. How are things going for you with employment? Here there is a lot of unemployment in the country. In Middelburg it is comparative, but nevertheless there are about 300 men unemployed, mostly seasonal workers. We are working at the Zuiderzee now but there are not many men needed for the time being. There are also big plans to widen and better the condition of the roads because of the tremendous increase in the number of cars and coaches. The roads are busy and there are accidents on the narrow roads. You wrote that you recently sent a letter to our address but we didn't receive it, which is a rarity.

The harvest was good in this country and everything is expensive, so it is a good year for the farmers. But the taxes are high and the leases and the farmland expensive. About the public sales of land: the money that was left in former days was spent in loans to other countries. The most were in Russia, but that country does not care a bit about its debts so about 1500 million Dutch guilders got lost and now farmers prefer to buy a piece of land. This land is very expensive, sometimes it costs 1500 to 2000 guilders per 3924 square meters or about an acre. They prefer this than to spend their money on stock. In the mean time everything stays expensive: butter 2,60 guilders a kilogram, meat 1,80, eggs 15 cents each, bread 20 cents per 800 gram, bacon 1,40 per kilogram, etc. We hope that better times are coming. There is still a row in Europe. The real peace will not be here for a long time. Now I end and wish you and the family all of the best for 1925 and kindest love from all.

Your cousin Jacob Joosse
Nederstraat O 222
Middelburg

Also greetings to the other relatives and to Jan Stroo.

◆◆◆◆◆◆

Middelburg, Zeeland   27 December 1926

Dear family,

Again we are at the end of the year so I thought it is time to write to my cousins Bruggink to wish them a good 1927. We wish you and your children a happy, healthy and prosperous new year; on behalf of our children too. And if you may see him also, to Jan Stroo. We have had a dark, wet Christmas day here. Till now we had a lot of cold. In November we had snow and in December frost. All over the country people could skate (on ice) and the Zuiderzee was totally frozen so you could walk over the frozen lake from the island of Marken to the other side, but now the ice has gone. Lately we have had many storms which caused a lot of accidents on the Zuiderzee, some boats sank. Among others, a ferryboat to Kampen named 'de Nijverheid' on which 4 people drowned. Last summer we had a tornado that went from Noord-Brabant on through Gelderland to Groningen, across the whole country. Borculo, in the province of Gelderland, was destroyed. The cost of the damage amounts to several million. Just in Borculo the sum is 3 million.

Otherwise it was a good year for the farmers, although the prices of their products are less than last year, but the harvest is good. Everything was and is good. Many a man has 17 or 18 hectoliter of brown beans which brought in 17 to 20 cents a kilogram. Peas, wheat, potatoes, beets, and also farmland and meadowland, are still very expensive. Farmers pay at public sale up to 3000 guilders a hectare, which is 2½ acres - and sometimes more. The reason for this is that people became afraid to put their money in the bank. They trust the value of land more than the bank. But this makes everything very expensive.

We wait till the balance of the world is restored because of the war (WW1). As far as I know my children are well, because two of them are far away from home. My eldest son departed on September 3rd to work as an engineer in the West Indies (Suriname). He is working there with an American company. They are taking aluminum ore out of the soil. At first they started with it on a large scale and now they have to build piers, warehouses and other buildings at the Colieu River. He has to plan and supervise it. We have received a few letters from him. He wrote that it is very warm there and they are busy with work but the nights are cool so he can sleep well. I hope that he can stick it out because it is a nice job. Our youngest son Jacob is married to a girl from Makassar (East Indies), so we'll have colored people in the family. I wrote to him that if you live a good life with her it doesn't bother me. We all are shaped in the same way and the other relatives are happily doing well. Give our love to your brothers Willem, Noach and Jacob and we send you our love too.

Your cousin J. Joosse and his wife
E. Gabriëlse and children.
Nederstraat O 222
Middelburg

♦♦♦♦♦♦

207

[Many families in Wisconsin sent packages to the Netherlands during World War II. Some went to distant relatives; many to complete strangers. This letter is representative of many thank yous that were sent to the U.S. One interesting example of the bond that was established between families during this time is that of Henk Voges of Winterswijk, Gelderland. His mother's family had received packages during the war and one had included a picture of the children. When Henk began taking trips to the U.S. in 1977 he carried the pictures with him and asked all he met from New York to Iowa if they recognized them. The address of the family had been lost over the years, so he was uncertain where to search. Although he had shown the pictures in Sheboygan County on a past visit, he tried again in 1991. This time the children were identified and within hours he was able to meet and thank the family who had been so gracious to his family during the war.]

Middelburg, Zeeland 15 February 1948

Dear Mrs. Walter Hesselink,

This week on February 10 we received a package in which a nice coat was sent to me. I was very glad to get it because I needed one very much. It suits me very well. Hereby I like to thank you very much and I hope I can wear it this summer. It is always good if a package from America arrives. We are totally helped by it and everything gets its own use. We can sew very well, so if it doesn't fit, you always can make something of it, isn't it? We also got a pair of child's shoes, which will fit my son in the future. He is 3 years old. And you Sjarel, (Sharol) thank you very much too, now Peter is going to wear your little shoes. We have 2 children, the youngest is almost 2 years old. In July we expect our third child. We hope so that it will be a girl. That should be very nice. How many children do you have Mrs. Hesselink?

Our home is on the Veerscheweg, the road to Veere, which is a small village. My husband is a policeman. We are living happily now after a long time of fear and misery. My husband was sent to Germany (during WWII), but we all were saved and are living by ourselves for one year. First we had to live with other people and had just one room. But now we have more room and we are very happy with it, because there are five of us. Yes, it goes without being perceived actually, you get quite a whole family. Life is very expensive here. Food and everything is very expensive and for everything you need tickets, so you do not get much of it. Everything you earn is needed to buy food so you cannot buy anything else like clothes and so on. Also the children need a lot. For everything like clothes or linen you need points (besides money) and there is a great shortage, so you will understand that when we get something (from you) that we are very grateful for it. The coat is very handy to me now because my own coat is too small and this style I can use very well now.

Again my kindest thanks for it.
We wish you and your family all of the best.
With many greetings, T van den Ouden-Kooman.

Fond du Lac and Dodge Counties

[Roelof Sleijster was born 25 December 1815 in Zutphen, Gelderland. He was a deacon in the congregation of Seceders at Velp, Gelderland and was a representative sent out in June 1846 to explore the United States for possible settlement by the Seceders. In Milwaukee Roelof was influenced by an earlier immigrant, Albertus Meenk, to consider the area of Wisconsin which was named Alto. This letter was written to Rev. Antonie Brummelkamp, a prominent Seceder who was preparing a group for emigration. In June of 1846, Roelof's fiancee, Johanna Liesveld, arrived and they were married in Milwaukee on 26 July 1847.]

Announcement in De Nieuwsbode of the death of the Sleyster's
young son Aron (Arend)

Waupun, Wisconsin   25 August 1846

Dear Brother in our Lord and Savior, Jesus Christ,
May it be well with you is the prayer of my soul!

From a letter which I wrote on the 13th of this month to my parents, you will have learned that I arrived in good health (in the Lord's goodness) in Wisconsin, and have chosen as my location or residence, Waupun, which is 86 miles north to the northwest of Milwaukee (three miles is equal to one hour), where Hallerdyk lives and nine other Dutch families.

It is fertile country here, heavy clay soil, little wood land in contrast to other places, but enough wood for lumber and fuel, so the land is much easier to cultivate than in other places; good water, a healthful climate; no taxes, no laws. The only taxes that have to be paid is one dollar on 80 acres for the support of schools for the children; two days of work a year on the roads, or two dollars for every 80 acres which a person owns. If a person sells land he takes two friends or witnesses, and is his own notary, no charges of any kind. When one marries, he goes to his priest and he is ready to perform immediately without asking for money. If a person leaves his wife, which happens very seldom, he is brought back at public expense, wherever he may be, and returned to his wife.

There are no road tolls here. Every farmer in the section must keep his own road in good condition. If here or there in a village or city is a poor mayor, he is deposed and immediately another is chosen from among the people. He does not receive a salary. When one buys land of 80 acres or more the fee is two dollars. If he goes to the land office himself, there is no charge, except the price of one and one fourth acres, but no charge for the description.

Ministers do not get a salary here either. Therefore it is not surprising that on Sunday a carpenter, miller or painter preach the glorious gospel. No minister can be recognized by his clothing on Sunday. The people are very friendly, much more cordial than the Seceders in our country. There are many Methodists here. The Sunday before I arrived in Milwaukee there had been a minister preaching in the street. If one says he is a Christian and conducts himself as a Christian, he is respected. The Catholics are not held in esteem. It is possible to get the most respect by preaching simply, without formality. Conducting church meetings are not approved, but preaching, not attempting to form a party, and not accepting a salary, but working for a living are approved.

Brother, I hope you will all remember me in your prayers. My needs are many, in that you will agree with me, for I hope this winter, if the Lord grants me health, to do a great deal of investigating for you people. Discourage anyone who wishes to go to live in another state, for those who have lived there, because it is much too warm there. Here it is still warmer than it is in Holland. Utensils are better here, except for spades and shovels. Housekeeping supplies a person brings along, especially Haarlemer oil, chamomile, elderberry tea and mustard plaster. You do not have to warn anyone about the night air. This is healthful wherever I have been.

I have purchased eighty acres, claimed 160. Claiming is placing a right to it for a year. A person must pay for it in a year and no one else can buy it. This also costs two dollars. One cannot claim more than 160 acres and must first become a citizen which costs ¾ of a dollar. So, brother, I have become an American citizen, and enjoy voting privileges in all matters, which is of great value for a Christian here, if he wishes to live as a Christian and to render Christian advice in school as well as in other matters.

In the summer the schools are taken care of by women, in the winter by male teachers. One who does not teach well is discharged and another is employed. The teachers in the villages receive from fourteen to eighteen dollars a month; in a city, twenty to twenty-five. In the month of May the children meet, and the teacher who has done the best teaching gets a prize.

There are many Christians here, also many who do not believe in a God, but there is no offensive behavior noticeable except the misuse of the name of God. On Sunday no business is transacted, and in no other places where I have been, except by those who have arrived recently. Very little strong drink is sold in the inns. In some states it is already entirely illegal. A person who wishes to do so must ask permission and gave the approval of his neighbors, or he may not do it. There are many temperance houses in America.

Those who have claimed land must build a house on it within 30 days, and live in it or his claim expires. If the Lord wills I hope to have my house finished in 8 days. I have earned my board for three days at carpentry, one painting and now once more plastering for 8 days. In the future I hope to work independently to bring my land and house in good order. As much as I am able, and the Lord permits, I hope to work out to earn some money, which is difficult here in the interior, for money to pay for work is scarce. One can exchange work or work for produce, but I hope to earn something, because now and then I have expenses to get letters into the mail. I cannot mail letters unless I pay postage to New York, and I must bring them to the post office in Fond du Lac, which is 24 miles from here. I would be pleased, brother Brummelkamp, if, when acquaintances come over to me, my expenses would be taken care of in part, since I have had more expenses traveling than others. We had to leave Brother Reusink and his wife and children behind in Rochester because he had an accident under a bridge. I loaned him two dollars because the Seceders we met there would not forward him money. If no provision can be made for expenses, that is alright too. I will not write fewer letters on that account, nor go to less trouble to investigate everything.

Land is not fertilized here, but people would have better crops if it were allowed to lie untilled for a seven year period. I do not know what advice to give a person without money. A person who has 1500 gulden to bring inland can in a short time become a big farmer. This helps many get started. To help someone across is wrong, for one must live here a year before he has an income, and everything is expensive here. It is true that a pound of pork in the inland costs nine cents but they are American cents. From money I can buy nothing but flour, pork, salt and vinegar. Everything is new here. There is plenty here for more than a year and it is cheaper, but, then when others come in they must go 30 miles farther, but then there is the same expense. If there are people who are well off they can feed those who came over and put them to work. That I find to the best plan. A person who wishes to start on his own must figure that he just have 1000 gulden for four times eighty acres of land, three yoke of oxen which sot 375 guilden, a wagon for 123 gulden, a plow for 40 gulden and four cows for 153 gulden. A year's living expense for a family of four for 400 gulden, and for small equipment 200 gulden. If more people come along it is a half cheaper for 3 yoke of oxen, a wagon, a plow is enough for four families. It is not possible to plow with 6 oxen they say.

Now, Brother Brummelkamp, I come to you with a request. Wherever I come, I am asked to preach. Up to this time I have not done it but I have read a sermon. Why have I not done it? Because I do not want to force myself in without your approval. You will probably say that if it is requested it is not a matter of forcing oneself in. That is true too, but later some may say so, or say, or men in your country that I stayed here for that reason. There is no money to be earned here in that way. So I have written to you, but I do wish to do it, that you know well. To work during the week and preach three times on Sunday is the custom here. I cannot do this, but I can make a speech, and the Lord can bless that also. I can't do this long, but church lasts for only an hour, and that is good for one who must make a beginning. Here it is a custom to have two ministers at the pulpit, and often the application and closing prayer are taken care of by another, but not always. Write to me whether you give me your approval. Until that time I plan to read a sermon as I have told those who have invited me. Greet all the students for me and tell them that I consider myself to be fortunate although I must cook my own meals every other day and do my own washing. Tell the students that it is not unusual for a minister to have preached four miles away, must prepare his own meals and the next day work hard again; well, not as hard as in Holland but still diligently for the Americans are faithful laborers. So for students who are brought up in a world of ease, this is no place for them. Working for a living is a proverb here.

My letters must be postage paid. I must also do this to New York and every letter I receive from you I would like to see accompanied by a note from J.L._____. Greetings to all of you from me, especially Mr. Veenhuizer (Assistant minister at Arnhem). And once more acknowledge my hearty and well meant thanks for your instruction and that received from Mr. Veenhuizer. Write plainly, otherwise it means nothing to me brother! Also receive my hearty and well meant greetings and wishing you the Lord's blessing.

Your loving and well wishing brother in Christ,
R. Sleyster

◆◆◆◆◆◆

[**Rijk Sneller was born 30 September 1816 in Oldebroek, Gelderland. In February 1850 in Elburg, Gelderland he married Maatje Juffer. Although they were an important part of the early settlement of Alto, WI, they felt the draw of cheaper land prices and the migration west. In February 1879 they had bought land in Sioux County, IA and Rijk Sneller died there on 18 July 1888.**]

New York 30 March 1866

Brothers, Sisters, Brothers-in-law, and Sisters-in-law,

We want to let you know that we arrived here this morning after a long, hard journey. While on the ocean we had lots of troubles. Many of the people had to spend most of the time in bed. I kept exceptionally strong and well and all the while I kept my clothes on. Seven people died at sea and one fell overboard. The first one to die was the wife of Bartus Boefe. Willem van den Berg from Elspeet and his child, the wife of Lubert Zandbergen, Janens van Dijk, and one other (unknown) and one from South Holland and a child of Evert Klomp. Our two young children had been ailing and the little one of Beert also, but at present seems somewhat better. The people got sick from those terrible drinks. They would drink too much and the water was awful, just like beer.

Be so good and send this to Gerrit Jan too. Greet all my friends and acquaintances, also Arend Brink. Hendrik has recovered and one need not bring a maid or servant to help. I had no rest day or night. I have written this in the dark.

Rijk Sneller

◆◆◆◆◆◆

New York 30 March 1866

Dear Brother and Sister,

With gratitude we can tell you the help we have experienced, we can report that we arrived here this noon in reasonable health except for our little one who has been very ill. At present the child seems not to appear worse and we hope that all will be well soon. We had a very difficult trip from Rotterdam all the way to New York. Everyone was seasick except me, Hendrik and Uncle Rijk, we all stayed well. All the little ones were ailing but are improving in the fresh air.

Much to our joy we immediately met Aalt van den Berg which was a good thing for without his help we would all have been cheated. Jannes van Dyk died, so be very cautious when you tell his mother. The wife of de Boefe also died and an Englishman fell overboard. The wife of Lubert Zandergen is dead too. In all, eight or nine persons, most Hollanders.

I beg you to give my best regards to all the relatives and anyone who inquires about me.

> Your dear brother and sister
> Beert van den Berg
> (Most likely a nephew of Rijk Sneller)

♦♦♦♦♦♦

(April?) 1866

My very dear Brothers and Sisters,

We are well and hear the same of you. I had promised to write you how things were here. We have two cows which give quite a bit of milk. These give enough milk for our own use and we sell some milk for a dollar and a half. Our containers are tin, as big as the tin saucers you have, but deeper. We have a churn as big as a butter crock that holds 70 pounds of butter. My churn is made of wood but my sister has a stone crock. We take the butter out by hand. We do not have sieves nor scrub brushes. We scour with a whisk made of hay and that works quite well. We have a stove on which we cook four things at a time and it has an oven. Then I can bake and cook at the same time. We have three beds on which we sleep. They are like sleeping couches which you have but at the head and foot ends there are frames like gates with hand turned knobs. We do not have a bedstead like you have. That seemed strange at first. We bought six chairs for $3.00 at a household auction. The seats are of wood, no woven mats, which are expensive here. The beds are expensive, too, but we were able to buy three at a sale for four dollars a piece. There were better ones for sale that were more expensive, too, but we were fortunate to get these nice beds. Everything is expensive except the printed cottons which are like they are there. The prices of the prints were reduced about 50% in price since last year. We pay 20 cents a yard and 25 cents for the best prints. A yard is 36 inches here so when people come here it wouldn't pay to bring new

213

material from there. I have not seen wool material in the shops in Waupun. Everyone here wears cotton prints and we always wear our farm clothes, but no bonnets. We all go bareheaded, which is handy. On Sunday we wear a hat to church. Bonnets are not worn here. The bonnets like we wore in Holland are not worn here at all. I wear the mourning hood under my hat, but I do not enjoy it, which you can understand. I cannot wear mourning clothes for my dear children because I do not have money. It cost so much for my family that there is no beginning to it. There are few who wear mourning clothes so I have not done it either. I had no desire to go the trouble of getting clothes because my grief was too great as you can imagine. First the dreadful loss of Gerritje, ten days later Dries died, and then three days later our new born little girl passed away. The other children were sick and I was worried especially about Driesje and Wichertje who were the sickest. Driesje had her legs so swollen that we had to carry her for fourteen days and she was so thin we afraid that she had T.B.

It is impossible for me to write and tell you how concerned I was about her and what I went through was terrible. Our troubles all started in New York when my husband and three children were lost. I and three youngest had been put on the wagon with others. The driver chased so fast that my husband could not keep up with them. Hendrikje had the measles on board the ship and was so pale and weak and Driesje could not walk, so they were left behind with father. When the wagon landed at the station, I had to stand while the others went inside and my sister Aaltje left me too. Gerritje was in the wagon with the girl and I called for my child. I couldn't get Gerritje and the wagon left. I called as loud as I could and there I stood with Dries in my arms and Wichgertje holding my hand. Then I went back to the house where we had been before and when they lit the lamps there was my husband. This was Saturday and on Monday we left arriving at Albany on Tuesday. There the others were waiting I asked my sister, "Where is the child?" (Gerritje) She said, "She has already been buried." What a shock that was for me. Dries had severe diarrhea, was wet and soiled and could not walk. Wichgertje had the measles and couldn't walk either. I had to carry one. There was no one to help me, so I could not rest. You can imagine how worried I was. I kept going till the last evening when I could go no more and I fainted. Then my sister took the child (Dries), otherwise she did not help me. Then they carried me to a baker. There we slept till morning when Lubbert got us. I was so glad to get to Alto on Sunday. On Monday I gave birth to a baby girl and remained quite strong. All the while Dries became weaker and he died on Thursday next to me on my bed. Thus you can understand what an awful time I had. When the baby was a week old, she also died because of my weakened condition. She had not gotten enough nourishment. This took away all my desire and pleasure. Otherwise I think I could enjoy being here. Now I'm well and strong, which surprised many people. I had to say, "The Lord gives strength to bear our cross." So many people came to call on me to console me in my grief and they brought plenty of food. How often I have thought of you, my dear sister. I cannot write any more because I am distressed by the loss of our beloved children. The others are well as they have never been. Driesje can sew everything, dresses and bonnets. I don't have to have anything made. Greet Jacob van den Berg, Dries Plak and Dirk Bos, Doornawaard, and especially Fenne with Gerritje and G. Koster and Labot van de Kerk. If Heine Chris were here he could make a good living. Tell him carpenters are expensive if you need them. Write and let me know how Apart Labot is and if he has to enter the service. Sister and children, especially from Driesje. Give our regards to all our friends in Elburz. Now I must end with my pen but never with my heart. Now sister will you send a small doll along with Bronkhorst for Wichgertje. There are not toys for children here. You need not send material. I would like to have some checked material for three pair of pants. I will pay Bronkhorst. Also send me the name of the design for the top of the butter mold that I left with Dirk.

Written by Maatje Juffer Sneller in 1866.

(Driesje referred to in the letter is Mrs. John de Zeeuw and Wichgertje is Mrs. Dirk Bos. Heintje is Mrs. Evert Vermeer)

♦♦♦♦♦♦

Alto, Wisconsin 14 June 1866

Dear Brothers and Sisters,

We want to let you know that we through God's goodness now are in good health and hope we may hear the same of you.

We had a very difficult trip which you perhaps know. Though all this was not what we intended to subject our children to, but the loss of our two children I could not forget and that will always stay with me and be a sharp thorn in my flesh. This has taken all our pleasure and enjoyment. If God did not give me the power and strength then I would collapse. It is impossible to describe how hard this has been for us. Those of you who have children can almost image what we all are going through.

As to our state of affairs we have rented a log house after we had been here fourteen days and we are living in it now. We have five hectare (about 12 acres) of arable land just like it is over there. We rent the land for $40.00. We bought two milk cows for fifty-seven dollars for the two. We have some for our own use and sell 50 cents worth of milk every week. There are places we can buy here and were offered to us almost before we got here. One place of 80 acres near Lubbertus Redeker with a good house on it, we could buy for $72.00 but I did not dare to risk it because I knew nothing about conditions here so we just rented this small place instead. This way we won't have the chance to gain anything but we don't have to lose either. If we find something better later, we can always leave here. In the fall, they tell me, one can rent larger places and I'd rather start on a small scale and not go into debt. You can imagine that it sounds good to buy such a large place but everything you need to buy for such a place is very expensive. Things are done quite differently here than in Holland. It's all done with machinery. It is easier to earn a dollar a day here than to earn four stuivers (20 cents) in Holland. Food costs are expensive here. We buy meat for 7 cents a pound, the best pork is 12 cents. Wheat meal is 3 ½ cents, buckwheat is 2 ½ cents a pound. Everything is according to American pennies. They way it seems I cannot notice things are

215

much different here than in Holland. If I didn't know how long the trip was coming out here, I would not be able to believe that we were such a distance apart.

The area around here is particularly nice and we are enjoying ourselves exceptionally well. The children are attending the American school. In the summer they are starting a new school sponsored by the church. The people are very friendly and helpful and come to visit us every day. Before we had our own cows or anything else, they provided us with everything. Everyone said, "Feel free to come if there is anything you need." When it comes to religion and worship, it is much like in Holland. We never get into a home where the Bible is not read and audible blessings and thanks are not said at every meal. On Sunday they are very strict to have all business places closed and they would rather not speak about worldly problems. I do not know if they are sincere because I don't know their hearts, yet I find it particularly edifying. A lot of Hollanders are living in these surroundings with few Americans, several of which are leaving and are glad to sell their farms. Yet there are many coming with money who will get along all right. Many who come without money find it isn't anything like they expected.

The young men who came with us are rather disappointed. Jan van den Berg had written about a man earning about $200.00 a year, but farmers here pay $100.00 and anyone who is slow will find it difficult to find a farmer who will hire him. In Holland people often spoke of farmers being able to pay good wages but I can give you a little hint. Everything here is done by machinery and horses such as sowing, mowing and threshing. Not too much work is done to the land. The land that grew wheat last year and had been mowed was still a stubble field when we came in April. They plow the fields before they sow wheat. The corn and potatoes are not planted until a week or two before the first of May. The land is plowed and the corn and potatoes planted. I have thought and said if we worked the land in Holland this way we wouldn't get anything. The straw is put on piles and burned. That is what is done with the wood. The bigger branches are sawed and used for fuel in stoves and the twigs are burned. How often I think if only the things that are burned here were in Holland. Oh, how many poor souls out there have to go to the woods with a sack and gather twigs. Here it is burned or they let it rot. I believe if people here would work the land the way it is done in Holland they would reap a lot more. Anyone here who works 80 acres of land can easily work the land with the help of one hired man, except in the busy season they sometimes pay someone $2.00 a day. On a farm like this they can harvest about 800 bushels of wheat if they grow 40 acres and they have corn, potatoes and hay and a pasture for their cattle. They do not keep cows, mostly five or six, that is cows and calves and two horses. Wheat is about a dollar a bushel and then you have $800.00 but you have to keep some to sow the following year which is about a bushel and a half, and then you have to keep some to eat. Then you can understand and figure what is left over. For those who have a good start, it is exceptionally good here, but those who come with little or no money, it takes some time to get a good start.

Thus brothers and sisters at the moment I cannot recommend too strongly and tell you to come, it would be so pleasant to have you here. I must first have more experience here and if later we are familiar with conditions, then I will write you more detail.

216

Tell Arend Brink that Hendrik is still with us and that he is enjoying himself and is well. He goes out working and is earning a dollar a day. Greet everyone from me. There are too many to mention names. Write soon and let me know if all is well. Also how the business with hay land has gone.

I remain respectfully you brother, namely
Rijk Sneller

♦♦♦♦♦♦

Alto, Wisconsin 5 July 1866

Dear Loved Ones and Friends,

Have read your letters and delighted to find out that all of you are well. In there I read that you have not received the letter that we mailed in May. That makes me very sad because in it I had written about experiences on our journey coming here. Later my wife wrote and now this is the third letter we are sending you. I note, too, in your letter that many things happened there and that several changed the temporal life for the eternal. Alas, dear brothers and sisters how much we have experienced in our trip out here and after we arrived here. Ah, the loss of our two dear children and also the one that was born here two days after our arrival. Oh, that loss is difficult for us to forget and it is something you cannot even imagine. I am not in a condition to even write you about it because if I dwell on that, then America is too small in spite of its being so large. Alas, if God did not give us the energy and strength I would long since have perished of grief. Thus far, all of us have been particularly healthy and strong and the children, too, are extremely healthy and strong such as they never experienced in Holland. After the circumstances my wife went through she has been remarkably health and strong. At first, Driesje was ailing a lot, but now is heavier than she ever was in Holland. The children are very happy here and have no desire to go back to Holland. When you consider the circumstances here, we are doing very well. We have rented a house with six acres of land and two acres of pasture. We can grow all we need for ourselves and we pay $40.00 rent. Land here is exceptionally fruitful. Hay land is cheap here. We have rented a piece for grubbing out the trees. We did this together in five days and then the wood is ours for fuel. We will have enough for the entire winter. We will have plenty hay for four cows. We have two cows that I bought for $57.00 and they produce well. Everything here is expensive but food here is not more costly than in Holland. Flour costs 4 cents a pound and buckwheat is 3 cents a pound and it's just like in Holland. Beef is 8 cents a pound, pork costs 12 cents. We live near a wooded area. During the summer we can pick up plenty wood for fuel. I'm concerned about troubles in the world just as we were in Holland. However, we do not seem to live in splendor. We live in a log house. I am not a farmer but am a day laborer. When I do not work on my acreage I work out and earn a dollar a day. For eight days now I have been shearing sheep. Then I earn a dollar and a half. There are some who have 800 sheep. There are three of us Hollanders who go out shearing together, always for Americans. I and Otto, son of Lubbert Redeker and Donkerschoot from

217

Putten work together. Donkerschoot has stayed with van de Berg. He left Holland fourteen days after we did and their trip was even worse than ours. They spent eight and a half days on an island. Of fourteen hundred, about half died. I want my brother-in-law van de Berg to go along shearing sheep. The Americans who can do it charge $2.00 a day and they cannot keep up with us, so they just leave. There are not many Hollanders who do it. Ah, dear brothers and sisters, you must not imagine that America is perfect. It is far from it. For much of life is trouble and vexation. We find it here just as we did in Holland that the righteous will scarcely be saved. (I Peter 4:18) that is to say not without difficulty and struggle. We certainly have found that to be true here. Over there it stayed mostly in our clothes but here it enters the flesh and blood. As you know so well I usually keep quiet. Often I cannot understand what they say but there are social evils here. Oh, if we could earn our salvation so easy. Seldom has anyone heard me complain, but just as I was there, I am here, but what I feel in my heart my pen will not write. I must profess with David when he said, "Lo, I have sinned and I have done wickedly but these sheep, what have they done?" (II Samuel 24:17)

But alas, dear brothers and sisters, friends and acquaintances, I may say with my heart and soul, even though I am in America and you in Holland, you all know that our reason for coming was not to create salvation. It was contrary to my desire and wish that we left Elburz and the neighborhood and especially the dear family of Dominee Callenbach and his relationship but my consolation is, "I know whom I believed (II Tim. 1:12). Nothing can separate me from the love of God which is in Christ Jesus our Lord." (Rom 8:39). It is in His strength that I shall overcome otherwise in this busy life we would have perished long ago. Not by my power because there is no strength in me. Oh yes, dear sister, from whom I parted, how bitter that was but I console myself that though we may not see each other's face on earth, we shall see each other again. We know our trust in God will not be in vain and He will answer us as we daily meet at His throne in prayer. We have His promise that He will be merciful to us and bless us if we will be faithful to Him. I have no time nor desire to write much about America. As to religion and worship in our area, it is much like over there. As far as outward appearance is concerned, the church is always filled on Sunday and I believe that the minister here would be in agreement with Callenbach. Sunday evenings we meet in our homes in our neighborhood and have fellowship together. Sunday night our house was filled. The people are exceptionally helpful, kind and friendly. As for our temporal needs, there is absolutely no want for anything. The poorest have bread but there is no time for idlers or those who are conceited.Anyone who wants to buy 80 acres of land must have six or seven thousand gulden. One can buy forty acres and can make a living if he will work the land well and if the season is good. If you in Holland would work the land the way they do there, you would not grow as much. Everyone says this has been an unusually fruitful year and the crops look particularly good, better than they have had for years.

Written by Rijk Sneller

◆◆◆◆◆◆

[Lubbert Redeker was born 22 September 1814 in Uttel, Gelderland the son of Otto and Ebertje (Schouten) Redeker. On 12 February 1847 he married Geeretje van Putten in Apeldoorn. She was born 2 February 1825 in Elspeet, Gelderland the daughter of Harmon and Jannetje (Mouw) van Putten. He became a lay preacher in the Hervormde Kerk and later in the Presbyterian Church in Alto. In 1865 he sailed with his wife and eight children for America. Their 10th, and last child, was born in Alto. This letter was written to his cousin, H. Van Asselt who had emigrated to Indiana. This letter is from the Dutch Immigrant Letters Collection, Archives, Calvin College, Grand Rapids, MI, Box 55, Folder 4.]

Alto, Wisconsin   28 April 1866

Dear Cousins and Relatives,

It was according to the will of the worshipful providence that I also arrived here in North America on October 17, 1865 with my wife and eight children in Fond du Lac, Wisconsin, Alto County, and we arrived in good health and are still able to enjoy the same privilege and hope we may hear the same from you folks. I have purchased a house and a barn on 180 acres of land at $34 per acre, and 4 horses, 7 cows, 3 hogs, etc., but all of these are expensive here. The horses $150 to $200, the cows $35 to $45. Here the crop is mainly wheat which brings at present $1.20 to $1.25, butter 25 cents.

So I have briefly told you about my situation. It would please me greatly if I could hear from you sometime, how you are getting along there and the situation in that area and its location, and the crops, because I am very eager to know about your welfare. And are there more Hollanders there? Here there are many Hollanders. We have two Holland ministers here. What is the situation there in regard to divine worship? Is the country hilly or level? Is there much woodland or prairie? Here it is not hilly, and formerly the land was covered with forest but now there are almost no woods; hardly enough for one's needs. There is a great deal of pasture land. In regard to your brother-in-law, John van de Broek, I have received a short letter from him asking me to send you the enclosed with the request to send him the money, but personally I have a serious objection because I do not know enough about that matter to make such payments. And besides, I do not understand the English language, so I think that if you could do as he requests you would be in a better position to send him the money than I. At least I would not know how to go about it when one goes to the bank which deals with the bank in Amsterdam and that one with Morgan and Sons, 39 Williams St. New York. Since I have no opportunity to get it there, you yourself will find a better chance than I, because I still do not know whether that office deals regularly with the office in Amsterdam in Holland.

So then my dearly beloved cousin, l I expect to receive a letter from you soon. Friendly greetings and also from my wife and children.

I remain,
Your cousin,
L. Redeker

♦♦♦♦♦♦

[Gerrit Alsum was born 1 May 1873 in Friesland, Netherlands and died 21 January 1943 in Friesland, WI. He married Dirkje Klaas Cupery on 7 November 1895 in Friesland, WI. She was born 10 May 1875 in Hiaure, Friesland, Netherlands and died 5 July 1958 in Friesland, WI.]

7 September 1890

Dear Friend,

I finally took my pen to give you an update about America. Today is a rainy day, so I have time for it. We have had a fantastic trip. For a young guy that is all alone, such a trip is quite a pleasure, a good living and always having fun. They danced and played sometimes until late at night – 10 or 11 o'clock, just like you are in Allerkellingen Fair, but now it was also beautiful as long as we have been on the boat. Otherwise it would not have been much fun. I think we have been at sea for 11 days. We entered the ship on Saturday and that Wednesday a week late we saw land for the first time. That was quite a noise and a hurray!! Now I must say that I have never seen such a beautiful sight as that first arrival in New York with hundreds of boats coming in that harbor and all kinds of vessels. And that was a beautiful city. We also waited there a couple of hours. We arrived at night at the railway station. There was also something to see the next day and we sat there for two days. On Friday night at 9 PM we arrived at our destination. Now I have informed you of something about the trip and something about here in America. It looks like I can earn some money here. I earn one dollar and 25 cents per day. You can get a lot of products here for that money, as much as you can get there with two guilders and 50 cents, so you can understand there is no poverty here. Most farm workers have a pair of cows and 50 chickens and they can almost live on that. The farmers here are not so afraid if they have anything to eat – like by you. A worker who works for a farmer and when he is busy he always eats with the farmer at the same table. Most farmers work here just as hard as a farm worker. Here there is not much difference between poor and rich as by you. A farm hand is honored just as much as a farmer. It is so busy here that every day I see farmers driving along the road looking for help. Now don't think that you can just get money for nothing, no, you have to work for it indeed! Work is mostly done by machine, even 15 to 20 acres grain is being cut, then a man comes and puts it in shocks, then the shocks are put in big stacks at the house. They do that with horse and wagon, the same as by you. Then comes the steam machine that threshes the grain real fast. That makes the grain also clean and brings the straw in a big block (stack). These machines can do about 40 acres per one day. There is a lot of straw here this year, so a very good harvest. Now I will finish my writing. Please let your parents read this letter also. Greetings to all of you.

Also greetings to my brothers and sisters and tell them that all is well with me. Also greetings to friends and acquaintances who are asking about me.

Gerrit Alsum

◆◆◆◆◆◆

Paesens, Friesland, Netherlands   December 30, 1896

Dear Brother & Sister & Niece,

We received your letter December 8 in good health. Jennie R. Joukema was by us with her husband and they stayed overnight. They are living now in Schengen close by Leeuwarden. Her husband came from there. He has a nice home there. They get along real well and are well satisfied. Greetings from them also.

Also greetings from E. Straatsma and his wife. You asked about them in your letter. My niece Tryntje Durk Zwart also stayed here two nights. Greetings also from them. She stays by her daughter and her husband and they have it good. Jan Wessel's – he passed away also. We read it in the newspaper. We read about nine weeks ago in the newspaper that Harke Douma from Lioessens, an old farmer, was walking from Lioessens to Morra and he drowned (they had a meeting in the tavern). This was sad as it was just before Christmas. There also was a farmer from Morra who hung himself – sad happening – It is sorry circumstance that they don't see any way out and therefore take their life. If only they would turn to the Lord in time of trouble.

We are blest from the Lord with good health. We have three cows, one we use for our milk, the other two are both with calf and that is also good. We have four sheep and we butchered a pig which weighed 314 lbs. We had some peas and oats which we sold, the prices were so low. We had some potatoes which were very good. Some other areas had disease in their potatoes. We raised flax which was also cheap. We got 19 bundles out of the garden. Now we are getting it from the field. We had seven shocks. Gerrit and Douwe harvested it and Lieuwe, he cleans it and Gerrit helps out too. Gerrit can handle 22 shocks and Douwe 8-9 and sometimes 10! They get along real well.

We (the women) do the chores and the housework, so we women are busy too. Aukje and Douwe – they pick up potatoes and Lieuwe and a daughter of van der Waagen on shares for us and the van der Waagens. And then Gerrit worked for four weeks yet by Klemstra. We rented land again which is close to our garden for 16 guilders. Last year it was 28 guilders, so that was much cheaper.

So brother we have nothing to complain, we are blest and we hope and trust the Lord will provide. Pieter and Tryntje and small child were here for three nights, the little one was very good and not afraid of anybody. They plan to move to the island. Pieter – he tried to buy a house but it was too expensive, so therefore they moved to the island. His sister and brother-in-law are living there too. We cannot walk there in one day. We must be content where the Lord leads us. Each day we are one day closer to eternity. The Lord has prepared a home for us, through grace I will be among them.

221

The children are all doing well. Lieuwe will probably stay here another year but things could change. Ulke visited here too for awhile. They came with horse and buggy. Pieter and Tryntje and child also came. That was a houseful, but there is always an empty chair.

Now I will finish this. Greetings from all your friends and also from us –

Your sister and children
Stiemsma

P.S. We wish you a blessed New Year
(Received by Newton Alsum from his mother Jennie)

♦♦♦♦♦♦

[Herman Beekman was born in Apeldoorn, Gelderland on 15 June 1888 the son of Klaas and Geertije (Bresser) Beekman. He died 20 January 1964 in Waupun, WI. He emigrated in 1890 with his parents. The mother of Geeritje Klein (Jacob van Beek's wife) was Catherine Beekman. These letters are from the Dutch Immigrant Letters Collection, Archives, Calvin College, Grand Rapids, MI, Box 76, Folder 7.]

Tonsel, Gelderland – Brandon, Wisconsin   2 March 1915
Jacob van Beek to H. Beekman

Dear Uncle and Aunt and Cousins,

You will probably think that we have forgotten you completely, but that's not the case. This has happened because of current circumstances. First they said that letters would not go to America, because the mail did not go as well as usual either, and now some more time has passed again.

All of us, and our relatives, are healthy and we hope to hear this from you as well. On January ninth we were gladdened with the birth of a daughter (Gerritje) and last Sunday she was baptized. As per August 1 Bart is in the service because of the mobilization. He comes home for a few days once every three weeks. This is not very pleasant, but many are in the same boat. At night Bart's wife is always with her parents who live close by, and she gets 6.60 guilders every ten days, 66 cents per day, so that's pretty good.

Fortunately, until now we live in peace, which is a big miracle and we hope that peace will soon return to Europe. Everything is very expensive here, but it is still available for your money. The corn costs fl19.20 per 150 pounds. The linseed flour fl8.50 per 100 pounds. The linseed cakes 16-17 cents each; and so, everything is more than 3 times as expensive as it used to be.

In our country there are many interned Belgians. On the field near Galgenberg, you still know where that is, there are 14,000 of them. Harderwijk looks like Amsterdam, that's how crowded it is. They live in large wooden buildings. You can imagine that they need a lot.

We have a mild winter with very little frost, and also very little snow. Just now we had some snow on the round for a few days, but that is also almost gone. Work is starting again. We are busy again on the potato fields. Gerrit is still an orderly at the Veldwijk Institute. He doesn't like farmer's work too well. We live in the living room and have a cow and a few yearlings. Bart lives on the farm and he is farming with a goat, two cows and two yearlings. W. Dekker and Hendrikje are doing like us; they live a bit further toward Ermelo. We still live in the parental home of Father Klein. Well now, dear family, the paper is filled and you are up to date about everything.

We hope to receive a return letter real soon. Herewith our kindest regards and our very best wishes and the Lord's indispensable Blessing.

Who calls himself   Jacob v. Beek
                                              Gerritje Klein

The address is:
J. v. Beek
Tonsel – Municipality Harderwijk
Province of Gelderland

Brown & Outagamie Counties

[Hermanus Vinkenvleugel was born 10 March 1804 in Dinxperlo, Gelderland to Hermanus Vinkenvleugel and Hendrina Oostendrop. He died 4 June 1889 in Wrightstown, Brown County, WI. His first marriage to Anna ten Haken produced 4 or 5 children. They left Gelderland in November 1847 and arrived in Boston 31 January 1848. There are three children from his second marriage to Theodora de Beijers. His third marriage was to Anna Marie Lauterbach and they had seven children. Hermanus was alternately known as Manus and Finkenvleugel and shortly before the Civil War the name was changed to Fink.]

Letter from Hermanus Vinkenvleugel
Translated by Loek van der Heijden

Wright Town   16th March 1885

Beloved family

I can not forbear just to let you know, how it's going with me here in America, because I have already passed my 81 years on 10 March, and now I should like to know how it goes there, whether my brothers and sister are still alive or not. There will probably be some people in the family, who will remember that I and my wife and five children departed from Dinxperlo 35 years ago. I then arrived at Boston. There I was a "koeper" (cooper) for 7 years. There I earned 700 dollars and with that I traveled to the west and bought myself 80 acres of land and that I sold three years ago.

I have my third wife and she has 7 children, from which one daughter has married last year. She was 18 years old. Furthermore I let you know, that I have a hundred acres of land, 5 cows, 6 head barren cattle, four horses, one 8 years old, one four years old, one two years old and one from one year old.

I am old and the children are young, but I am doing the most with machines. I have a grass mower and a seed mower, a sowing machine and a rake machine. They cost a lot, almost 300 dollars, because the wages are also more expensive than in Holland. Here one can earn good money.

If it should be, that in the family there are people who want to come over to live with us, whether married or not married, they can work by me. And if they are married I will let them live on the sixty acres. Here they would plant half, then the owner gives nothing more, but I will provide the machines and also two horses and everything belonging to the use of horses like the horse harness on the horse wagon, plough, harrow, etc.

224

Firewood, don't you think about it, there is plenty.

Now I will just request that you let me know who cultivates the land on the "Brinkenveld." I do not know better that that it is still mine, because I have sold the house, but not the land. Furthermore I do not know much news to write than that I personally am determined to once come over to you if the good Lord lets me keep my health. The land that I sold three years ago I miss, but where I am now, it goes good without.

Now I end with the pen but not with my heart and greetings to all my friends and acquaintances, for I hope that you will receive this letter in good health.

In expectation I remain your brother or uncle, who calls himself,

Hermanus Finkenvleugel

Not I expect an answer soon please.

Furthermore, O yes, I had almost forgotten my children from my first wife. The oldest son has been married in Boston, but he died and has left a wife and three children, Johanna is in Oregon, Gertruida is in New York, Hendrikus died in the war and therefore I receive a pension of 8 dollars each month. The youngest daughter is in Arkansas. Those who live are all married. The youngest daughter has 13 children, from which two are married. (LvdH: I assume he is speaking of Maria Magdalena?)

The address is listed as Herman Fink (not Finkenvleugel), Wrights Town, Brown County, Wisc.

◆◆◆◆◆◆

[Arnoldus Verstegen was born December 1820 in Zeeland, Noord Brabant to Johannes Hermanus and Adriana Laurens (Bevers) Verstegen. He died 30 October 1900 in Little Chute, WI. On 14 February 1844 in Erp, Noord Brabant he married Anna Maria Biemans. She was born 21 April 1821 in Erp, Noord Brabant to Egidius (Delis) Arnoldus and Anna Maria (van den Elzen) Biemans. She died 18 December 1863 in Little Chute, WI. Arnold, Anna and their first 4 children arrived in New York on 25 May 1850. They possibly had 6 more children and Arnold and his second wife, Maria Catharina van der Aa, supposedly, had 12 children. These letters are from the Dutch Immigrant Letter Collection, Archives, Calvin College, Grand Rapids, MI, Box 87, Folders 12-13.]

Arnold Verstegen to Delis Biermans   16 June 1852
Little Chute, WI to Erp, Noord Brabant

Dear Parents,

Your letter of April 24, received here May 23, afforded us great pleasure. Not getting an
answer sooner, we were afraid that perhaps our letter might have been lost. You tell us that
Mother has been sick but is now improving; we wish her a speedy and complete recovery.

While I was reading the rest of your letter, tears came to my eyes. You suggest that we take
our inheritance at this time; and I read between the lines that you are under the impression
that we are living here in great poverty and are too proud to ask for help. We are happy to
hear that we still have a place in your heart, although undeserving of it, since we came to
America against your advice. But Father, we are not poor, we are rich! We have more and
better food than we ever had in Holland; we live in a warm house and have good clothes; we
have Mass in our church each Sunday; and the children go to school and catechism. The
little patch of land which we have cleared is sufficient to supply all of our wants. No, Father,
don't give your money away; rather keep control of what is yours as long as you live, and
may that be for many more years.

If, however, you have some money lying idle in the house, and wish to invest it, that is a
different proposition. I need a few more horses and cows, and have no money on hand to
buy them. My credit is good, and I can borrow the money here, but not for less than 12
percent; some moneylenders charge as high as 30 percent, although the legal limit is 12
percent. Two hundred dollars is all that I need, and I will promptly pay you 6 percent; in this
way we both will make a profit.

The best way to send money is to buy a money order from a bank in Rotterdam which has
connects with a New York bank. They will give you three drafts if you ask for them; mail

them to me, one at a time, about a month apart; one out of three will always reach its destination. Storekeepers in Appleton are glad to give me cash for them. Instead of going to Rotterdam in person, you could ask Doctor Van Loo in Veghel to arrange that matter for you; his first wife was a sister-in-law of Mr. J. Wap; the banker in Rotterdam.

It has been two years now since we arrived here, and we are becoming accustomed to the country and its people; so I shall give you my impressions. The country is still in the making, and much of the improvement is of a makeshift character. The land, after clearing, is left full of tree stumps, which will be removed as soon as the roots have decayed enough so that they can be pulled out. But in the meantime we must plow between them the best way we can, and everything grows without fertilizer. The buildings are mostly constructed of logs; there is not beauty about them, but they are warm and serviceable. The roads are rough, and during a wet spell heavily loaded wagons have to keep off, lest they sink into the mud up to the hub.

This is a free country where only a few necessary and useful laws are made. Ordinances and restrictions which would benefit only a few, and would be a burden to the people generally, are wisely avoided. And with few laws and few officers to enforce them, the people have respect for the law and like to see it enforced; as a whole the people cooperate with the officers so that transgressions are few.

There are policemen in the cities, but we never see one; still we don't have to lock the house or the stable or keep a vicious watchdog to frighten burglars away. You can leave a spade or any implement or tool in the field after using it, and it will still be there whenever you go back to use it again.

Is there a kommie (revenue collector) in Little Chute? Of course you think that no town should be without one, to watch everyone's every move, to prevent illegal butchering, brewing, or baking, etc. No, we have no kommies, and that is another reason why I like this country!

There is no compulsory military service here. Every state in Europe maintains a large standing army because each country is afraid of its neighbor. The United States has no dangerous neighbors, and the quarrelsome nations of Europe are too far away to cause any serious concerns. We have only a small army of volunteers, and no compulsory service.

There are no game laws; you can go fishing or hunting whenever you please. There is plenty of game, big and small, in the woods; the rivers are full of fish.

Do we pay taxes? Certainly we pay taxes, and enjoy doing it! I am paying taxes on 160 acres of land and I am highly assessed because my land is of the best; yet I am only paying twelve dollars a year, and that includes school tax. My brother John has been elected tax collector, the highest paid office in town; he receives 5 percent of all the money taken in, and it will bring him the neat sum of $80.00 a year, but he must go from house to house to collect it.

Now, Father, you will understand why we love our new country, and you will not be surprised when I say that we have made up our minds to make it our home for the rest of our days, bringing up our children to become American citizens. But to come over to Holland for a visit and spend a winter with you is what we are wishing and praying for. However it will take at least two more years of hard work before the conditions of our farm will allow us that luxury.

Now for a bit of local news. The Fox River, a river as big as the Meuse, is shallow and fast-flowing, because Lake Winnebago, its origin, is seventy-five feet higher than the Green Bay, into which it empties, and the distance is only forty miles. A plan has been adopted whereby the river can be made navigable. Dams are being built at several points to retard the flow and raise the water to a higher level, and locks will be installed at each dam to help the boats from one level to another. One of the locks will come right opposite my land. Water transportation will be a great boom to towns along the river. At this moment the work has stopped on account of a dispute between the contractor, Mr. Martin, and the Governor of the state. They say that will come to a lawsuit, and that may be some time before the work will be resumed.

Another public work, now in progress, is the paving of our main road with planks. They want to straighten out the road, and run it through my land, which will necessitate the moving of my house. There is also a dispute her between a certain road boss and one Mr. Verstegen, governor of this manor! They have not come to terms yet about the cost of moving the house, and the price of the land. In the meantime they have skipped my land and are already two miles beyond it, grading the road and making a bedding for the planks. The planks have been laid for a distance of five miles, up to the house of brother John, and that part of the road is open for traffic.

The price of produce is as follows: wheat, per bushel, 75 cents; rye, 60 cents; buckwheat, 60 cents; oats, 30 cents; beans, $1.60; peas, $1.00. Flour is $4.00 a barrel (200 pounds); salt pork, per pound, 10 cents; butter, 14 cents; coffee (not roasted), 14 cents; rice, 8 cents; and eggs, 12 cents per dozen.

Father is still with us. Adriana and Anna Marie are going to school to learn English, and are beginning to read and speak it quite well. J. Van Lisshout says that he will pay his share and that you can go ahead.

With best regards, respectfully, Your children,
Arnoldus Verstegen

Anna Maria Verstegen (Biermans)

♦♦♦♦♦♦

Arnold Verstegen to Delis Biermans
Little Chute, WI to Erp, Noord Brabant   30 August 1857

Dear Parents,

Arnold Hurkmans, a friend and neighbor of ours, will be leaving in a few days on a visit to Holland. We would like to go with him in person, but that being possible, he will bring you our portraits. They have been made by a new process, not painted by the slow brush of an artist, but by a clever device which does the work quick and neat, although the pictures are small. It must be a new American invention, because I never heard of it in Holland. There is a man here in Appleton who knows all about it and gets many customers because he is doing wonderful work. A few weeks ago I went there with Ma and the two youngest children, the ones who were born in America, Anna Maria and Egidius. The machine that performs the mysterious work is simple enough – just a square box that has a big glass eye in front. I was told to sit down a few feet away from the machine and hold the little girl on my knees. Next he told me to look pleasant and to try not to move. Then he removed a cover and let the magic eye look at us for a few seconds, and that is all there was to it. Ma and the baby were next. A few days later we got the pictures and they were just wonderful. When I look at mine, I seem to be looking at myself in the looking glass. It is too bad that the children's faces didn't turn out so well; they are a little foggy.

Are we not living in a wonderful world? One marvelous invention looms up after another. It took us two months and a half to come to this country, and that is only seven years ago, and now your letters reach us with a month.

The wild land we undertook to tame a few years ago has seen a great change. We have almost forty acres under cultivation, a nice herd of cattle, and can take life a little easier this year than any previous year. But Hurkmans will tell you all about that. He knows us and our circumstances. Just ask him, and he will tell you everything. In Holland they think that visitors coming from America are fond of telling tall stories, that they like to make things look twice as big as they really are. However, Hurkmans is not that kind of a man; everything he says can be taken at its full value.

Hoping to receive an answer with Hurkmans, I am your obedient son,

Arnold Verstegen

P.S. We recommend Hurkmans to your kind hospitality.
Arnold Verstegen to Delis Biermans

♦♦♦♦♦♦

Little Chute, WI to Erp, Noord Brabant   28 October 1858
Dear Parents,

We received your letter of October 20 of last year, but did not answer because Arnold Hurkmans was on his way to Holland with a letter from us and would bring all the news personally. In the meantime there has been an increase in our family. On the 15th of September a baby boy arrived. His name is Hermanus. That brings the total again up to five, three girls and two boys. The baby is doing fine, but the mother suffers from cramps in the legs, although she is otherwise in good health.

Hurkmans tells us that you liked the pictures but that you would sooner have seen us in person. It has always been our plan to come to see you as soon as the condition of our farm would allow us, but we overlooked one thing and that is the children. For no money in the world would Anna leave them to the care of strangers. A few years from now it will be different; Adriana, who is a willing and handy worker and already does much of the housework will then be able to take the place of her mother, and then you can expect us. We left Holland, not because we disliked the country, but to give our children better opportunities. Here I will be able to put each of them on a farm, something I never would have expected to do in Holland. But if it is God's will we hope to see Holland once more, and walk the streets of Erp and Boekel and Uden, and meet our old friends and have a happy family reunion.

Hurkmans tells us that he spent many hours with you, and that you were delighted to hear of the progress we have made on our farm. He told us, too, how he had to draw maps of Little Chute and point out the location of our house, and the house of John, and of the church. I am sure you now have a pretty good picture in your mind of the entire town.

Late in the summer an unusual sight was noticed in the sky; it was a star with a tail. As weeks passed by, the tail grew longer and head grew brighter, and it seemed to come nearer the earth. In the month of October it began to look so threatening that people began to fear that something was amiss, and that the end of the world was coming. One Sunday our priest talked about it in church and said that it was a comet and that similar stars had been seen in the past; that it was a friendly wanderer of the universe, not intent upon any mischief, and that it would disappear noiselessly, just as it had arrived. The papers tell us that it was seen all over the world; you must have seen it in Holland too.

Father has been very sick this summer and hasn't been in the church for three months; he was anointed, and for a few days his condition was such that any moment he was expected to pass away. To the surprise of everyone, he recovered, and is going to church again, although he is not quite as strong as he used to be. Next summer he will again be seen working in the garden and doing odd jobs around the house and taking the children for a walk.

Now a little about the weather. There was so much rain this spring that the work in the field was much delayed. The horses would sink in the mud as deep as the land had been plowed before. It was July before all the seeding was done. Then a dry hot spell came, once the thermometer registered 105 degrees; and the latter part of the summer was wet again. Wheat is only 85 cents a bushel, so that farmers in some states, considering the low price and the poor quality of grain, have set fire to the crops, not thinking it worthwhile to harvest them. I myself have two acres of wheat still standing in the field; it has plenty of straw but little grain, and even that is infested with smut.

The money you have sent I have put on interest. Home breeding has taken care of the increase of my stock, so that I need not buy any more. When I see a good piece of property I will buy it.

I was told two years ago that Cornelius Elsen was married. Is it true that Uncle Cornelis of Boekel is also married? Give my best regards to all relatives and friends.

Yours truly,
A. Verstegen

♦♦♦♦♦♦

Arnold Verstegen to Delis Biermans
Little Chute, WI to Erp, Noord Brabant   2 January 1860

Dear Parents, Brothers, and Sisters-in-law,

Anna has been telling me right along that the new year was coming fast, and that it was time to look for pen and ink and send our New Year's greetings to Holland; and I kept on saying that there was no hurry, for no other reason that I know of, except that I dislike the mention of pen and ink; that puts the blame on me for their coming so late.

Accept our sincere wishes for a happy New Year. So far God has been kind to you and given you a good share of the blessings of this life, and we pray that you may enjoy the same happiness for many more years.

Your welcome letter of January 8, 1859, found us all in good health, except that Anna is still suffering from cramps in the legs; it is four years since she began to complain, and now it is so bad that she has difficulty in walking, otherwise she is in good health.

Wheat, rye, and oats were fairly good last year, but most of the winter wheat had to be seeded over in the spring. Early in the month of July a severe frost did much damage to Turkish wheat, buckwheat, and potatoes and another killing frost the last days of August aggravated the damage done earlier in the season. That is the climate of Wisconsin - impetuous extreme cold and long winters, and short, hot summers; everything must grow in four months' time; and it is surprising what a wealth of grain and fruits can grow in so short a period. Buckwheat seeded the latter part of June is ready to be cut during the week of the Boekel kermis. All in all we did fairly well this year.

The prices of produce are as follows: wheat, $1.00; oats, 30 cents; potatoes, 50 cents per bushel; flour 5.00 the barrel; butter, one shilling per pound. I have two fine work horses for sale and three milk cows; that would leave me seven horses and as many cows; but although grain brings a good price, livestock is cheap and I don't like to sell at the prevailing price. I think I have told you everything worthwhile mentioning and we remain as ever, with respect and love, your son and daughter.

Arnold Verstegen
Anna Maria Biermans

◆◆◆◆◆◆

Arnold Verstegen to Biermans Family
Little Chute, WI to Erp, Noord Brabant   20 August 1860

Dear Mother, Brothers and Sisters-in-law,

We received your May 30 letter in good health and learned that father died. I am still thinking about his soul. That's why I have asked for a Mass every month on the date of his death. At this time we do not have a priest here, but on this coming Sunday we were promised to have one again.

Now it is all right with my wife that I shall come for a visit around All Saints Day. So when I come I hope to see you again, so we can talk to each other. So keep the money there and if I cannot come I will let you know.

The end of July my wife delivered a baby daughter, her name is Ardina and both are doing fine except her old ailment. Those were the reasons you have not heard from me in so long.

We had a good harvest: the wheat is in, the straw is very coarse, oats and other fruits are looking very good. But we had a lot of thunder and rain this year. I bought a threshing machine in the middle of the year, which cost me 100 dollars and I can thresh about one hundred bushels a day with it.

There is no more news here. So, our greetings to all friends and acquaintances also the ones in Boekel.

Always with our best regards.
Your son and daughter,
Arnoldus Verstegen

Arnold Verstegen to Biermans family
Little Chute, WI to Erp, Noord Brabant   1 June 1862

Dear Mother, Brothers and Sisters,

We must bring you some very sad news. Adriana our eldest daughter is dead. You know her well; the nice little girl who was of school age before we left Holland, and came often to see you and you like her sweet disposition. Here too she went to school a couple of years and learned so well that she could talk and read English as if she had been American born. When she grew up she was a favorite with everybody because she had such winning ways, not proud or selfish, but satisfied with the humblest place, just like her mother.

Now she was a grown up lady, a stout and healthy looking woman. She started young to help her mother with the housework, and the last couple of years she did practically all the work alone, until she got married two weeks before Lent, February 16th. We could hardly afford to lose her much needed help, but her companion, Arnold Hurkmans, was a nice young man and they seemed well matched; and it would have been unwise to interfere with plans concerning her own future happiness. On the wedding day there was much feasting and rejoicing and well wishing, in which nearly the whole of Little Chute took part.

Two weeks after the wedding Adriana took sick; on Ash Wednesday the doctor was called and he found it to be a serious case, an infection of the liver. She grew steadily worse and wasted away so fast and so completely that the friends who came to see her towards the last said that she did not look any more like the Adriana they had know so well. As soon as she realized that her condition was hopeless she became reconciled to God's will, and suffered patiently asking only for our prayers. She died peacefully on Saturday, May the 24th.

Eighteen hours after Adriana had breathed her last, her mother gave birth to another girl. Mother had looked forward to that event, expecting to have Adriana at her bedside; Adriana was always happy when she could wait on her frail mother. Her ways were so gentle, and as by instinct, she would always do and say the right thing; her presence along gave her mother a feeling of security and comfort.

And now preparations were being made for her funeral, which was to be held the next day. We felt great anxiety for Mother; but her trust in God, and her calmness and patience in the most trying situations did not desert her this time; she is doing well now. The baby was baptized on the day of her sister's funeral, May the 26th, and named Adriana, to honor the memory of our first Adriana, hoping that she will grow up to be as fine and virtuous a woman as her predecessor was. Of the four children which we brought from Holland, Johanna is the only one left; she is not thirteen years old. On our farm we have done well since we came here, but misfortunes on our family have been too many and too severe. But it is God's will, and we must carry our cross no matter how heavy it is.

The war between the North and South is still going on with great fury; the papers bring news every day of new battles being fought, more soldiers being killed, more property being destroyed; and we don't seem to be making any headway. The end is not yet in sight. Only volunteers are being asked for, to raise an army of over 600,000 men.

With best wishes for you all, and asking you to remember Adriana in your prayers, I remain with love and respect,

Arnold Verstegen

♦♦♦♦♦♦

Arnold Verstegen to Biermans family   19 June 1862
Dear Mother, Brother, and Sisters,

Only two weeks ago I wrote you about the death of Adriana, and the arrival of a new baby girl. Now I am writing again to let you know that mother has stood the ordeal well and that the baby too is doing fine. However, we still miss Adriana and I don't think we will ever forget her; but it is God's will and we must carry our cross with patience.

Now I want to tell you about the great works which are here in progress. The railroad is coming to Little Chute. Already for some time trains have been running as far as Fond du Lac and Oshkosh and now the line is being extended through Appleton and Little Chute to Fort Howard and Green Bay. At first the road had been surveyed through my land, but now it will run between my two properties, and will pass within 500 paces from my house and 300 paces from my land. A big crew of men is working with shovels and pickaxes and scrapers drawn by horses, making a perfectly level roadbed. It is surprising that in these times of uncertainty, funds can be found to finance so big an undertaking, and that with so many young men joining the army enough labor is available. But the work is progressing nicely and we expect trains to be running soon. This will be a great boon for our part of the country; it will mean markets for our produce and merchandise for our stores; factories may locate here and Little Chute may become a big city. When we want to go to Appleton on business or for pleasure, the train will bring us there in less time than it takes now to hitch up a team of horses.

It is also rumored (and rumors of this kind are usually based on good authority) that the canal will be widened to one and one half its present size, to accommodate the big lake steamers, which cannot now pass through the locks. That also will give employment to many workmen so that there will be jobs for everybody for a long time.

The other items that will interest you is that we are building a mill. Of course you think of a windmill, which is a common sight all over Holland; you can look at one in Erp without leaving your house. That kind of a mill is not known in America, although Little Chute came once very near having one. When I first came here the notion came to my mind to build one. We farmers had to sell our wheat cheap and buy flour at a high price. A windmill would have solved the problem nicely, just as it does in Holland. I spoke to my neighbors about it and they all encouraged me; the sight of it alone, they said, would be worth a great deal and would cure the homesickness of newcomers. Brother John, however, ridiculed the idea and wouldn't listen to my arguments. "Don't you remember," he said, "that our miller in Erp often was sitting in the doorway of the mill scratching his head, watching the weather, when stacks of grain were piling up waiting to go through the grindstones and that the wings of the mill with all sails spread stood motionless, as if paralyzed, because there wasn't the slightest breeze to turn them around? Why don't you put a water wheel here in the river? The river never stops flowing; and the water that goes over the dam here in Little Chute has more power than all the windmills in the whole of North Brabant combined." From then on we started figuring and planning and negotiating, with the result that today the foundations for a mill to be driven by water power are finished. We cut through five feet of limestone on the bank of the river, to make room for the installation of up-to-date machinery; enough stone has been excavated to build the foundation walls, the lumber for the superstructure is on hand, and it won't be long before we will be ready for business. We call it the Zeeland Mill, after our home town. Little Chute has now a railroad, a canal, and a factory. Watch her grow from now on.

The newspapers every day are filled with accounts from the battlefront. If I wanted to repeat all that, I would run out of paper before I had half done; I am sure that your papers carry the news too. Everybody here would have it over with.

The crops are generally good; the winter wheat is excellent. Best regards from Anna, and greetings to all relative and friends.

Yours very truly,
Arnold Verstegen

◆◆◆◆◆◆

October 1871
Dear brothers and sister-in-law,

On this occasion I feel obliged to report about our health, because of the terrible disaster, which struck our state with fire. The fire was in the forests everywhere. However you cannot imagine those forests, you probably look at your heather as forests. These were not forests for coppice, but all kinds of trees, which were all on fire. Every afternoon the wind rose and spread the fire. But it was not enough, on Sunday, October the 8th at 10 o'clock in the evening it broke loose in Chicago. The morning after we heard about it, I was in Appleton that day where every minute news arrived via the telegraph. By evening 2000 acres or 1000 double acres were reduced to ashes and many people lost their lives.

The city was very beautiful and it was in the centre of the city. Most of the houses were fireproof, that's what they thought. The stone in the walls did not melt, but the iron columns, which were under the houses, melted as this as water. They tell us that some of the houses had cost a million dollars and also much of the goods in them, so that the damage up till now has not been calculated.

But that was not all, there was still (at Peshtigo), which had already burnt, except a boarding house. On Sunday evening on October 8 the fire came through the air as a cloud, like a heavy snow squall. Everything burned in four hours, houses and 800 people, as far as is known now, they find more every day. To tell you everything is almost impossible but I myself leave it up to God. We have to carry our crosses like you do yours.

It was not only our state that suffered, but also Michigan and other states. Our state during the first week in October, every day there is so much smoke that we have to put grease into our eyes to be able to stand it. Johannes van Rijsingen from Uden is also reported burned. Others die every day, which were burned halfway. Those had saved themselves by hanging on to trees that were drifting in the river. They had to stay under water to the neck and still the hairs on their head burned. I even talked to such persons. They told me that they had to sit in the river for four hours and had to put their heads under water all the time or keep it wet or they would have burned. Even the trees, lying in the water, but not totally under water, burned. Well I have to stop. I could keep on writing the whole day. As far as I and my family are concerned, we are all well and healthy, thank God.

We had a dry year. The wheat did not grow well. The rest of the harvest is pretty good and also the hay, but that which was kept outside, what is done here a lot, is burned.   Concerning my work: I am checking the mill and my oldest son Johannes Egidius Verstegen is working now also.

I ask you to answer me. Is it because my wife is not rich enough? She sure is a good mother for my children as a rich one and is tough. I shall not talk about this anymore, but hope for an answer.

P.S. If there are other circumstances, just ask and I shall answer. Greetings to all from me, brothers and sister-in-law, and next of kin (if they are with you).

A. Verstegen

♦♦♦♦♦♦

Little Chute to Erp   September 1882
Dear Cousin Johannes J. Biermans,

I would like to write a few lines to you about myself and my children. All of us are healthy again but my children were sick the most. From what we read in the newspapers it is the same sickness that you had in Europe, but hardly anyone died from it and at my house everyone is restored.

Regarding my trip, I boarded the ship in Antwerp on August 10 and arrived in New York on the 21st. So we were at sea for eleven days and then one and half days to my home. That would be a nice pleasure trip for you too and I would welcome you with pleasure. Then you would see something of the world and the difference between this place and your place. My absence from my family passed by quickly. They made more money (in my absence) than I spent on the trip. For many years now I have saved more than $2,000 every year. That is a large sum to save in the short time of a year. Anyone here, who has money and who watches his expenses with care, earns money. At the moment, however, it is to so good for farmers because everything is so cheap – $25 to $20 (per acre). Horses are expensive; a good horse can cost as much as $200 each but not many are buying them. Wheat here is 65 cents to 75 cents per bushel. A bushel is equal to two containers (type and size not specified). Hay is 20 cents (per bale). Employment is generally very weak. But more people are at work locally because two paper mills were built here last year but they only use half of the workers that they could (at full employment).

Now, greetings from my wife and children and also to your wife and your father and mother.

I remain respectfully yours and willingly at your service.

Your cousin,
A. Verstegen

♦♦♦♦♦♦

Marinette and Racine Counties

[Willem Nicholas Wezenaar was born in 1845 in Noord Holland to Willem Wezenaar and Maria van der Boom. He married Minnie Boerner. Minnie's sister Mary Boerner was married to Johannes Cornelis Wezenaar, Willem's brother. The sisters, both German, survived the Great Peshtigo Fire. Johannes Cornelis Wezenaar was born in Amsterdam, Noord Holland on 24 June 1850 to Willem Wezenaar and Maria van der Boom. He emigrated with his parents and his brother Willem ca. 1852 and by 1856 they were living in Marinette, WI. He died 16 October 1927 in Marinette, WI. He married Mary Elizabeth Boerner on 3 November 1873. She was born 21 March 1856 in Marinette, WI the daughter of Frederick Boerner and Fredericka Gottslaff and died 25 February, 1923 in Marinette, WI. These letters are from the Dutch Immigrant Letters Collection, Archives, Calvin College, Grand Rapids, MI Box 88, Folder 38.]

Marinette, Wisconsin – Voorschoten, Zuid Holland, Netherlands   21 March 1886
Willem Wezenaar to relatives

Dear uncle and aunt and cousins,

Because I have learned from Jan that you are still in the land of the living I am taking up the pen to write you once, hoping that you might find yourselves in the best of health just like us at the time this letter is mailed. That is my best wish. Well uncle, it is hard work for me to write in the language of the fatherland. This is the second time since we came to live in America. So you must not take offense if I make some mistakes. You probably have heard from Jan that I am married so I don't think I have to write about it. Jan and I have married sisters, German women. I have the youngest and Jan the oldest. Also I have two children, Neeltje, a girl named after her grandmother and Klaas, who is named after his grandfather. Also we have two children who are dead; two boys. Well uncle, I actually do not know what I shall write to you. I think that the best thing is to let you know about my circumstances and how things are with me. How it would please me if I could speak with you once, that is better than writing. But that cannot be because I have to work hard for my bread. Because here in this land the situation is such that a bachelor is a gentleman compared to a married man. He receives his room, board and wages. And if he saves, then he doesn't have to spend on anything other than tobacco and laundry. So then I have 35 acres of land, two cows, a bull, a horse, two hogs, chickens, and a couple of calves. I have lost two other horses, which caused me much financial harm. And this spring I have to buy another one in addition to my old jade. Now you people will think that Willem is not doing quite so badly, but that is wrong because I am just barely able to make a living but nothing more. We still must be thrifty; and now you will say, why is this so? Then I will say to you, the land is not fruitful here. It is sand land just like the dunes at Haarlem. One must fertilize it heavily otherwise a person doesn't get any fruit. This is a great place for a man who has a trade. He can make money here. A carpenter's wage is two to three dollars per day. A dollar is two and a half guilders. Bricklayers earn two to four dollars per day, and this is the same for all tradesmen. They get high wages, but that doesn't help me. I have already worked in a sawmill and there

238

the wages are not so high because I was father's first help he had and God knows that my dear father had tough times in America…. In the beginning when we came here everything was expensive and uncultivated but now this has developed into a large village. Well, uncle, has Jan written to you already? Mother has told me that he would send you some money. She thought that you could use it for your family. Well uncle, I am ending with pen but not with my heart. Give greetings to all your children and greetings to you as well, my uncle. So I call myself your Willem Wezenaar.

> If you are willing, be so good to write back once.
> Willem

♦♦♦♦♦♦

[These letters are from the Dutch Immigrant Letters Collection, Archives, Calvin College, Grand Rapids, MI, Box 29, Folder 3. No further information is known about the writer.]

Twin Lakes, Wisconsin   25 June 1917
William Hilbrands to relatives

Dear children and grandchildren,

This is to congratulate Johanna, and also all of you, with the addition of another year to her age, in the hope that she may celebrate many more in happiness and contentment. We send to her, and also to Elisabeth, a handkerchief, dividing the remaining ones as you will. This only to please you all, and a little reminder of your mother and grandmother.

Hoping you are all well and happy. The outside world does not appear very flourishing, water, water, wherever one looks, and nothing grows. The corn is still in the bags, and so are the potatoes and beans. The Lord only knows what the summer will bring; we humans can do nothing to change the situation.

At present I am a little better, but do not know if this will remain so. I have been very ill; this was a week before Friday. At that time I did not think I would be here anymore when morning came. I kept thinking how father always said that the anxious and oppressive feeling he had (benauwdheid) was much worse than the most severe pain. One who has not experienced this cannot understand it. I think it may be an illness by itself, maybe you do remember some of this.

I wish you could all come here so I could see you once more. However, I feel a little better, and hope for the best. I hope that, if God would call me to Himself unexpectedly, you will think back with love of your mother and grandmother who always love you.

In the meantime we hope we may all live for many years yet, even if we cannot see each other. However, if it is possible, do try to come here, because it does not seem we will be able to come to you for awhile. Write back soon to let us know how things are by you.

♦♦♦♦♦♦

Twin Lakes, Wisconsin   14 April 1918
William Hilbrands to relatives

Dear children and grandchildren,

It is Sunday again and already a week ago since Dominee Kolkman was here. Time does go by so fast one does not know where it goes. Dominee, likely, will have told about his experiences. He was here only a few moments due to the confusion in regard to the train. So I did not talk much with him. He did, however, (and this made me feel very sad) say that Letta had been ill. But added immediately that you were better now and attended church again. I suppose it happened after you wrote your last letter because you did not mention it. I hope with all my heart that you may be spared illness.

As he further told us, you were going to work on the road and leaving the farm alone. Well, we too are doing very little to the farm. Corn is so expensive, and almost impossible to get. We have only a few potatoes and besides not much horsepower, so we do as little farm work as possible farm. It is something these days but we must not lose heart, after this another time will come.

Yesterday they bothered us for money for the "freedom landing," Well, we said that first we had to take care of ourselves and our animals to keep alive.

We received a letter from the Old Country, from Titial Schuth. The future does not look so good, especially for the farm help, like her husband. As Jan wrote, Tiddo's Minnie is in the hospital again and very weak, so much so that nobody may visit her. Is that not sad? I did visit her in October, but then she seemed very poor to me. It is a heavy burden for Tiddo to carry. Yes, dear children, so do we all have our crosses to bear. The one is heavier, the other somewhat lighter, and I thought it to be so true what the enclosed poem states. I thought to send it, maybe it will comfort you a little and bless you.

The rough winter is now again behind us and one begins somewhat to forget all the suffering one went through. The farm animals cannot take care of themselves. As you write, you have a nice bunch of farm animals and a young horse. Well, that is nice. We did not have much luck this past year, and now we experience the results of that. We got a cow who just calved two weeks ago, for $96.00 and now a Holstein heifer, born in July, for $62.00. What a lot of money, but we had to. Receive for now the heartfelt greetings from your loving mother and grandmother.

Father and myself